To my writer friends,
Tom & Mary

FeatureWriting.Net

All the best in your
writing pursuits.

Timeless Feature Story Ideas in an Online World

Best. Michael Ray Smith

By Michael Ray Smith
Campbell University

Episte*logic*
Bloomington, IL

FEATUREWRITING.NET: A GUIDE TO WRITING IN THE ELECTRONIC AGE

Publisher and Editor: Stephen D. Perry
Copy Editor: Rabeya Merenkov
Printer: Data Reproductions, Inc.
Distributor: AtlasBooks
Cover Design: University of Mauritius Press

Library of Congress Cataloging-in-Publication Data

Smith, Michael Ray
    Featurewriting.net: A guide to writing in the electronic age / Michael Ray Smith
    Includes references and index
    ISBN 0-9748319-2-1 / ISBN-13 format 978-0-9748319-2-3
    1. Journalism. 2. Writing. I. Title. II. Smith, Michael Ray

Manufactured in the United States of America
10   9   8   7   6   5   4   3   2   1

To order copies of this and other Epistelogic products, contact our distributor
    AtlasBooks
    1-800-Booklog or 1-800-266-5564
    order online at www.epistelogic.com or through
    www.atlasbooks.com/atlasbooks/index.html
Permissions to reproduce portions of this work may be obtained by contacting us at:
    Phone: 309-826-4808
    Email: publisher@epistelogic.com
        (include "permissions request" in the subject line)

47 White Place, Bloomington, IL 61701 USA

For the tender one who makes life joyous, Barbara

Table of Contents

Acknowledgements

Thank you to all my writer friends, the ones who have poured out their prose for years and those who are just beginning the editorial journey. I'm grateful to webmaster and brother Stanley Smith and cheerleaders such as John Lawing and Dennis Bounds. Others are just good friends and include Michael Graves, Dennis Fulk and James Wendell Curtis. Copy-editor Jill Darling read countless drafts along with other writers and proofreaders Rabeya Merenkov and Kay Lynn Perry. Thanks to Stephen Perry, my publisher. He underscored what I wanted to say and helped me say it better. And I'm grateful to Barbara, Shannon and Taylor, who endured photographs and countless rewrites. Acknowledging these people seems to be so little for all that I received.

Introduction

Write it in plain English
FeatureWriting.Net/GettingStarted

Chapter at-a-glance

- ➤ Philosophy of the text
- ➤ Overview of this text
- ➤ Navigating the text

Philosophy of the text

For too long writing of any kind was the gorilla in the closet. If you let it out, only damage could ensue. *FeatureWriting.Net* is the secret weapon for writers who have the passion to write but need some ideas to irrigate their thinking. The following ideas are from professional writers and writers on their way to publication. I've tried to distill their very best counsel to give you workable ideas on getting into print and using the Internet to make your work as competitive as the best wordsmiths in the nation. In many cases, the participants in writing workshops and students in university writing programs offered their suggestions to make the book accessible. One critic said the textbook was "too accessible," but the editors and I are convinced that too easy

Writing. Is there any more solitary activity? Some books are designed to demystify the process of writing. We hope this textbook is one of them. Our goal is to break it into manageable steps to help you keep your fingers on the keyboard and stay with the task, to write with confidence and some days, with a bit of flair.

may be a strength in the case of getting your feature article published.

Here are some of the compelling features that make *FeatureWriting.Net* your best tool to unlock the writer in you.

Overview of this text

- **Clear, concise coverage of the skills used by writers.**
  This step-by-step guide is your crash course in identifying a topic, gathering   information on it, getting started writing it and finishing it with panache.

- **Clear objectives, summaries and boldface words to aid the writer in learning the craft at a glance.**
  FeatureWriting.Net is designed to be accessible to new writers of all ages.

- **A format that helps students focus on key concepts.**
  Informative side notes and a clean, easy-to-read design help highlight key ideas and make the text navigable and accessible.

- **Designed for use in your personal classroom.**
  FeatureWriting.Net provides examples and exercises from a variety of articles to stimulate writers.

- **Practical helps.**
  Helps include profiles of successful writers and examples of their work to encourage new writers with stories and practical advice on improving their prose.

- **A unique approach to developing articles.**
  New writers can use an easy-to-understand formula to learn the best way to package their writing. In addition, *FeatureWriting.Net* has nearly 70 specific article ideas in an A-to-Z list to give the new writer a map from article idea to article angle to specific web sites that will amplify the topic. Writers can use part or all of the formula to develop the article.

- **Visuals.**
  FeatureWriting.Net includes examples of web sites and other visual art to make its use enjoyable as a guidebook and reference book that new writers will refer to over and over.

Navigating the text

Each chapter begins with bulleted highlights, phrases that will help summarize the key goals. The chapter also uses a webpage subtitle, a repeated motif for this project. Those pages don't actually exist but you can use the suggested idea to stay focused on the chapter's goal. The web page idea is another way to suggest the quotidian approach to frequent but responsible use of the Internet to research your article. Words that are important to know are in boldface. You can find footnotes of sources at the bottom of the page. Section headings divide up the material to help guide you from main point to main point. As stated earlier, each chapter showcases at least one feature writer. In some cases, these writers work for newspapers; in other cases, the writers are book authors. Some of the featured writers are columnists and conference speakers. Others are editors and freelance writers. The goal is to present a variety of writing voices, their philosophies and their approach to collecting and writing articles. Background on the writer, a question-and-answer interview of the writer, and a sample of the writer's work is included in each chapter.

The last chapter may be one of the most useful. It is meant to give you feature writing ideas and specific strategies to get the story. These ideas are meant to be timeless and not tied to any geography. The list is alphabetical with more direction early in the alphabet. As you gain confidence, you will develop your own feature story ideas and this list will seem, oh, so quaint. For now, use it to jumpstart your thinking and set a goal of writing one feature article each week.

Chapter 1

The chocolate-covered almond
FeatureWriting.Net/NoConflict

<u>Chapter at-a-glance</u>

> ➤ Understanding conflict is essential in story-telling
> ➤ Identifying the news peg or news angle in an article
> ➤ Using the 5 W's to answer questions that are important in an article

In many ways, writing for publication is like foil-wrapped chocolate.

The foil wrapping can be viewed as the central idea of the story. Beneath the foil is a luscious piece of chocolate, detail that supports the main idea. But inside that hunk of chocolate is a sweet almond, a colorful expression that makes your writing sing.

This chapter will provide an overview of the steps writers use to unearth the sweet spot that's part of every story assignment. These techniques will serve writers well, whether it's crafting a news release in public relations, creating a tight argument in advertising or writing a crisp new story. Good writing begins with selecting the main idea.

Some tools such as the versatile hammer are used more than others. For the writer, finding the conflict in the story and using it in a compelling opening is among tools that may be most essential.

5

The main idea

Find the **conflict**, and you'll find the main idea.

Imagine that the library is installing a new system that will allow students to scan books for check out if they have an identification card. What's the conflict? The conflict could be the time and inconvenience needed to make the change. Or, the conflict could be the amount of money the system will cost. Maybe people are just fond of the old system and don't want to see it abandoned.

Literature, film, life. All require conflict. Where is the sparkle without conflict? The same idea is true in media writing, but don't be deceived into thinking that a writer imposes conflict where none exists. Don't make up the conflict; just ask yourself, "What issues does this story suggest?"

Throughout this book are **Tips**. TIP, an acronym meaning "to insure promptness," once was the payment given to someone in advance of his or her service. For our purposes, **TIP** can stand for **"To Insure Publication."** The tips that you will find in the pages ahead are ideas that may help you refine your editorial edge, to become the writer that is only a byline away.

Tip: To gain an appreciation for news writing. Type . . . literally, type . . . the first three paragraphs of a news article from a newspaper. *Drug arrests are on the rise but burglary and other property crimes fell for the third year in a row, says a federal report.* That's what is called a lead, a first sentence.

Now note the lead from the Dec. 14, 2004 *Wall Street Journal* on page one under the headline "Making waves, New luxury goods set super-wealthy apart from the pack," a piece by Robert Frank on luxury goods:

> *Don Weston used to feel special cruising the world in his 100-foot yacht. Yet on a recent morning at the International Boat Show here, the retired Cincinnati businessman stood on his upper deck, overshadowed by giants.*

Frank goes on to develop a feature article that explores the boat-envy of millionaires.

Find a lead that you like and type it and the next two paragraphs! Most people will ignore this technique, but for those who try it, they will gain a greater appreciation for the rhythm and cadence of good writing. The old master Benjamin Franklin taught himself the beauty of a well-turned sentence by copying and then rewriting essays that he found highly readable. It worked for Franklin, inventor, statesman and writer, and it will work for you.

The interview and conflict

A typical assignment for news reporters and writers is to interview a person. Those making assignments, called **editors**, don't randomly assign writers to interview just anyone. People are interviewed because they've done something notable or can provide information about someone who has. The job of the writer is to unlock as much relevant information on the issue as possible while meeting that crucial deadline. Some assignments will require extensive preparation on the person's background and demand additional interviews with the subject's friends and peers. Other stories don't merit this attention and can be completed with a thoughtful but quick telephone interview. In all cases, the writer must find the conflict that makes this article worth the reader's effort. Joseph Pulitzer told his reporters in the 19th Century he wanted to read articles that caused him to say, "Gee, whiz." To surprise the reader, the writer must work hard to mine for a conflict that is appropriate for the article and interesting to read.

Like the chocolate candy, conflict may have many layers. Imagine, for instance, you were in a community where two retired men spend the better part of two summers carving a 40-foot totem pole, complete with colorful depictions of bears, turtles and an airplane. You hear about the enterprise, contact an editor in your area and sell her on a feature. The editor assigns you to write the article, and gives you a firm deadline.

> **Tip:** Should your interview lag and you need to juice it up, try some of ABC TV's Barbara Walter's sure-fire questions.
> What was your first job?
> When was the last time that you cried?
> What would you like your tombstone to read?
> Did you ever... build a weapon, sing at a wedding, fall out of a tree? Ask any silly question that comes to mind. Usually, these questions get nothing but a laugh from your source; however, sometimes the source comes back with something very unexpected.
>
> A news reporter speaking to a university class on these questions had one member of the class turn the question on him. The class conducted an interview as part of the host teacher's assignment. "What would you like your tombstone to read?" the student asked. The speaker paused and finally said that he wanted to be remembered for his faith in Christ. That answer surprised the class and it opened up a number of follow-up questions that no one had anticipated. This tip worked for them, and it will work for you.

What's the conflict?

For this article, you make an appointment to meet the men and you show up on time, feeling relaxed, but curious. As you think about the totem pole carving, your mind toys with the question, "What's the **conflict**?" The natural conflict is the men could have spent their days sipping hot tea and pondering the heavens, but they chose to use electric grinders to make a totem pole. Find out the reason for the labor and you've found the natural conflict.

The fact that no one paid them to work day after day on the pole, once an ordinary utility pole, is another layer of conflict. The conflict could include that choice of sites to show off the work of art; in this case, the finished totem pole will be erected near the parking lot of a butcher shop.

Let's say one of the carvers is related to the owner of the shop and carved a vulture on top of the pole as a joke. That element also suggests conflict between the businessman who wants his customers to value his meat and an artist who finds humor in a predator associated with decaying animal carcasses.

Whatever conflict the writer chooses must be one that can be sustained throughout the article. If the article is meant to be humorous, the vulture conflict may be the best pick, but if the men hope to make a political statement about Indian art in rural Pennsylvania, the vulture idea may interfere with the overall concept.

The goal and news qualities

Keep in mind that the conflict is supported by other demands of the article. All articles must satisfy readers' questions. In short, relevant articles possess **news qualities**.

When you pick the conflict, consider the characteristics of news qualities.

Ask yourself...

Is it timely? Some event happened and people are talking about it. The emphasis here is on the currency of the information. A tragedy last month is dated as a report for a daily newspaper; however, a feature writer with a creative bent can find a fresh angle to write about the situation. The September 11, 2001, disaster is of interest today as writers reflect on new angles such as the role of buildings as symbols of capitalism, security issues vs. personal freedoms, and the call to fire fighting and police service as an act of commitment to a noble truth.

Next ask yourself . . .

Is it close? The nearer the event to the audience, proximity, the more interesting the audience will find that information.

Will it affect a lot of people? The more impact, the newsier the story.

Is it unusual? About once a decade a man will bite a dog... and it's always news but the reverse isn't news. Dog bites are common and aren't typically reported unless the attack is particularly severe such as the case of an animal hurting a child. As you write, keep these ideas in mind as you refine the article's most salient point. So, news is characterized by timeliness, proximity, impact and unusualness. News is about the human condition and involves conflicts.

The news peg

By ruminating on the timeliness, proximity, unusualness and other aspects of the ideas, you will help yourself find a **news peg**, the reason this article is being written now. Sometimes an anniversary is all that is needed to make an article idea fly. Sometimes it's a matter of pairing three ideas such as restaurants along the Susquehanna River that are available by boat. Other times the news peg is a general awareness that the topic is hot such as the trend to wear face masks in Asian countries during the Severe Acute Respiratory Syndrome panic of mid-2003. Many approaches are available for the news peg. Part of your job as a feature writer is to isolate the strongest news peg and use it to build a memorable article.

Here's a series of TIPS for your consideration.

Tip 1: Ever meet a person who clips funny sayings or illustrations and gives them to her friends? A women's magazine might be interested in an article on a person who entertains her friends with cut-out phrases and illustrations. This idea is meant to be fun and the writer would use a light tone to explain a playful person who shares humor in this way with friends, but does this story meet the requirements for news? What would you say?

Tip 2: In the November 1991 issue of *Campus Life* magazine, Nancy Ricker Hoffman suggested that writers emphasize a central point, another name for conflict.

Instead of writing about the list of activities with which a person may be involved, try capturing the central meaning of those activities.

Not: I spent the summer painting houses...

Better: With each stroke of the paintbrush, I learned the truth about myself.

Hoffman also suggests that writers use concrete detail by showing the reader, not telling her.

Not: The car is attractive . . .

Better: The fire engine red Renault convertible gleamed in the afternoon sun.

The 5 W's

Feature writing is a subset of writing that is meant to be more timeless, and, in general, more entertaining. Nonetheless, among the qualities all the articles share are answers to the **5 W's**. Master raconteur Rudyard Kipling said:

> I keep six honest serving men.
> (They taught me all I knew);
> Their names are What and Why and When
> And How and Where and Who.

Answer these questions and you'll have the basis of an article.

In constructing your article, particularly a feature article based on a news story, the writer must answer all those questions, but not necessarily one at a time or all at once. The "what" question is important. To open your article, you may answer the question, "What's new?"

Answering the what question

Here's an opening from *Christianity Today* magazine about a public school district in Central Pennsylvania that stopped Bible reading and prayer in late 1993.

For nearly 40 years, students in Pennsylvania's Warrior Run School District began classes with Bible reading over the intercom system. In December, the practice stopped.

Although it took two sentences to do it, this beginning, called the lead, tells us that a Bible reading practice-*the what*-stopped in December-*the when*. The Question could be, "What's happening with the Bible reading?" The lead answers that question.

Another useful question is to ask, "Who did what?" In this case, the writer can plug in the correct answers.

For the Bible reading story, the lead could have been:

A Pennsylvania community school board official stopped Bible reading in his public school in late 1993 to avoid a lawsuit.

In this lead, part of the "why" question is answered. Why did the school board stop the Bible reading? The school board feared a lawsuit would ensue if it didn't stop the practice.

Here's your crash course in writing an article in list form. Some of these ideas have been covered in the chapter; others are new.
Your feature story needs a main idea or theme.
1) Look for the natural conflict in the story. Tell us in one sentence what the story is all about. Summarize.
2) Be brief. Be concise. Be terse.

10

Sentences can be 12 to 15 words long or longer, but alter the length for variety.

3) News and magazine columns can be narrow, sometimes a little more than two-inches wide, so each paragraph should be short to avoid looking too gray when a story is published. No more than two sentences per paragraph.

4) Use quotations. Use lots of quotes.

"The new scanning system will make checking out a book easier for all the library staff," said Library Director Betty Bookbinder.

Make sure you punctuate the quote in the same way as the example.

Paragraph one is your lead. Paragraph two amplifies the lead and explains some of the feature components. Put a quotation high in the

---

Tip: Avoid trademark woes.

A warning!

Beware of the power of words, not just to uplift and comfort or inform and entertain, but to violate the law. Note the precise language of this letter regarding trademark misuse. A general counsel for Kransco Group Companies in San Francisco, California, spotted a reference to one of its products in a little known community newspaper in Shippensburg, Pennsylvania, a town near Gettysburg. The attorney wrote, "I am writing to you because one of our company's registered trademarks (Frisbee) appears in the above mentioned," a photograph captioned, "Frisbee frivolity."

The letter went on to give three guidelines to mentioning Frisbee. The common name "disc" should follow the trademark Frisbee, as in Frisbee disc. The attorney also suggested that the symbol for registered trademark be used, but acknowledged that some publications do not have that symbol on the keyboard.

Finally, the attorney urged the publication not to use Frisbee as a noun as in "Let's play Frisbee," because the word is an adjective describing a specialized disc.

You may be wondering, so what's all the huff? The problem is that promotion of trademarks is costly, and if they aren't protected, the trademarks can become generic names. For this reason, it is important for mass media writers to refer to products by precise names.

For instance, you may want to take two Bufferin tablets, or you may settle for two aspirins. Notice the capitalization. If you want to photocopy this page, you would use a photocopy machine or a Xerox machine if it's available. You don't want to make a Xerox. You can reach for a carbonated beverage but be sure you want a Coca-Cola if you ask for this product using the formal name.

story at about paragraph three. End your story with a quote and put some quotes in between.

5) Interview at least three people about the story.

Get quotes and background information from them. Ask at least three people about the issue, but don't necessarily ask each one the same question.

6) Always double-check the spelling of names. Even the name Smith can be spelled Smyth, Smythe, Smithe and so on. Misspelled names are inexcusable. For students, include class status and major. Senior Joyce Mills, a psychology major, said, "I'd give the president a B for his foreign policy because it's always late and not very neat." For adults, provide some identification of their profession or vocation and address. Often, the person's age is included because readers tend to rank others in terms of their age.

7) Always type your story notes as soon as you finish the interview. You will think more clearly and write with more ease by following this simple edict.

8) Meet your deadlines.

9) Watch mistakes such as spelling, comma splices and pronoun agreement. Use the spelling checker function on the computer.

Biography of George Archibald

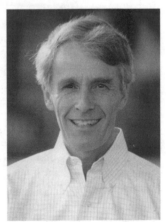

George Archibald has covered Congress, the federal government, and national politics in Washington for 22 years and has been a senior investigative reporter for *The Washington Times* since he broke the Geraldine Ferraro financial ethics story in 1984.

He is the newspaper's national education reporter. He has been nominated for the Pulitzer Prize in journalism four times. He reports as a former government insider, having also run a congressional office, served as a budget policy staffer on the

George Archibald

House Appropriations Committee, and briefly as a deputy assistant secretary of education during the Reagan administration. His 28 years as a newspaperman include six years as editor and general manager of college, military, and community newspapers.

Archibald's first job out of high school in 1962 was as an assistant for the late national Mutual Network radio news commentator Fulton Lewis, Jr. He went on to be editor of his college newspaper at Old Dominion University in Norfolk, Va., where he earned a degree in political science and history. He was editor of an Air Force newspaper while stationed at a pilot-training base in Arizona for four years during the Vietnam era. After military service, he was a staff writer, letters editor, and editorial pages makeup editor for *The Arizona Republic* in Phoenix from 1970 to 1973.

During the remainder of the 1970s in Washington, D.C., he was a press secretary, legislative assistant, chief of staff and Appropriations Committee aide for two Republican Arizona congressmen. In 1976, he opened and managed the Washington office of the American Legislative Exchange Council, a conservative state legislators' group, and helped produce ALEC's first book of suggested state legislation. Archibald served on President Reagan's Transition Team at the National Science Foundation and co-authored the education chapter of the Heritage Foundation's heralded report to the incoming president, *Mandate for Leadership*.

In 1981, he was budget specialist for President Reagan's assistant secretary for legislation at the U.S. Department of Health and Human Services. Archibald joined a pre-publication team that started *The Washington Times* in January 1982 and was the newspaper's first reporter hired for the national news desk.

He covered federal budget and Social Security reform battles on Capitol Hill before becoming an investigative reporter. The paper nominated him first for the Pulitzer Prize for breaking the Ferraro story the day she was nominated for Vice President in July 1984, and again with Paul Rodriguez for breaking the Barney Frank-Washington scandal in 1989.

Following Clinton's election, he left Washington from 1993-94 to return to community journalism as editor-general manager of *The Warren Sentinel* in Front Royal, Va., a weekly owned by Byrd Newspapers. Among many awards, he personally won the Virginia Press Association's first-place editorial writing award and second-place for a community news series on fire and emergency services.

With a greatly improved news product, he also dramatically increased *The Sentinel*'s circulation and advertising revenue before *The Washington Times* recruited him back to investigative reporting. After rejoining *The Times*, he covered waste, fraud, and abuse in the federal government and has been the newspaper's senior education reporter since 2002. Archibald has four daughters. He is listed in *Who's Who in America*.

Editor's note: George Archibald has made a career of writing on deadline. His story follows this brief introduction.

Writing on deadline leans on 5 W's and a passion for news

George Henry Archibald brings passion to the business of writing. He's from the old school that sees the role of a writer as a kind of poet who serves no master. Writing, and journalism in particular, is a noble calling to right wrongs, set the record straight and give voice to the powerless. It sounds a bit sentimental, but it is based on an experience George Archibald's father, George William Archibald, encountered that shaped his worldview, and ultimately, the thinking of the junior George himself. George's father raced horses for most of his life. At the onset of World War II, George Sr. found himself in Great Britain in a country with war fever.

Although he was an American, George's father joined a tank corps and distinguished himself throughout the liberation of France, Belgium and Holland, and was mentioned in King George VI's dispatches for valor during the Battle of the Bulge. His medals included two British bronze stars and the King's 1939-1945 campaign medals. He proudly wore his uniform and medals on horseback in June 1952 as leader of Queen Elizabeth II's Coronation celebration in Newmarket, the headquarters of British thoroughbred horseracing.

By the end of World War II, however, when the senior Archibald was ready to return to the United States, the American consulate refused to honor a request for a renewed passport. They said George Sr. had pledged an oath of allegiance to a foreign power, England. No amount of paperwork or rationale would sway the leadership and citizenship was denied.

For journalist George Archibald, the system with all its checks and balances is a marvel, but one that can choke when the bureaucracy swells with rigidity that suffers no exemptions. His father's painful encounter of doing his duty at the expense of his citizenship provided the motivation to hunt down government inefficiency and expose it. After a career in government reporting, George Archibald sees his mission as informing others on public policy issues. He knows that the best feature writers have internalized the ability to arrange the facts of an article from most important to least important while keeping a lively tempo. News reporters often arrange the facts like Dominoes, one after the other. The feature writer keeps this order in mind while working to weave information throughout in a kind of web.

In late 1997, his editor asked him to pen an obituary on a political figure. George knew he had to write fast, but resorted to a feature story approach to include quotations, anecdotes and the kind of background that will help readers who are unfamiliar with the name L. Brent Bozell understand his impact in the world of visceral politics. His article is a sophisticated combination of the Domino approach woven together with a theme that this fallen figure, while controversial, was a person who is worth remembering for his influence in the shaping of the political landscape.

In preparing for the article, George called Bozell's friends to get their reactions. For conservatives, this ordinary obituary served as a kind of eulogy to a movement as well as a man. The following is a Question-and-Answer piece on George Archibald's feature article, **L. Brent Bozell dies.**

Interview with George Archibald

Q: Sometimes the 5 W's have to be asked over and over again as new topics are introduced in an article. What main questions did you want to answer in this piece?

A: The most important question to answer was, "Who was Brent Bozell?" That's a name most readers wouldn't know, a strong-willed American Catholic who was at the center of most important political events from the 1950s to the 1980s. What did he do? He wrote Joe McCarthy's pivotal, undiplomatic, in-your-face speech that doomed him in the U.S. Senate; founded *National Review* magazine with his brother-in-law, Bill Buckley, in the 1950s, the seminal magazine for American conservatives; and went on to ghost-write Barry Goldwater's pivotal book, *Conscience of a Conservative*, which led the way to Ronald Reagan's love for Goldwater conservatism and a TV endorsement in 1964 that paved the way for the Reagan Revolution of the 1980s and 1990s. What was his impact? This largely unknown, tall, thin, red-headed, strongly traditional Catholic intellectual with a gift for writing common-man's prose was, perhaps, the most important "who" of two or three political generations.

Why, how? Because he knew how to transmit generations of political wisdom and culture in a few well-chosen words, imparted by others who had star-power, and made the words resonate throughout the public. Most quotable quotes of the libertarian-conservative Goldwater-Reagan era of 1950 to 1980 came from Brent Bozell's pen or typewriter.

Q: Openings are crucial to articles. Other than the standard opening for an obituary, what did you want to emphasize in your lead, your first sentence? And why?

A: The death of an icon, who helped birth an era of freedom and prosperity for people throughout the world. I wanted to draw readers into the story–people who knew this man, and loved him, to know that his place in history was recognized. And for those readers who had never heard of this man, to help them realize and appreciate the important contributions he had made and the reasons we were all better off for his life's work.

15

A lead is supposed to draw people into your story, and you want readers to stay with the entire story, so every sentence must be carefully written to provide details and keep the reader. I also hoped this piece would sow seeds among younger readers and help motivate them to a personal commitment, in their own way, to help continue this man's fruit through the written word. Knowing Brent Bozell's vital legacy, I closed my eyes after writing and refining each sentence, thinking of the next generations of writers and media professionals who will hopefully continue growing the crops of freedom and prosperity for people throughout the world, transmitting our culture through the written and spoken word, perhaps more motivated by his one life's example.

Figure important to conservatives[1]

By George Archibald,
Copyright © 1997 News World Communications, Inc.
Reprinted with permission of The Washington Times. This reprint does not constitute or imply any endorsement or sponsorship of any product, service, company or organization.

L. Brent Bozell, a founder of the modern conservative movement who propelled Sen. Barry Goldwater to national political prominence in the 1960s, was buried yesterday in Washington.

Scores of conservative leaders throughout the country flew to the nation's capital to pay their last respects and eulogize Mr. Bozell, 71, who ghost-wrote Mr. Goldwater's *Conscience of a Conservative*–which launched the Arizona Republican on his way to the 1964 GOP presidential nomination–and co-founded *National Review* magazine with William F. Buckley Jr.

Mr. Bozell died Tuesday of pneumonia and was buried yesterday at St. Mary's Cemetery on Lincoln Road in Northeast after a Roman Catholic Mass at Our Lady of Carmel Church.

"He was one of the most brilliant and bravest of the young lions of the first generation of modern conservatism," said Pat Buchanan, former Republican presidential candidate and co-host of CNN's "Crossfire."

"And the longer time went on, the stronger he got in the faith," Mr. Buchanan said, "and he never compromised."

---

[1] Archibald, G. (1997, April 19). L. Brent Bozell dies; helped start modern conservatism; Was powerful force behind Joe McCarthy, Goldwater. *The Washington Times*, p. A2.

In the early years of Soviet communist expansionism in the 1950s, Mr. Bozell was a close friend and key adviser of Sen. Joseph R. McCarthy, Wisconsin Republican and anti-communist firebrand censured by the Senate for obstructing the legislative process.

In fact, Mr. Bozell wrote Mr. McCarthy's 1954 speech that tipped the tide against him, Mr. Buckley recalled yesterday.

"Edward Bennett Williams, who was defending McCarthy, thought it was pretty well fixed so the Senate would vote against censure, and then came McCarthy's thunderous speech that senators for censure would go down in history as 'handmaidens of communism.' It was utterly undiplomatic," Mr. Buckley said. "I just thought it was a hell of a speech."

Mr. Bozell was married to Mr. Buckley's sister, Patricia. "He was the most incisive political orator I ever knew," said *National Review's* founding editor and host of public television's "Firing Line" interview show. "His mind was sharp and he had consummate skills in organizing thoughts in readable and persuasive language."

Mr. Buckley and Mr. Bozell co-authored *McCarthy and His Enemies*, which publisher Alfred Regnery said is still "one of the primary sources of the history of the McCarthy controversy." Still in demand, the book was republished last year, Mr. Regnery said.

Mr. Bozell gave conservative ideas widespread popularity in the early days of the movement, said William A. Rusher, founding publisher of *National Review*.

"Thirty-five to 40 years ago, Brent Bozell was the political golden-boy of conservatism–far more so than his brother-in-law Bill Buckley, because Buckley was primarily an intellectual and Brent had marvelous gifts as a political personality," Mr. Rusher said.

"He was a towering figure for those of us who grew up in the late '50s and early '60s, a great writer," said Kenneth Y. Tomlinson, former editor in chief of *Reader's Digest* and director of Voice of America during the Reagan administration.

The Goldwater book was "the bible of the early conservative movement" that provided "the philosophical and rhetorical framework for the building of the political movement that culminated in Ronald Reagan's election," Mr. Tomlinson said. David A. Keene, a co-founder of Young Americans for Freedom and later national manager of George Bush's presidential primary campaign against Mr. Reagan in 1980, said the Goldwater manifesto remains the movement's "most influential book."

"It not only catapulted Barry Goldwater to the GOP presidential nomination and therefore facilitated the conservative takeover of the GOP. If you asked 50 conservative Republicans of my generation today what was the most influential political writing that they had read, 45 of them are going to say *Conscience of a Conservative*." Mr. Keene said.

"It stands up pretty well 43 years later, which can't be said of many books from any point on the spectrum."

"Even though illness forced Brent Bozell to drop out as an active participant in the conservative political debates, I never cease to be amazed how many college-age political thinkers in the '90s are familiar with his legacy and writings," said Jeffrey Nelson of the Intercollegiate Studies Institute. "His criticism of the judicial usurpation of the political process was ahead of its time."

Exercises

Re-read the article. Think about George Archibald's article and compare it to the crash course list on page 8.
1) What is the conflict in this article?
2) This article is an obituary written in a feature style. What's the main idea of the article?
3) What is the shortest sentence? What is the longest sentence? Does the piece have a good variety of long and short sentences?
4) What is the best quotation in the piece?
5) If you had been assigned to write this article, what would you have done differently?

Here's another feature article by George Archibald. How does this tone differ from the first article?

Lynne Cheney touts books for children[2]
By George Archibald
Copyright © 2003 News World Communications, Inc.
Reprinted with permission of The Washington Times. This reprint does not constitute or imply any endorsement or sponsorship of any product, service, company or organization.

Lynne Cheney invited 33 D.C. schoolchildren to her home yesterday to talk about the importance of courage.

"What do you think courage means?" the wife of Vice President Dick Cheney asked the 8- and 9-year-olds who surrounded her on the front veranda of the vice-presidential residence at the Naval Observatory.

"Bravery," said Brenda Perlera, one of the third-graders from Marie H. Reed Learning Center in Northwest.

---

[2] http://www.washtimes.com/national/20030603-115716-7328r.htm

"Not to be afraid and to stand up for oneself," Roberto Reyes responded.

Mrs. Cheney introduced a list of 15 books on the theme of freedom that leading historians, authors, and librarians say should be on every youngster's reading list.

The fiction and nonfiction selections include Stephen Crane's *The Red Badge of Courage*, Frederick Douglass' account of his escape from slavery, Mark Twain's *The Adventures of Huckleberry Finn*, Laura Ingalls Wilder's *Little House on the Prairie*, Harper Lee's *To Kill a Mockingbird*, and John F. Kennedy's *Profiles in Courage*.

Yesterday's event was part of a $100 million "We the People" program started by President Bush through the National Endowment for the Humanities to teach youngsters more about American history and culture.

Mrs. Cheney read the children Langston Hughes' poem *Dreams*, with its famous line, *Hold fast to dreams*. She asked the children what dreams they have.

"To be president," Diego Fuentes said.

"That's a great dream to have," Mrs. Cheney said. "But I also think that even if you just have a high goal like that, and maybe only get to be vice president, it's OK."

Ali Malik said he dreamed of being an archaeologist. "That's a great dream to have," Mrs. Cheney said, "and you can find out how things were a long time ago."

The NEH's "We the People" Bookshelf Program will offer the books to 500 libraries across the country, said Bruce Cole, the endowment's chairman.

The aim of the program is to encourage young people to read classic literature and explore the ideas and ideals of America, he said. Mrs. Cheney was NEH chairman during the first Bush administration.

Teachers Angela Sims, Sammy Ferguson and Principal John B. Sparrow joined their children at yesterday's event.

"The books they have chosen are definitely age-appropriate and should be in any child's library," Mrs. Sims said in an interview.

She said the event with Mrs. Cheney was "a spectacular experience" for the children, "very much up-close and personal; she was a great storyteller."

"Books not only feed our minds, they steady our souls," Mrs. Cheney says in NEH's literature about the program. "They show us how people in other times and places met adversity and triumphed over it."

Mr. Cole, an art historian, accompanied Mrs. Cheney.

"Books are really important because they can take you to all sorts of places," the NEH chairman told the children. "They take you into the past, say 200 years ago, and they can take you into the future. And you can meet through books all sorts of interesting people, animals and other neat things. If you have a book, you have terrific companionship. You're never alone when you have a book."

Sidebar on Cheney's suggested reading list.
By George Archibald
Copyright © 2003 News World Communications, Inc.
Reprinted with permission of The Washington Times. This reprint does not constitute or imply any endorsement or sponsorship of any product, service, company or organization.

Readings on courage.

Lynne Cheney, wife of Vice President Dick Cheney, and the National Endowment for the Humanities yesterday released a recommended list of books for children and youth on the theme of courage. They are:

Kindergarten through grade 3:
- *The Cabin Faced West* by Jean Fritz
- *Anansi the Spider* by Gerald McDermott
- *Sylvester and the Magic Pebble* by William Steig

Grades 4 through 6:
- *The Matchlock Gun* by Walter D. Edmonds
- *The Dream Keeper and Other Poems* by Langston Hughes
- *My Side of the Mountain* by Jean Craighead George
- *Little House on the Prairie* by Laura Ingalls Wilder

Grades 7 and 8:
- *Johnny Tremain* by Esther Forbes
- *Narrative of the Life of Frederick Douglass* by Frederick Douglass
- *The Hobbit* by J.R.R. Tolkien

Grades 9 through 12:
- *The Red Badge of Courage* by Stephen Crane
- *Invisible Man* by Ralph Ellison
- *Profiles in Courage* by John F. Kennedy
- *Adventures of Huckleberry Finn* by Mark Twain
- *To Kill a Mockingbird* by Harper Lee

Which article did you prefer? Why? Is there something you noticed in each article that can help you as you write? Here's another example of a feature story that uses the 5 W's. Can you identify them?

A couple of cutups in Central Pennsylvania
By Michael Ray Smith

SHIPPENSBURG, Pa.–The eagle has landed on the totem pole in front of Crider's Meat Market in Central Pennsylvania.

But, wait, that's no eagle–it's a vulture with an uneasy eye on the products at Crider's.

"I call it Mr. BuzZARD," says Joe Kelso, who worked with Bill Commerer to carve the 1,000-pound totem pole just off Interstate 81 in Shippensburg, a community 50 miles south of Harrisburg.

The vulture is just one of Kelso's good-humored jabs at his cousin Jake Crider, president of Crider's Meats.

"I'm just glad it's pointed toward town," said Crider.

The totem pole was erected in December and customers are delighted.

"One lady told me that she wanted to take it home," said Crider. Another contacted Kelso's co-carver Commerer about carving a mailbox post for her.

Kelso and Commerer, both of Shippensburg, worked nearly two summers carving eight faces, the vulture, and even an airplane on the cedar pole, once a utility pole for Crider's Market. When he upgraded his electrical service, a new utility pole was installed and Crider kept the old one.

"I told Joe that I was going to carve a totem pole," Crider said. "That's when Joe said, 'No, I'll do it!'"

Totem poles were once used by Native Americans to honor a high-ranking member of the group who died. Although the poles vary in function, many displayed crest figures.

"I wanted to be faithful to the Indian art," said Kelso, 66. Although the faces and designs on the pole reflect traditional Indian art, Kelso also managed to include a design of something modern, the airplane. A small airport is located near the meat market.

Kelso and Commerer used wood grinders and small power tools to produce a bear with a cub, an Indian mask and other intricate designs, painted in colorful patterns.

"Joe's related to Tonto way back," quipped Commerer of his friend. Both are members of the Cumberland Valley Wood Carvers, a group that meets each month at the nearby mall to talk about their hobby.

Commerer started carving more than 20 years ago when he whittled while camping. He produced decorative walking sticks.

"I love carving," said Commerer. "You take a cedar log and see a knot or a hole and think to yourself what you can make of it. You look at the wood and try to see what may be there."

Although Commerer has been whittling for more than two decades, he didn't begin the kind of elaborate carving he does now until 1991. It began when he carved a small dog and he joined the wood carving club.

He used his father's old Barlow and Shrade penknives, but has moved on to professional wood-carving tools. He likes to carve in the open air beside his apartment or use a basement shop as a retreat.

Commerer keeps his tools in wooden cigar boxes or lovingly sprawled across an old rug. The air of his workshop is redolent with wood aromas. On the bench are wooden figures running track, toting lunch pails or smoking cigars. Wizards with peaked hats and waterfalls of beards stand sentry on his shelves.

"The best way to learn about wood-carving is to join a club," he says. Club members teach each other using techniques they study and practice between meetings.

Since retiring from a ball-bearing manufacturer, Commerer says woodcarving keeps him active. His wife, Peg, also works with crafts and the two of them manage some good-natured rivalry.

"I sell more than he does," Peg said proudly of her plastic canvas crafts.

Both Kelso and Commerer are preparing for a new totem pole project.

"This time we'll settle for a six-foot pole," Kelso said with a wink.

Exercises

1) Re-read this story. What is the conflict in this feature article?
2) Identify some of the parts of the article. Find the dateline. Datelines contain the city name, entirely in capital letters, followed by the name of the state. New writers often consult the *Associated Press Stylebook and Briefing on Media Law*,[3] better known as the AP Stylebook. Large cities such as Atlanta, Baltimore and Chicago can stand-alone.
3) Find the byline. A byline identifies the writer.

---

[3] Goldstein, N. (2000). *Associated Press stylebook and briefing on media law with internet guide and glossary.* New York: The Associated Press. The book is available through other publishers.

4) Find the headline. A headline is the partial sentence that sums up the article. Use the present tense when composing one.

5) A version of this article first appeared in the May-June 1995 *Chip Chats* magazine, a publication of the National Wood Carvers Association. This is a specialty magazine for wood carving enthusiasts. Can you think of an article that you can write for a specialty magazine?

Rookies and prose:
Words to master

Affect, effect

These are troubling words. The best approach may be to avoid them. One way to remember which is which is to memorize that affect, when used as a verb, means to influence. When affect is used as a noun it suggests an emotional state, but writers should avoid this usage.

- Verb: *Eating fatty foods may adversely affect your health.*

Effect can be both a verb and a noun. As a noun, it means result. As a verb it means to cause, which is why I use the cause and effect mnemonic.

- Noun: *The effect of too much running was blisters.*
- Verb: *Avoiding fatty foods may effect an improvement in your health.*

Allude and elude

Allude is different from the word refer and the word elude. Allude means to make an indirect reference without specifically mentioning it.

- *Joe alluded to the poor grade.*

Refer means to say something directly.

- *With a sign, Joe referred to his mass media writing grade.*

Elude means to evade or escape.

- *When Joe saw his teacher coming, he eluded him by ducking into the men's room.*

Advertisement, add

An advertisement is a paid message. In general, the person or organization placing an advertisement may print the message exactly as he or she wants the message to appear, short of libel or bad taste. An advertisement, commonly called an ad, is different from news. The staff writes news copy except in the smallest of newspaper operations. News includes feature articles.

- *The display advertisement depicted an elephant in a swimming suit.*

The word "add," meaning to increase, is sometimes erroneously written when the writer meant the abbreviation for advertisement or "ad."

- *The ad manager added the number of column inches in the section.*

Addition, edition

This pair also causes confusion in mass media writing. Again, addition is the process of adding, but edition refers to a publication.

- *Addition is the best way to gain loyal readers and well-edited editions are the means.*

Aid, aide

Aid is a verb and means to help.

- *Editors aid writers in the process of crafting good prose.*

Aide is a noun and means an assistant.

- *The aide will finish the chore.*

Editing symbols to master

- ☐ Indicate "abbreviate street" by circling it.
  He lives at 12 34 Ross Street.
- ☐ Close up the space between 2 and 3 by using sideways parenthesis marks.
  He lives at 12 34 Ross Street.
- ☐ Use a caret mark to show insertion of a dash between "two" and "story."
  He lives at two story on 1234 Ross St.
- ☐ Delete the 4. Use a loop mark.
  He lives at 12344 Ross St.
- ☐ Indent at the word "He." Make a right-angle mark.
He lives at 1234 Ross St.
- ☐ Insert space at the number 4. Use a tic-tac-toe mark, #.
  He lives at 1234Ross St.

☐ Indicate paragraph. Use a backward P.
He lives at 1234 Ross St.

☐ Indicate period at the end of the sentence. Use a caret symbol with a dot inside.
He lives at 1234 Ross St

☐ Spell out street. Circle street.
He lives on Ross St.

☐ Indicate stet, which means "ignore the edit." Write the word, "stet" after the word, "One."
He lives at One Ross St.

☐ Indicate transpose. Use a serpentine mark to separate letters.
He lives at 1243 Ross St.

☐ Indicate the end by writing 30 or ###.

Now, check yourself below and see how the editing symbols should really look. When an editor makes corrections, it will look a lot like this.

☐ Indicate "abbreviate street" by circling it.
He lives at 1234 Ross Street.

☐ Close up the space between 2 and 3 by using sideways parenthesis marks.
He lives at 1234 Ross Street.

☐ Use a caret mark to show insertion of a dash between "two" and "story."
He lives at two story house on 1234 Ross St.

☐ Delete the 4. Use a loop mark.
He lives at 12344 Ross St.

☐ Indent at the word "He." Make a right-angle mark.
He lives at 1234 Ross St.

☐ Insert space at the number 4. Use a tic-tac-toe mark, #.
He lives at 1234 Ross St.

☐ Indicate paragraph. Use a backward P.
He lives at 1234 Ross St.

☐ Indicate period at the end of the sentence. Use a circle symbol with a dot inside.
He lives at 1234 Ross St.

☐ Spell out street. Circle street.
He lives on Ross St.

☐ Indicate stet, which means "ignore the edit." Write the word, "stet" after the word, "One."
He lives at One Ross St.

☐ Indicate transpose. Use a serpentine mark to separate letters.
He lives at 1243 Ross St.

☐ Indicate the end by writing 30 or ###.
–30–

Try your hand at using editing symbols in the following article.

In my twenty-seventh year, while riding the metro in Leningrad, I was over come with despair so great that life seemed to stop at once, preempting the future entirely let alone any meaning. Suddenly, all by

25

itself, a phrase appeared: Without God life makes no sense.. Repeating it in astonishment, I rode the phrase up like a moving staircase, got out of the metro and into God's light and carried on living. Faith is the only trust and the rarest ofgifts. Exaggeration without faith dangerous is whether man recognizes the existence of God or denies it. If man does recognize it, his misinterpreting leads him down the path of idolatry so that he ends up idolizing both the random and the particular. If man denies God, he is certain to take the particular for the whole and the random for the regular, becoming imprisoned by the logic of denial.

Andrew Bitov, Soviet novelist, in *Life* magazine's issue on The Meaning of Life.

1) Use the symbol for indent to show a paragraph at the first sentence.
2) Use the symbol to close up the space in the word "overcome."
3) Insert a dash after "entirely" and before "let."
4) Delete the extra period after "makes no sense."
5) Insert a space between "of" and "gifts."
6) Transpose the words "dangerous" and "is."

A final word on conflict

Among the salient points in this chapter is the idea of conflict as a necessary part of any media artifact, particularly news, and that includes a feature article. Fictional newspaper editor Bob Miles Jr. of *The Harmony Herald* learned that his small town of Harmony wasn't much interested in conflict. "So Bob decided to get out of the news business and confine his reporting to weddings, graduations, church happenings, and gardening. A doomsday cult could poison the New York City water supply and kill a million people, and Bob would write about Bea Majors having Sunday dinner at her sister Opal's house."[4] Bob is meant to be a humorous caricature of a hard-driving editor to underline the idea that conflict may be overrated. That content may appeal to some readers, but most of us want some edge on our news.

It doesn't take much; just enough to make flesh-and-blood people wonder about the contest of life. Who is winning, who won, who should win? This simplistic idea of winning and losing is just another way to frame conflict. If it doesn't help you internalize the concept, discard it. Instead, retain the idea that your audience expects you to give them information of value. Be sure to ask yourself, "Why does this information matter?" Once you've written the piece, ask yourself, "Would I read this piece if I hadn't written it?" If the answers to those questions aren't

---

[4] Gulley, P. (2000). *Home to Harmony*. Sisters, OR: Multnomah Publishers, p. 31.

satisfying, rework your piece. Don't settle for second-rate work, if it's not up to your high standards. All writing is re-writing, and no ink spot is satisfied with submitting a first draft for the audience she loves too much for second-rate prose. You will succeed, but you have to invest the sweat equity to make the article work well. You may never write the perfect book, perfect article or even the perfect sentence, but with perseverance, you will go from mediocre to half-bad to better than average, and with time, words that seem to have a home in harmony.

Summary

The chapter examined the role of conflict in an article. Without **conflict**, an article has no depth charges and is pinched and narrow. It is weak and likely to take a break just to catch its breath. An interview with a source can help a writer identify the inherent conflict by thinking about the timeliness, the proximity, the impact, the unusualness, even the human interest of the topic or event. These elements also lead the writer to select the best **news peg** or **angle** to frame the article. Once the conflict has been identified, a writer can use a series of questions, better known as the 5 W's, to collect the pertinent information that is necessary for all articles. An article by George Archibald served as an example on using the **5 W's**. Another article on woodcarving provided an introduction to the use of a valuable reference guide, the AP Stylebook, as the default style in most feature writing. The chapter concluded with some tricky words to know and a list of editing symbols. Conflict is not something that we seek in our personal lives, but it is essential in writing for the mass media. Inhale it through the mouth, and let readers enjoy a deep cleansing breath.

Chapter 2

Getting started and mastering the lead
FeatureWriting.Net/NowWhat

Chapter at-a-glance

> ➤ Examining the summary lead
> ➤ Selecting the appropriate opening
> ➤ Considering fictional techniques in non-fiction writing

Writing for mass media is different from fiction, yet the best non-fiction relies on fictional techniques such as drama and dialogue. The most outstanding difference is that mass media writers never suffer from **writer's block**, the inability to formulate a developed idea. In mass media, the material for the assignment is defined by the assignment; therefore, the writer won't have to worry about what to say, only how to say it.

Throughout this book, feature story ideas and approaches will be explored in the context of news. Ideas abound and part of your job will be to recognize them. Online enterprise alone allows any of us to formulate an idea and trot it out without a deep investment. One writer made a modest livelihood by writing about his experiences living on the street. Writer Kevin Barbieux's web site is www.TheHomelessGuy.

The hardest part of writing is getting started. Where do you begin?

net.[5] Barbieux calls himself the homeless guy and says his web site received 15,000 hits one day after Yahoo.com mentioned his site on its new-and-notable list. Barbieux blogs - online talk for a free-form diarist style of Web logs - from Nashville about his efforts to get off the streets and build a normal life. He talks about what it's like in the world of the homeless and offers his ideas on finding good meals. The site includes a "tip jar" button that allows visitors to use their credit cards to deposit money in his bank account, and he once received a donation of $1,000.

Another challenge to traditional writers-for-hire are the ubiquitous web sites for personal information such as photographs. In mid-2004, moblogs became popular. According to The Dallas Morning News, moblogs (pronounced *moe'logs*), combine the features of the Internet with photographs taken with a cellular telephone. Users take the photographs and post them on a web site.[6] A modest deviation from this idea is the video blogger or vloggers, writers who use the Web to post personal articles supplemented by video clips.[7] The problem with these kinds of stream-of-conscious sites is that they are raw and unedited. As a writer, you bring to your audience your own filters of good humor, good taste and good writing.

Writing can pay, but you must be ahead of the curve. Take a lesson from Dr. Norman Vincent Peale of *The Power of Positive Thinking* fame. He suggests that all of us spend 15 minutes a day in quiet. The idea is to make your mind still. When the mind becomes like a tranquil pool of water, deep and creative thoughts can form. His counsel is to avoid thinking; instead allow the mind to rest. Out of this restive state may come ideas that you can use in your career, not just to write, but to soar with the angels.

As a writer, you are ever vigilant for article ideas. Next, you must think about the story that you are crafting and make the decision on how best to write it. The first portion of this book will examine the conventions of writing news to prepare you to take the feature approach, often considered the supplemental way of learning about topics, events, places and people. A feature story can be the second view, often read or watched because the audience chooses this content. The news approach can be a warm up for the main event, the feature article. For this reason, an understanding of news writing will be examined as the foundation for all the concepts that follow.

---

[5] Kornblum, J. (2002, October 3). A homeless guy finds a refuge on the Internet. *USA TODAY*, p. 10D.

[6] Bebell, D. (2004, April 7). "Moblogs" could give rise to new journalism. *The (Raleigh) News & Observer*, p. 6F.

[7] Ressner, J. (2004, April 19). See me, blog me. *Time*, p. 98.

The concept of NEWS

One ancient idea about **NEWS** is that it stands for North, East, West and South,[8] the intelligence from all points of the compass. News may be defined as reports of information of interest to an audience. One of my editors liked to say news is what she said it was. True, but news can be generally understood to be concerned with people in high places, people in low places and those in between – you and me. News concerns events, issues, the little known and overblown. It is about correcting false or distorted reports, and reminding audiences of information that was lost or forgotten with an attempt to set the record straight. News is more about recent history, the now, rather than the past – timeliness. It's about events closer to home, rather than farther away – proximity. News is about the unusual and the controversial of the culture, along with the celebration and defeat of the human condition. It is about celebrity and celebrities, as well as conspirators and consequence.

That last category is the one that feature writers often consult to write profile articles, how-to pieces, or a different view on a topic that is in the news. As you craft your feature article, remember that you are still providing news – you're telling an audience

> **Tip:** When a media writer talks to a source, the first question that he or she should ask is the person's name. If the person won't give you her name, any other information is nearly useless. After you ask for the person's name, write it down and show what you've written to your source. Ask, "Is this correct?" The person will spy any misspelling. People who use this technique will never have a source accuse them of shoddy work, but be advised. Even veteran reporters can get careless.

something that is new to them. Often the news is event-oriented. A speaker comes to town and you get an assignment to cover the speech or interview the person. In either case, the writer selects the information he or she wants to use based on an understanding of news. The article may take the form of a **profile** on the new mayor after her first 100 days in office, or it may explore a family who must endure loneliness as a parent fights in a war thousands of miles away.

Getting started means examining the essence of the assignment to determine the best angle for the presentation. Regardless of the form,

---

[8] Hoffman, D. (2000). *Who knew? Things you didn't know about things you know well.* New York: MJF books, Pine Communications, p. 141.

whether it's a speech story or a personality profile, the writer will be asking herself, "So what's new?"

What's new?

The best way to answer the **"What's new?"** question is to role play with yourself or a friend. Pretend you just went to a government meeting or met with a prominent businessman who is giving $10,000 to build a new shelter for homeless people. Your notebook is brimming with pithy quotes and descriptions of the scene.

You have so much information that you are hard-pressed to get started. That's when you turn to a friend and have him or her ask this question: "In one sentence, tell me, 'What's new?'" Getting a friend to ask this question will force the writer to clearly articulate a response; however, a writer can play this game in his or her head. Pose the question, then answer it.

If this question doesn't do the trick, try a variation. Have your accomplice ask: "In one sentence, tell me, 'What happened?'"

If you are still fumbling to reduce the information to a statement, try yet another variation, this one a directive rather than a question. "In one sentence, tell me the most interesting action, fact or idea that you just heard."

By compressing the story idea into one sentence, you are fashioning a crude lead, the first sentence of your report. The lead, also known as the lede, is the hook you hope will make your reader, and listener, want to stay with you. The lead is crucial to your report. These days readers often abandon an article after only six paragraphs, so it's our job to make them want to read on.

Leads

Leads are like tools in a tool box. A tool is designed for a specific job. While a screwdriver may be used to hammer a nail, it isn't recommended. In some cases, the wrong tool just won't work. Try using a claw hammer to remove a sticky screw. Nonetheless, some tools just get more of a workout by virtue of their usefulness. Hammers, for instance, fulfill a deep desire in many of us to strike objects, even when we're not trying to be constructive. This tool is used over and over and over again. In the worst case, a person with a hammer sees every article as a nail.

The hammer may be compared to a type of lead known as the summary lead. This lead packs the sentence with all the essential information to understand the article.

Summary leads

A summary lead provides preferably a one-sentence, and not more than a two-sentence summary of the article. Summary leads may be up to 35 or 40 words in newspapers such as *The New York Times*, considered the premium newspaper in the United States. *The New York Times* is known for its international news coverage and its coverage of public affairs including reprints of speeches.

These summary leads are long because they are trying to answer all the questions mentioned in chapter 1, "The chocolate-covered almond," *who*, *what*, *where*, *when* and sometimes *how* and *why*. The *why* question is particularly difficult to integrate into a lead. Imagine reducing the reason something happened to a short phrase. Generally, it will take a separate sentence or a paragraph to provide the most rudimentary explanation. For instance, answering the question, "Why did the fire begin?" may be answered briefly by saying, "an electrical short sparked a fire," to a more complicated explanation on the nature of charged energy and friction.

A more common approach to the summary lead is to say who did what. The lead could be a kind of formula where two or three of the W's are answered ... but not all of them.

Who-did-what lead

Who did what? The idea is to put a person's name in the first spot and the action in the second spot.

Virtual reality artist Brenda Bennett won first place today in an art contest.

Who? Virtual reality artist Brenda Bennett.

Did what? Won an art contest.

This type of summary lead only answers two of the 5 W's yet it does the job. When writing these leads, select a strong verb that conveys action or your lead will be limp.

For instance, avoid summary leads such as this one with a weak verb.

An alcohol-dumping party occurred over the weekend at Glendale's oldest college.

In this case, the *what* is the first element followed by the *when* answer.

What? An alcohol-dumping party.

When? Over the weekend.

The verb *occurred* is very weak. In addition to being the language's most frequently misspelled word, *occurred* doesn't convey specific action.

By substituting a stronger verb, the writer sometimes can solve other problems with the lead.

For instance, take our friend Bennett. You could write:

Virtual reality artist Brenda Bennett spoke Monday night.

33

The lead answers three questions.

Who? Virtual reality Brenda Bennett.

What? Spoke.

When? Monday.

The problem: The lead doesn't tell me the topic. Since none of us know anything about Bennett, knowing what she had to say in one abbreviated phrase would be a big help.

Revised lead:

Virtual reality artist Brenda Bennett denounced the lack of sacred images produced by the majority of artists in a speech before Colson College students.

In this case, the lead tells us who said what and gives the reader some context for the remarks. This lead has the following arrangement:

Who said what?

Examples from new writers

What kind of lead would you write if you were assigned to cover one elected official's criticism of her organization? Here's the background. This happened at Franklin College when junior Deanna Barthlow published a letter to the editor of the student newspaper, criticizing her student organization for its ineffective approach to conducting business. At a meeting following the publication of her letter, the other members of the group known as the Student Senate of Franklin College, listened to her read the letter and then responded. Some agreed; others didn't. Senate President Bob Tyson responded by listing a number of accomplishments of the senate in the last six months. He went on to say that the senate exists to improve student life and suggested that the letter might be the motivation his group needed to excel.

Here's one possibility for a lead.

Junior Deanna Barthlow stirred up some controversy around campus with her letter written about ineffective student government in the Jan. 20 issue of the Express student newspaper. (For news and feature articles, the month is abbreviated when written with the day.)

While that lead sounds good, it's missing the latest news – that Senate President Bob Tyson then wanted to use the critical letter to improve his organization.

See the difference?

By playing the game, "What's new?" the writer can focus on the latest and most important development of the story in the very first sentence.

Here's a better lead.

Student senate President Bob Tyson is denying that apathy lurks within his organization in response to a negative letter published in the recent issue of the student newspaper.

This lead is an improvement over the first one because it provides a partial answer to the "What's new?" question by saying that the president doesn't agree with the letter writer. However, this lead still fails to give the reader the absolute latest in the article – the idea that the president, despite his misgivings about the letter, hopes to use it to improve the senate.

Here's a lead that puts the latest news in the lead and uses an economy of words.

The student senate is running a negative letter to make some positive changes.

The story went on to say that the senate president urged the members to return to the next meeting with a fistful of ideas to rid the organization of its inefficiency.

Regardless of the type of lead or sentence word length, a lead must be supported by the rest of the article. An article that begins with a dispute about a critical letter must maintain that focus and not veer off into some unrelated issue such as a problem with dormitories, pollution or the coming drought.

> **Tip:** While the lead above, 13 words total, may not look like the same kind of lead in *The New York Times*, it is. It summarizes the new story and gives the reader a clear idea of what to expect in the following paragraphs. Future chapters will describe other types of leads, other tools, and situations that demand an approach other than the summary lead. However, a good rule of thumb is the shorter the lead, the better. A corollary to that rule is to strive for 12 to 15 words to jumpstart your article.

All the leads about the critical letter were written by students, writers who knew no more about publishing than the person who has read thus far in this book. By concentrating on answering the "What's new?" question, you, too, will be ready to write summary leads. Tell the most important information first and the summary will be both efficient and appropriate. For practice, read a newspaper such as *The New York Times* and identify 10 summary leads. Then type, literally type, those 10 leads on a typewriter or personal computer. Feel the rhythm of the words. Notice the syntax or the word order. After typing those leads, read them out loud and get accustomed to the sound that this kind of writing makes.

Be advised. Summary leads, like any tool, work best when they are used for a specific purpose. In breaking news – news that is unexpected and ongoing – the summary lead is very useful. A news story about a kitten who survived being sucked through the city's leaf-gathering equipment, while news, lends itself to a non-summary lead. In the case of the kitten, the maintenance crew adopted it and named him–you guessed it–Hoover. More information on non-summary leads will be given in the next chapter.

Exercise

Read a publication.
1) Identify five "who-did-what" leads.
2) Write them out in longhand along with the next two sentences.
3) Now type them on a computer.
4) Study the leads. Sense the cadence. How does it sound?
5) Write a lead based on some experience that you had today.

Biography of James Watkins

James Norman Watkins has worked as an actor, author, college professor at Taylor University in Fort Wayne, Ind., construction worker, door-to-door salesman, dormitory parent at Indiana Wesleyan University, editor/editorial director at Wesley Press, factory worker (put raisins in Kellogg's Raisin Bran), graphic designer, hairstylist, magician, minister, puppeteer, singer/songwriter, speaker, truck driver, unicycle dare devil, Webmaster, and all the jobs any writer should experience to succeed.

James Watkins

These days, Watkins writes a syndicated newspaper column and speaks nationally and internationally. As an author, Jim has sold more than 1,500 articles, devotionals, editorials, hard-news stories, poems, reviews, scripts, short stories and song lyrics, and more than 100 color and black/white photographs. His work has appeared in *Time, Campus Life, The Door, Leadership* and many other national periodicals. He's written eleven books including *Characters* (comedy/dramas from Lillenas, 1993) and *Death & Beyond* (Tyndale House, 1993), which received an award of merit in *Campus Life's* Book of the Year contest. In addition, he has contributed to 10 other books.

Watkins is married to Lois and has two adult children and one son-in-love. An ordained minister in the Wesleyan Church, Watkins is a graduate of Indiana Wesleyan University with graduate work at Ball State University's School of Journalism and Purdue University's School of Communications.

Watkins crosses over from journalism to literature

Writer Keisha Hurst conducted the following interview with writer James Watkins over the Internet. Her angle is Jim's various identities. He's an ordained minister, fiction writer, journalist and syndicated columnist. Her interview examined the intersection of faith and craft as Jim writes for various audiences. An example of his work follows the interview along with his biography.

Hurst's work has appeared online. A teacher of English, she works as a writer and actor from the West Coast. She has a bachelor's degree in Speech Communications from the University of South Carolina and a master's degree in journalism from Regent University.

Interview with James Watkins

Q: What do you think of interviews over the Internet?

A: Actually, I've done a few e-interviews. As an interviewee, I love them as I can carefully choose my words and have time to do some revising. As an interviewer, it does lose a lot of the spontaneity and loses all the body language and vocal tone that add so much to an interview.

Q: Talk about *literary journalism*.

A: First, if we're defining literary journalism as telling the truth using fiction technique, then I think it is a great genre. My problem – especially with "celebrity" auto-biographies – is that the truth isn't actually honestly told, but embellished – dialog and entire scenes created ex nihilo. But, when used with honesty and integrity, it's a wonderful way to put the reader right into the story. I've used the technique in both my articles and books.

Q: What does it mean to be a Christian and a writer or a Christian and a journalist?

A: If Christian writers fit the category of "teachers" in scriptures (and I think they do), then they have a lot of responsibility. "Not many of you should act as teachers … because you know that we who teach will be judged more strictly" (James 3:1). As a journalist who is a Christian, I have a responsibility to "speak the truth in love" (Ephesians 4:15). I need to be truthful, objective, and balanced in my reporting. And I need to have a pure motive in my writing.

Q: How has your faith impacted your work?

A: I love Madeline L'Engle's answer when someone asks, "what is a Christian writer?" It is reported that she said because of her faith, what she writes is going to be Christian, whether she mentions Jesus or not. And if she is not, in the most profound sense, Christian, then what she writes is not going to be Christian, no matter how many times she invokes the name of the Lord.[9]

For instance, as a stringer for a local paper, I covered a sewer system coming to our little town. I think I covered the story from a "Christian" perspective as, again, I tried to be truthful, objective, and balanced in my reporting. Another paper covering the same meetings, often showed its prejudice on the issues and played up the community leaders' conflict over the issues. The other paper also printed a lot of errors. So, I guess you can cover sewage from a Christian and unchristian perspective, from a truthful, objective and balanced perspective or not.

Q: How has news writing affected your style of literary journalism?

A: Being schooled in journalism's "5 W's and an H," it was a bit of a stretch to incorporate good character development, setting, and conflict in literary journalism pieces. I've enjoyed the experience as I believe good literary journalism, rather than reporting simply the facts, actually takes the reader with the writer to the event or interview. I'm still more a journalist than a novelist, but I think my writing has come alive using fiction techniques to present nonfiction truth.

Q: Is there such a quality as total objectivity?

A: Never trust a reporter who claims not to have any bias on a story he or she is covering. We all have a point of view. As a Christian who is trying to be a person of integrity, I need to be aware of that bias and overcome it.

Q: Do you feel that your faith has affected what you write or write about?

A: Definitely! As a reporter, you really don't have a choice of subjects. As a columnist (which I enjoy most), I have the freedom to choose what I write about. Because I'm writing for a secular paper, I try to limit "religious" subjects to about once a month.

As a person of faith, I also knew I had to "speak the truth in love." Another passage, that has sort of become my "mission statement" for a Christian who is writing in the secular media is Colossians 4:2-6: "Devote yourselves to prayer, being watchful and thankful. And pray for us to, too,

---

[9] For an outstanding feature article on Madeleine L'Engle, see Zarin, C. (2004, April 12). The storyteller. *The New Yorker*, pp. 60-67.

that God may open a door for our message, so that we may proclaim it clearly, as I should. Be wise in the way you act toward outsiders; make the most of every opportunity. Let your conversation be always full of grace, seasoned with salt, so that you may know how to answer everyone." We must balance the truth with love and grace. I've not always done that perfectly, but at least that's my goal.

Q: What writers inspired you?

A: This answer is going to sound really schizophrenic, but St. Thomas à Kempis for his work, *Imitation of Christ*, and humor columnist Dave Barry.

A good wordsmith can switch from fiction writing to fact reporting. How? The basis of all good prose is the detached style used by reporters. In this next example, writer Jim Watkins demonstrates his ability to move gracefully from fiction writing to the style of a journalist telling a news story. Notice the similarities but also notice that the journalist tries to strike a neutral tone. Tone is how the writer feels about his own work. Tone may be subtle but it bleeds through the copy to the reader. For this piece, the writer wants to achieve a tone of impartiality as a disinterested observer.

LaOtto streets to be repaired next summer[10]
By James N. Watkins © 1998
Used with permission

The chip and seal streets of LaOtto may be widened and paved with asphalt pending a meeting among the LaOtto Sewer District, state Sen. Robert Meeks, R-LaGrange, and the County Highway Department.

Recently county commissioners agreed to tear up and replace the current chip and seal streets damaged by the sewer project. The sewer district will contribute its $35,000 budgeted for street restoration with the county adding a "comparable" amount, according to sewer district president Phil Troyer. If state monies are available, hot asphalt would be used rather than new chip and seal.

The work is not scheduled until next summer to allow for any additional settling of cuts repaired following sewer construction. The following streets will be repaired: Tamarack, Vorhees, Simon, Collins, Miller, Bilger, Woodlawn and C.R. 450S.

---

[10] Watkins, J. (1998, Sept. 8). LaOtto streets to be repaired. *The News-Sun*. p. A12.

The recent public meeting of the sewer district discussed five residences and two businesses that have not connected to the new sewer system. Jack Chronister of the Noble County Health Department will be sent the names and addresses of property owners who have not complied with the mandatory hook-up. In 1993 the health department had planned to condemn 11 properties within the district for raw sewage seepage, but delayed action since the sewer was planned.

Four of the five properties already have liens against them for non-payment of monthly sewer charges. According to clerk Linda Keister, one property owner "hasn't paid a penny." The delinquent amount will be charged to the owner's property taxes.

The board also voted to allow 20 property owners 30 days to meet inspections on their taps. Most properties that did not pass inspection had sinks or showers emptying into the storm sewer rather than connection to the new sanitary system. Those names and addresses will also be turned over to the health department if not in compliance within the 30 days.

The only disagreement at the meeting came over whether "heavy cast iron" is acceptable material for connection to the sewer system. Ken Ryan, the appointed inspector, interpreted the ordinance to read that only SD 35 plastic was to be used, while Troyer argued that cast iron is used in high pressure systems and so is acceptable. Jeff Bartels, the district's pond operator, agreed that the heavy-duty cast iron doesn't pose a problem for the community system, but does allow for roots to grow into the homeowner's section of the pipe.

Ryan also relayed concerns of some residents that discharging treated water from the pond may cause flooding. Bartels assures residents that the absolute maximum mixture of creek water to effluent is 10-1. "Normally it's a 200-1 ratio between creek water and effluent," so the rise in the level of the creek will be negligible.

Fiction for a juvenile audience

In this example, writer Jim Watkins moves from the detached style used by journalists to the literary style used by fiction writers. The fiction writer has the luxury of invented quotations. The news reporter must faithfully quote a source's exact words. The fiction writer can create a beginning part, middle part and dramatic conclusion for his piece but a non-fiction writer often must be content with a beginning part and middle part but no formal ending. Alas. In this fiction article, notice the way Jim Watkins includes the background material that is necessary for the reader to understand the drama.

Exaggeration, hyperbole and just plain lies
By James N. Watkins © 2003
Used with permission

"So, Brandon, how'd you do on Power Planet? I got 100,000 points and got to level fifteen."

Inside, Brandon sensed a war greater than the battle for the "neutron energy source" in the latest video game.

"Uh . . . I didn't do too bad," he replied to his best friend Shane.

"Come on. How many points did you get?"

Before Sunday school the previous day he would have taken Shane's score and added 50,000. But something about the session on honesty had pierced Brandon's conscience like a "neutron torpedo." Now he felt as if a band of "planet plunderers" were pressuring him to return to his old habit of exaggerating facts.

"You got disintegrated before you ever got close to the energy source, didn't you," Shane continued.

"Ok, I kept getting zapped in the anti-matter maze," Brandon finally admitted. There, he had overcome that challenge, but he braced himself for Shane's attack.

"Too bad. Why don't you come over after school today and I'll show you how I got through it. It's pretty tricky."

Brandon was shocked that Shane hadn't made a big deal out of his trouble with "Power Planet." Maybe being honest wasn't such a bad idea.

"Stu-dents! Students." Mrs. Stuart's voice interrupted the post-weekend conversations in eighth grade class. "How many of you read your assignment in *The Old Man and the Sea?*"

Come on, Brandon thought. *How much am I going to be tested about my promise to God to be more truthful?* He had spent most of his spare time Saturday playing "Power Planet" rather than reading some guy's fish story. Most of the class members' hands were in the air, but Brandon sheepishly kept his on the desk.

"Well," Mrs. Stuart seemed to growl. "I see some of you must have been in front of the TV instead of in front of the book this weekend." *How do teachers know these things?* Brandon wondered.

"That will be an *F* for reading today for those who didn't read their assignments," his teacher continued.

So much for "honesty is the best policy," Brandon grumbled to himself.

At lunch Brandon and Shane's friends couldn't wait to hear all about "Power Planet."

"I hear it's got some really cool graphics and sound effects," Kevin half said and half asked.

"Yeah," Brandon answered. "Screen 15 is the coolest."

Shane glanced at him as if to say, "You've never been to the fifteenth screen." But Brandon told himself it really wasn't a lie. *I never said I got to fifteen, just that it was really cool.*

"Is the anti-matter maze as hard as everybody says it is?" Jonathon wanted to know.

Shane stared at Brandon again, but it didn't matter. Brandon's reputation as a video wizard was being questioned.

"Yeah, it's tough," Brandon continued, "But there are some tricks to get through."

"Why don't you tell us how to do it?" Shane taunted.

Brandon realized his less-than-honest talk was getting him in trouble. "Well," he said as he looked for a way out. "You're the one who figured it out. You go ahead."

Shane smirked at Brandon, and then began telling how players have to jump to "warp speed" just as they turn each right corner.

"Thanks for bailing me out," Brandon told Shane later.

That week Brandon struggled with the idea of honesty. Sometimes it just didn't seem worth the effort – like getting an *F* in reading class. At other times he saw how much trouble dishonesty can cause.

Brandon also discovered how much of a habit dishonesty had become. He seemed to naturally add a little extra to video game scores, grades, the number of CDs he owned, the memory capability of the hard drive in the family's home computer, the distance in softball throw–everything! By Wednesday, he was back in the same habits.

Then came Sunday. "So, how did you guys and girls do after last week's lesson on honesty?" his Sunday school teacher asked.

"Lousy," Brandon blurted out without thinking.

"Now there's an *honest* answer," Mr. Spencer replied. "Changing old habits can be tough. But here's an idea – try to ease into honesty. For instance, you've made a habit out of lying – or anything else. And let's say you tell ten lies a week. Ask God to help you cut that number in half the next week. And then when you're down to just five lies a week, ask God to help you knock off three more incidents.

"Now," Mr. Spencer quickly added, "that doesn't mean that you set out deliberately to tell five lies a week, and then two lies the next. It just means you give yourself some slack if you do fall short. If you try to go from ten lies to zero overnight – and then fail – often you'll just give up and say, 'It's impossible.'"

That Monday during lunch, talk once again turned to "Power Planet."

"So Brandon, how's your game coming?" Shane asked.

"Well, I've decided to give myself some slack if I don't get to screen 15 overnight. But I made some good progress this weekend," Brandon answered – honestly.

Humor column

Writers tend to excel in one area of writing over another. In the case of Jim Watkins, humor writing is his forte. (For fun, look up the word forte and note the pronunciation. Most people pronounce it incorrectly.) Jim Watkins uses the conventions of a journalist to parody the style of a news writer. He sounds serious. His tone suggests that he is sharing information as an important part of the public's right to know; however, he is kidding. Nonetheless, the information that he shares in this column is accurate. Since the web sites are real, the column is all the more comical. Humor writing that works is very sophisticated and it requires just the right touch or it falls flat. Tone is the key. Read this piece and note the fun-loving tone that Jim uses.

A totally useless column on totally useless web sites[11]
By James N. Watkins © 2003
Used with permission

As a professional journalist, it's my job to bring you useful and helpful information on a variety of socially significant subjects. Well, that's not going to happen this week!

Presenting a totally useless column on even less useful Websites. But these aren't those "create a free Website" like geocities.com sites and the ubiquitous "blog" sites on UFO abductions or dental floss fetishes! Nope, someone has actually gone to the expense of buying a domain name for, well, who knows what reason. (Perhaps operating a computer and credit card while under the influence!)

First, the totally useless sites with absolutely no content: www.something.com See the word "Something." That's it, folks! Just "Something." www.zombo.com See the Zombo.com logo and hear

---

[11] This column was from James Watkins's "Spam of the Month Club" in July 2003.

"Welcome to ZomboCom" in a really bad James Earle Jones impersonation.

www.purple.com is simply a purple screen! With some experimenting I was able to find www.purple.com/faq.html where I learned that I may lease sub-domains of purple (other than www) for $2000 per month or buy the domain name for just $500,000!

Second, are the sites that do have content, but you suspect these people are in serious need of a www.life.com!

www.itsmytie.co.uk/ Scan your ugly tie and send it as a .jpg to this virtual closet of nasty neckwear. (The perfect virtual Fathers Day gift?)

www.DearHeaven.com and www.DearHell.com offer to send email to the dearly (and not so dearly) departed.

www.iowafarmer.com allows you to watch corn grow on the live "CornCam."

Really! But wait, there's more. Watch cows being milked live on the "DairyCam."

www.menwholooklikekennyrogers.com Well at least it's not "The Dull Men's Club" at www.dullmen.com/.

www.theshotgunrules.com is the virtual "Book of Hoyle" for claiming the passenger seat in the car. Over twenty rules for avoiding embarrassing "Shotgun" faux pas. It's a good thing! Third, in the category of disturbing social trends:

www.subgenious.com offers membership and even ordination in the Church of the Subgenius. The site includes this quote: "If you are what they call 'different'; if you think we're entering a new Dark Age; if you see the universe as one vast morbid sense of humor; if you are looking for an inherently bogus religion that will condone superior degeneracy and tell you that you are 'above' everyone else; if you can help us with a donation, then this is the church for you."

www.dailyconfession.com offers virtual Catholics online forgiveness.

www.[censored].com – Type in any of the Federal Communications Commission's seven dirty words and you'll find sites that have absolutely no redeeming social value. Judging by the X-rated "spam" that slithers through my Internet filters, I've seen more romantic photos in medical text books and autopsy reports.

However, for some sites that are actually useful and helpful, check out my list of favorite reference sites at:

http://www.jameswatkins.com/references.htm

Sorry, no "CornCams" here!

Exercise

Re-read the news article, the short story, and the humor column written by James Watkins.

1) Find similarities in each article.
2) Find differences in each article.
3) Compare the quotations used in the articles. Are quotations in news articles handled differently than in fiction articles? How about a humor column?
4) Which style do you prefer? Explain.
5) Can you spot the 5 W's in each piece?
6) How do the leads on these articles differ?

Summary

This chapter explored the classic opening to articles, the summary lead. While the summary lead is used most often for breaking news, it is considered the basic opening for writing; however, the lead is dependent on the type of article that you are constructing. The creative writer considers the goal of the article and fashions the appropriate opening. Among the leads that are available to writers is the summary lead, which often can be reduced to the phrase, "Who did what?" Be advised. The first draft of the article, and the lead, will need some work. Revise it until it is a lean, trim statement packed with relevant detail. To illustrate the idea of the summary lead, an article by writer James Watkins was included. In an interview, Watkins discussed the goal of spirited writing in all types of prose. As a journalist, author and writer, Watkins knows that good writers can adjust for many assignments, from humor writing to essays and feature articles.

Chapter 3

Free the writing spirit
FeatureWriting.Net/B1withtheWord

Chapter at-a-glance

- ➢ Exploring free writing
- ➢ Using creative openings in articles
- ➢ Developing the habit of journaling

In most newsrooms around the nation, editors, reporters, writers and producers keep in touch using electronic messaging, where one person sends a typed message to another person using the computer system. These days that idea is practiced internationally with electronic mail systems using the **Internet**, a global information network.

A typical day for most writers begins with checking for messages in what is sometimes called the **messages cue** or **in-basket**. That's where an editor may send a message assigning a reporter to cover an event that day.

This system is so convenient that some editors send electronic messages for anything, even urging the reporter to check on a bomb threat heard just that minute on a police scanner. The editor might flash a message to the reporter that suddenly appears at the top of a computer screen or send a longer version that shows up as "message pending" on the top of the screen. The point is that the editor might save some time by resorting to the old-

Swing into the story by freeing the writing muse.

fashioned method of alerting a writer about a story – yelling across the room.

Free writing

Old-fashioned methods survive because they work. Among the techniques that hold promise for callow mass media writers and veterans alike is a method of writing known as **free writing**. Some writers remember penning essays where they wrote the first idea that came to mind, then the next and so on until the idea reservoir was dry. This crude convention didn't produce memorable prose but it freed the writer to get on paper a bevy of thoughts. That's *free writing*.

Here's how it works. Let's say your editor flashed you a message to bolt to a fire at the historic church on Center Square. You grab a notebook and two lead pencils, sling a 35mm camera over your shoulder and break for the door. Within a few minutes, you're at the scene watching the spectacle.

Six firefighters wrestle hoses off an engine. Flames peek through a second story window. A crowd of shoppers forms at a safe distance. An elderly woman holds the arm of a man in an overcoat, crying silently. In the distance, you see a single-engine airplane veer toward the west and you suddenly become aware that a wind tosses your hair from side to side and the rank odor of smoke assaults your nostrils.

In short, your senses are bombarded. You want to capture the moment as a rough draft of the event, but you know that the story demands quotations from authorities, including the church leadership, firefighters and eyewitnesses.

Back at the newsroom, you must select a lead that captures the tragedy of the moment including the color appropriate for a fire that destroys some property but doesn't cause any personal injuries. You may be writing a breaking news story, sometimes called **hard news**, but the technique works for both **hard, tragic** news and **soft news**, or **feature news**. This occasion suggests *free writing*. You take a long pull from a bottle of mountain water or hot beverage and get to work. For five minutes you write non-stop. You dump all your impressions on the page. Stray thoughts are allowed.

"Flames bright orange and white-yellow. Get Honda brakes checked. The woman's crying sounded like a tinny toy sound. Confusion. Sadness. The fire chief spits when he talks fast."

You write and write and write or type and type and type until five minutes passes. Then you look at these random observations and mine for the one gem that could sum up the story as a summary lead might do, but with some passion and spirit.

In some cases, this process yields a winner. The goal of the exercise is not, repeat *not*, to edit the words as they appear. The goal is to reach deep into your mind for images, pictures, impressions that help reveal the story that you want to tell.

Once the words can be seen and read, the writer can eliminate most of them – but those rare, rich phrases that fall lightly from the lips and ring true in the ear may be the ones that will make the article sing. This technique is worth trying on occasion, for no other reason than it can be liberating. Should it produce no powerful results, slide the idea into your mental toolbox with a reminder to try it another time.

Variation on the summary lead

When it works, free writing may lead to a phrase that you want to stamp into the first sentence. Perhaps it's one word.

Determination.

That's a one-word lead for an article on a basketball team that fought back from a dismal season to snag a place in a tournament.

Delicious.

That's another one-word lead on a feature story about ice cream.

These leads are examples of **creative leads**, which work best for feature stories but can be used anytime. An article about a 10-year-old girl who writes reviews of children's books for an out-of-town newspaper is the kind of story that doesn't become stale if it isn't printed or broadcast right away.

These kinds of stories are known as soft news stories and tend to focus on lighter topics that entertain. Many depend on **human interest**, unraveling the human condition. Since this quality covers the spectrum of behavior, many of the approaches are considered standards and are written over and over again. Often, feature news is considered more **timeless**. It's even referred to as **evergreen**, news that holds up no matter the calendar. It is always fresh and in bloom.

For instance, a person who rescues another person is the substance of dramatic stories. While the event can be written as hard news – news that must be printed or broadcast immediately or it loses its value – a more complete story would require a longer, feature touch.

Word play and creative leads

More will be said about the feature story in future chapters. For now, let's return to the technique of fashioning a creative lead. These leads can draw on word play, but the goal is to suggest more than one meaning and intrigue the reader.

When the world closes in on you and your head feels a size too small, what you need is a piece of mind.

That lead is from *Mademoiselle* magazine in December 1993. Ordinarily slang terms are avoided in mass media writing, but creative leads allow the writer to slip one in on occasion as this writer did:

Those clever Brits – they've discovered that having a belt or two every day can increase your resistance to the sniffles.

The *Williamsport Sun-Gazette* carried the following lead from the Associated Press wire service using vernacular on February 3, 1995.

In the City of Brotherly Love, even dead men can get ripped off.

The same paper that same day, carried this lead about feuding elected officials:

The Lycoming County commissioners are acting like a dysfunctional family.

Word play relies on clever use of words that suggest the theme. An article on meals could use a food term such as the verb *cook* as the writer did in this *USA Today* lead February 6, 1995.

Taco Bell has cooked up a new menu that could change the way fast food is sold.

Even without this special brand of word play, strong verbs can make an opening sentence sparkle as the writer did in this March 1995 lead in *Sassy*.

Claire Danes was just about to tell me the wildest thing she's done lately when her car phone crackles, sputters and dies.

Perhaps the master publication of creative leads is *USA Today*, the pioneer of the short, breezy article topped off with a pithy lead. Note the

50

lean but creative words in the following six-word lead from September 12, 1994.

NBC could get a second parent.

Here are some other creative leads.

Foreign food marketers are gobbling up U.S. food and beverage markets – again.
– USA Today, September 10, 1993

Imperative leads

Another useful lead in opening an article is the **imperative** or **command lead**. Ordinarily mass media writers avoid telling people what to do. Too directive. In some cases, however, the command lead drills the point home. The command may be a soft one as in the case of this lead.

Look into the refrigerators of single men and women and you'll come away with some significant indicators of gender spending differences.

The reader can barely sense the command, but it's there. The writer said, "Look," but the lead reads more like a suggestion than a command. Subtle imperative leads are useful to aim your reader in the direction that moves the story flow in the direction the writer wants. Consider this lead in *Time* from February 7, 1994.

Imagine the five-and-ten on the corner.

Do you see the store in your mind? Eight words. Words can be powerful to evoke pictures. The beauty of mass media writing is that a wordsmith doesn't need an elaborate vocabulary, just an inner voice that suggests strong verbs for the thought you want to convey.

The imperative may be used for effect as Jennifer Whitlock did in *The* (Allentown, Pa.) *Morning Call.*

Listen up, Bub. You don't mess with the Friggs. 'Cause if you do, they might write a nasty song about you.

That's a much stronger command. No subtlety there. This type of lead is rare. More likely, the writer who chooses the imperative will go for a more paternal tone as the *USA Today* writer did in this February 3, 1995 lead.

Do what works.

Here are some more examples of imperative leads.

Don't ask whodunit in the 'X-Files.' Ask what.
– *USA Today*, September 10, 1993.

Recycle your cans and shorten your showers.
– *Seventeen* August 1991.

Get ready for lower PC prices – and more choices on store shelves.
– *USA Today*, February 6, 1995,

If you can't beat them, steal from them.
–*The New York Times*, February 3, 1995.

Forget the kiss! It comes late in the movie and the world keeps turning.
– *The* (Harrisburg, Pa.) *Patriot*, February 6, 1995.

Try if you must, but Fox's an institution you can't deny.
– *USA Today*, February 3, 1995.

The question lead

As you can see, the variety is endless, but the rule is to select the best lead for the article. News reporters sometimes joke with one another that somewhere in the universe is a big book of leads made-to-order for the article that is underway at this moment.

Someone once suggested a Dial-A-Lead telephone service where frustrated writers could order a specialty lead using the keypad: "Press one for a feature lead, press two for a summary lead and press three for the question lead." I'm afraid such a device still doesn't exist, but the idea sounds good, doesn't it?

The question lead, also known as the interrogative lead, is one of the easiest leads to write. In this case, the writer just poses a question. The trick is to be sure to answer the question in the next paragraph or so. Never end the story unless some kind of answer is provided or the reader may feel cheated. *The Williamsport Sun-Gazette* reported a story Feb. 4, 1995 by asking,

A 12-story mountain?

Does that question make you want to read on? If not, the writer missed. (What's that number for Dial-A-Lead?)

The biggest disadvantage to the question lead is that writers must discipline themselves not to overuse this tool. I know a reporter who once became hooked on song titles and lyrics as a way to start all his news stories, even hard-news articles! The editors chuckled to themselves whenever they fielded one of these leads that were cute the first 100 times but became trite after awhile. The same can happen with the question lead. Use it sparingly and it will brighten up the report.

Here are some more examples of question leads.

The Texas Rangers in the pennant race? After Aug. 1? Believe it.
– USA Today, September 10, 1993.

The political upheaval of 1994? They saw it coming two years ahead of time.
– Williamsport Sun-Gazette, February 5, 1995.

What are kindergartners through third-graders learning in some of our public schools these days?
– Reader's Digest, February, 1995.

Is O.J. Simpson's trial a high-tech lynching?
– USA Today, February 3, 1995.

Looking to buy something quickly and cheaply, but you don't know anyone who can get it for you wholesale?
– The Patriot, February 6, 1995.

Putting the creative lead to work

Here are some facts for you to consider. Review them and try constructing one of the leads mentioned in this chapter.

FACT 1 The Office of Residence Life is proposing a charge to unlock dormitory room doors when students lock themselves out.

FACT 2 Each day the Office of Safety and Security must unlock as many as six doors for forgetful students.

FACT 3 Each year safety and security unlocks nearly 1,500 doors and spends nearly 260 hours responding to these calls.

FACT 4 The Resident Life Committee proposed the change to help reduce the number of these kinds of nuisance calls and to encourage students to be more responsible.

FACT 5 The proposal calls for no fines for the first and second "lockout," where the safety and security office is called to respond to a locked dormitory door. Fines may be charged for the third and each succeeding lockout. The fines will increase as the number increases.

Armed with these facts, start with the stand-by lead – the summary lead. Answer the main questions of who, what, where, when, and, later, how and why. Here's one attempt.

Students who lock themselves out of their dormitory rooms may soon have to pay a penalty as part of gaining access to their rooms.

The lead tells the reader all the information that he or she needs to know to decide if it's worth reading on, but the article warrants a creative touch.

Students who forget their room keys must remember to carry their wallets.

That lead, written by a student, is having some word play fun with the idea of forgetting and remembering. Working with duality often makes for a memorable lead.
Here's another memorable lead from another student.

Use your keys or lose your money.

Here's a lead that retains this idea, but presents it as an imperative lead.

The next time you lock your keys in your room, try to remember your wallet.

The idea can be reworked as a statement.

The Office of Resident Life is installing a price on lockouts.

This lead is another statement.

For Franklin College students, financial planning could soon include remembering their keys.

Here's the same opening using the question lead.

What's the price for forgetfulness?

That lead sounds reminiscent of the old "What price ignorance" slogan from broadcast TV. These next two leads are moralistic yet they convey the same idea.

Should students have to pay for their forgetfulness?

Students getting punished for obviously unintended accidents?

The lead as a springboard

The emphasis of this chapter is getting started. Many times a well-crafted lead will suggest the remainder of the article. In other words, nail the lead and nail the story. In the following example, student Sean Kirby starts his article with a clever lead and develops it in the article.

Here's his draft without the corrections. Read it once through without any editing. Then read it a second time for errors. Mark the errors or ways that you think might improve the piece. Check yourself on the next page.

Lockouts could be the key to more money for security.

The Office of Residence Life is proposing charging students for getting security to let them back into their rooms, which is a major problem.

"This proposal is something I am in favor of," said Jeffrey Brown, director of the safety and security office.

He said that security spends too much time on this problem. Security has already dealt with 1,034 lockouts in four months, which may pass the 1,587 of last year.

Rookies and prose:
Words to master

Compliment, complement
"Complimentary" suggests praise or courtesy.
* *The professor complimented the student on the presentation.*
* *News organizations sometimes receive complimentary tickets.*

"Complement" is used to suggest completeness.

- *The scarf complemented the suit.*
- *The couple have complementary careers.*

Complacent, complaisant

"Complacent" means self-satisfied or bored.

- *Director Alfred Hitchcock's characters begin his films as complacent figures.*

"Complaisant" is used to describe an eagerness to please.

- *Many workers aren't like cocker spaniels, too complaisant.*

Irritate, aggravate

"Irritate" means to excite or provoke.

- *The student's constant tardiness irritated the professor.*

"Aggravate" means to make worse or more burdensome.

- *The lack of sleep and poor diet aggravated my illness.*

Damage, damages

"Damage" means an injury or harm to a person or thing – a loss.

- *The storm damage amounted to $70,000.*

"Damages" is a legal term used in connection with compensation for injury or losses in a lawsuit.

- *The court awarded $50,000 in damages.*

Legal terms

Legal terms must be translated for readers. For instance, "habeas corpus" is a petition seeking the release of someone in custody. Rather than writing, "The lawyer sought a habeas corpus," say, "She filed a petition seeking the prompt release of her client."

Practice exercise using the creative lead

Use the following facts to construct an eight-paragraph news brief. A summary lead will be provided as part of the facts.

SUMMARY– Alternative media organization Paper Tiger urged college students and others to challenge mainstream mass media Thursday in the Heim Building at the opening of a two-day Media and Technology Symposium.

FACTS 1-2 Paper Tiger is a group of volunteers in the New York City area who produce broadcasts that criticize mainstream mass media for its support of the status quo. The group hopes that the programs will provoke audiences to fight back against mainstream mass media.

FACTS 3-4 Paper Tiger shows its programs on a public access channel, a cable channel available freely to anyone who signs up to use it; however, only some cable companies around the country have public access channels.

FACTS 5-6 Michael Eisenmenger and Lina Iannacone showed videotapes of programs that they produced using a low-budget production.

FACTS 7-8 The tapes criticized mainstream mass media because it is too concerned with capitalism, ignoring disadvantages of big business including pollution and monopolies. The message also criticized the mass media business and those who write the messages and the content of the messages.

FACTS 9-10 "We are part of the struggle to get television into the hands of the people," said Iannacone. "We critique the information industry," said Eisenmenger.

> **Tip:** Apostrophes may be used to indicate a letter is missing, hence the phrase "rock 'n' roll." The "a" and "d" are missing, and the apostrophes are used to show the omitted letters.
>
> Remember this rule when you are grappling with the use of *its* and *it's*. *Its* is the possessive pronoun but it doesn't need an apostrophe to indicate possession as in the case with the word *man* and his hat – *man's hat*. On the other hand, *it's* uses the apostrophe to indicate a contraction for *it is*.
>
> Here is a sentence using both words:
> *It's a dirty cat that scratches its fleas.*
> The apostrophe can solve other problems, too. Have you ever written *your* for *you're*?

Here's a synthesis of three student stories.

Paper Tiger TV showed its stripes Thursday at Franklin College.

The alternative media organization challenged the audience of 60 to question the creators and content of mass media. The program was part of a two-day Media and Technology Symposium.

"We critique the information industry," said Michael Eisenmenger, one of the two Paper Tiger representatives who spoke.

Paper Tiger is the name of a group of volunteers in the New York City area who write and produce TV programs that are shown on a public access channel in Manhattan. The group hopes that the programs will provoke audiences to fight back against mainstream mass media.

Public access channels are open to the public and furnished by some cable companies in the United States as part of their community service responsibility for operating a cable franchise.

Linda Iannacone, another Paper Tiger representative, joined Eisenmenger in showing videotapes produced by their organization.

The tapes criticized mainstream mass media for their focus on the benefits of capitalism and neglect of the inequities associated with this economic system.

Eisenmenger said Paper Tiger uses a low-budget program to comment on media monopolies and other issues.

"We are part of the struggle to get television into the hands of people," said Iannacone.

This chapter has emphasized the news approach to help you sense the cadence of straight news. As you become familiar with the organization of ordinary news stories, you will be better prepared to develop your rhythm in a feature article. Examine the ideas below from editor Marvin Olasky on starting an article, then read the feature article opening used by John F. Kelly in his article on restoring cars. What approach did he use? Could he have used another feature lead to open his article? If so, try your hand at composing one.

> **Tip:** Sometimes an article has so many facets that it is begging for additional treatment. What to do? Use the **sidebar**. Sidebars are often associated with the idea of a feature article, soft news. In this sense, the sidebar is used to humanize the story by providing information that the main story, the **mainbar**, can't include. For feature writers, the sidebar can provide more human interest material in the form of a long anecdote. It can be used to provide helpful information such as directions for travel, useful telephone numbers and valuable Web sites. Sometimes the sidebar can provide analysis and other angles that would otherwise crowd the main article.

Here's your crash course in writing a lead.

Take a page from Marvin Olasky. In his "Telling the Truth,"[12] Olasky, the crack editor, urges writers to use one of the feature leads in opening an article. What are they?

1. **Anecdotal lead.** Give a mini-story with a beginning, middle and end. The ending is like a punch line.

---

[12] Olasky, M. (1999). *Telling the truth*. Wheaton, IL: Crossways.

2. **Descriptive lead.** Describe the scene using a wide-angle lens. End with a close up.

3. **Situational lead**. Provide a look at this situation that sets up the rest of the information in the story. Discuss in narrative form the typical situation that exists. For instance, what series of events typically occurs during a police stake-out? Do the officers get coffee, record the weather, count cars on a street or what? A writer uses this type of lead to set up the situation to suggest that the events that she described represent a typical stake-out.

Olasky also suggests writers avoid summary, quotation leads and the dreaded essay lead.

Next, insert the **Nut Graf**, the background paragraph that tells the significance of the story. The Nut Graf tells the reader the reason you are writing this piece. Typically, it provides the essential background and basics the article needs to make sense. Essential background usually includes the history of the issue in a sentence or two. See Chapter 10, *SHOP talk for writers*, for a more complete understanding of the history required for a feature article.

After the Nut Graf, add quotations, anecdotes and the other information you need to complete your feature article.

When John F. Kelly of *The Washington Post* examined a rural automobile refurbishing shop and told a story headlined, "Where vintage cars go for salvation," he used an anecdotal lead.

WHITE POST, Va.–A year and a half ago, Julie Moore of Fremont, Calif., sent her beat-up 1962 Plymouth Valiant to this tiny Virginia town 60 miles west of Washington.[13]

Kelly went on to note that White Post Restorations removed each part from the car, restored the ones that were in poor condition and transformed the Valiant to look like new. Kelly used a story of one customer's experience to illustrate the kind of restoration work this shop has been doing since 1940.

The **little story** suggests the **big story**. By personalizing the business of grease, pistons and wheel covers, the writer helps the audience appreciate the novelty of a shop that has made its reputation on detailing the details.

---

[13] Kelly, J. F. (2003, Feb. 14). Where vintage cars go for salvation, At small shop in rural Virginia, restorers use brand-new old parts. *The Washington Post*, pp. B1, B6.

To break through the clutter of boilerplate approaches, writers must reject the sterile writing of the stenographer in favor of experimentation. Good writers study language, read poetry and gain a sense of playfulness with syntax. They want to be creative and think about ways to take an existing approach and bend it into a new form. They reach for imagery to make readers, listeners, and viewers see the emotion, the power of the moment. Good writers compress and use words with rhythm but sparingly. The goal is to be clear but with boldness, excitement and style. When done well, the audience will see the world from the writer's pen. Ah, but the view! It will be so compelling that the audience will be unaware that words transported her mind from the cellar of the ordinary to the rooftop where the air is clean and the view panoramic.

Journaling

A technique used by writers, particularly feature writers, is to include **personal impressions** in the prose. This technique should be used with care; otherwise, the remarks that you mean to be candid quips fall flat and sound amateurish. Nonetheless, good writers can follow the lead of Tom Wolfe's *The Electric Kool-Aid Acid Test,* Hunter S. Thompson's *Hell's Angels,* Norman Mailer's *Armies of the Night* and others from the **Gonzo School,** where the writer deliberately inserts opinion into the article. This approach must be cleared in advance by an editor and should be used judiciously. Most readers aren't concerned with what the writer thinks unless the comments are dry, novel, cogent and insightful. This style of writing, also known as **new journalism**, became fashionable in the 1960s. "Earlier work by Lillian Ross – and much earlier by George Orwell – is clearly situated under the creative-nonfiction umbrella," wrote Lee Gutkind, professor of English at the University of Pittsburgh.[14] Gutkind commended creative writing and said, "Creative nonfiction – writing techniques like scene, dialogue, description, while allowing the personal point of view and voice (reflection) rather than maintaining the sham of objectivity – is hardly a new idea. For new writers, however, the personal approach should be reserved for articles that require the treatment. Be judicious and discerning about the goal of your prose. Failing that course, check with your editor!"

To prepare for this kind of writing, keep a **journal**, a diary. A journal is the place for your personal reflections. Avoid reminding yourself of your meals and other routine activities. Instead, use your journal to capture that emotion that ebbs and flows with each sunset.

---

[14] Gutkind, L. (2003, November 14). Stewardship as survival; brilliant nonfiction. *The Chronicle of Higher Education*, p. B4.

One writer captured this kind of introspection when he wrote, "I entered a period of listlessness, spurred neither by love of self nor love of God. During this journey through the desert, I drifted from one diversion to another, committing the worst deeds of my life along the way. Looking back, I think it would have taken just one Christian friend to have spared me all those barren years, a friend who could have explained to me that although religious feeling had gone, the reality had not; that the Christian life depends not on the Christian, but on Christ; and that our inability to lead a perfect life does not condemn us to lead a bad one. I started out well, but had stumbled and fallen. I hadn't known that the point of the race was not to win, but to finish."[15]

Can you hear the emotion in those honest words? Those are the kind of deeply personal thoughts that can be recorded in a journal, but hard to locate when pressed to write them on demand. The journal works much like a photograph album. It can be used to jumpstart a memory that links to other memories. The chaining may help you develop a series of thoughts that advance the article. Clearly, this technique works best for the personal narrative, but the Gonzo gang used it liberally to castigate a source for sloppy thinking, criticize someone mentioned in the article for a fashion faux pas, and, in general, tee off at someone else's expense. Clearly, this technique should be reserved for those rare times when your intellectual antennae are wiggling beyond control and you feel compelled to weigh in.

Biography of Georgia Shaffer

Georgia Shaffer

Georgia Shaffer, M.A., is a licensed psychologist in Pennsylvania, a professional speaker, author, life coach and radio personality. She produces *The Mourning Glory Minute* for radio and also was the producer and co-host of Faith is Alive, a talk show airing on a radio station in south central Pennsylvania.

Her work has been featured on national television, and she has spoken at national conventions as well as from the West Coast's Crystal Cathedral in California to Sandy Cove on the East Coast. *Living Solo* magazine named her book, *A Gift of Mourning Glories*, to its Top 10 List

---

[15] Hale, T. (1986). *Don't let the goats eat the Loquat trees*. Grand Rapids, MI: Zondervan.

for 2000. Georgia is the founder and Executive Director of Mourning Glory Ministries and is also on the teaching staff of the Christian Leaders, Authors & Speakers Seminar.

Georgia writes regularly, keeps a journal, and penned a book on the topic[16]. The process of writing helps improve her craft and monitor her thinking. She calls the writing in a diary, journaling, and this next section is an excerpt from her first book, *A Gift of Mourning Glories*. Notice Georgia Shaffer's journal entry from March 5, 1997 that is included in the piece. This technique should be used sparingly. It works well here and suggests the benefits of journaling, a practice used by writers for centuries.

Interview with Georgia Shaffer

Q: How long have you kept a journal? What made you begin to record your thoughts?

A: For me, I began the habit after reading the *Diary of Anne Frank.*[17] Anne's honesty and transparency captured me. She was real about her struggles in hiding as she grappled with the uncertainty of life. Although my life wasn't threatened like the Jewish people in Europe during World War II, I still identified with Anne's fears, her sadness and her anger. Somewhere, while I immersed in the pages of that book, it hit me that I, too, could keep a journal about my own heartaches and celebrations. And maybe, just maybe, someday others would read what I had penned.

My first diary was a pink padded one with a poodle on the front and a lock and key. I don't know what I wrote (I've never been able to find it), but I do know I poured out my heart on those pages never realizing the profound effect it would have on my life.

I stopped journaling during high school and it wasn't until my son was born, 15 years later, that I reestablished the habit.

Q: What three tips do you share with new writers on keeping a journal?

A: Here are three tips.

1.   While it may feel very awkward at first and you may be tempted to believe journaling is not for you, make the commitment to do it and don't give up.

2.   I found it to be one of the best ways to discover your true writing voice. As a licensed psychologist and college professor for many years, I had to journal my way through my "teacher voice" and my "thesis voice" in writing. I still remember the thrill I had one morning when a colleague

---

[16] Shaffer, G. (2001). *The journey inward.* York, PA: Mourning Glory Ministries.
[17] Frank, A. (2003). *The diary of Anne Frank.* New York: Doubleday.

read something I had written and said, "I could hear you saying that – you've finally found your true writing voice." Journaling enabled me to do that.

3. Don't make journaling a "have to." Some days you may write a few sentences. On other days you may write several pages. And there will be those days when you may not write anything at all.

Q: Are you concerned that a passage that you write when your are out of sorts may be read by someone else who may not understand? What can a writer do to protect her privacy, but keep a journal as vigorous as possible?

A: It is a real concern for me. I have heard horror stories about journals being "used" against the person writing it. One lady said her husband used her journal entries in their divorce hearings. I live alone so it is not an issue for me, but I would recommend a safe hiding place or write the issue haunting you and then tear it up and destroy it, if it will deeply hurt someone you love.

Q: What's the biggest mistake new writers make in keeping a journal?

A: Editing their writing and trying to write with the idea that they are producing publishable material. You write out of your heart and soul. If you can later use it in an article or book, then that's great, but don't write with idea of publishing it as your main focus.

A Gift of Mourning Glories, Eliminating the "Someday..." and "If Only..."[18]
By Georgia Shaffer
Used with permission

"It's about the size of a grapefruit," the doctor said after my ultrasound test. He was referring to an ovarian tumor that had been discovered during my annual exam. Given my history with breast cancer, the doctor did not paint a pretty picture. We scheduled surgery, and I cancelled a speaking engagement in California.

As I drove home that day, my head throbbed. I hadn't seen this coming. The only possible hints were that my jeans fit more snugly and I was experiencing more fatigue.

In spite of the report, though, I felt a peace that came from knowing I had tried my best to focus on the things that mattered most to me. My

---

[18] Shaffer, G. (2000). *A gift of mourning glories*. Ventura, CA.: Gospel Light/Regal Books.

relationships, especially with Jesus and my son, had grown deeper and richer over the last few years.

I could not have always made that statement. Eight years earlier I had a stack of unfinished business that reached the ceiling. It was a pile of "somedays."

"Someday I want to see the cherry blossoms in Washington, D.C. Someday I'm going to sit down and write my son a 'Did-I-ever-tell you' letter. Someday I'll…"

With the recurrence of breast cancer my "somedays" had turned into "if onlys". "If only I wouldn't have taken my job so seriously. If only I would have spent more time with my family. If only I wouldn't have felt the need to get straight A's in my graduate studies. If only…"

When I arrived home from the doctor's, I pulled into the garage, propped my arms on the steering wheel, buried my head, and prayed for strength and wisdom.

As was true years earlier, I knew I needed to plan for the worst but continue praying for the best.

Almost immediately, I felt an urgent need to write a letter to Kyle. Rather than a "cold" will I wanted him to have something warm and caring – a handwritten note containing a permanent record of my love, faith, and values. It would be something that he could read over and over again, in case I wasn't around to tell him myself.

But first, I had to share the devastating news with him. Since he was still at swim practice, I had some time to gather my courage. My vision blurred with tears thinking of what we had gone through over the last several years. How I dreaded what I had to do.

I had just finished dinner when I heard the garage door open. Immediately, Kyle leaped up the steps to the living room.

"What's going on?" he barked loudly, his eyes filled with concern. "This afternoon a doctor kept calling here every fifteen minutes asking for you. What did he want?"

I sighed, evading eye contact, and motioned for us to sit down. The tears I had been determined to hold back gushed down my cheeks.

"Kyle, I had a routine checkup, and they discovered another tumor. I'm scheduled for surgery in a few days."

"How serious is it?" Kyle asked, visibly cringing.

"Only God knows the answer to that."

I paused to gather more strength, blew my nose, and whispered, "Kyle, I won't be able to go to your state swim meet."

"But you have to," he pleaded.

"Believe me, I want to, but I'll still be in the hospital."

I blew my nose again. Taking another deep sigh I asked, "Kyle, will you pray with me?"

He jumped to his feet.

"I'm not praying with you," he raged. "You picked the worst time for this to happen. Now I don't even know if I can swim at states, let alone win."

He stomped off to his room and slammed the door.

Stunned, hurt, and alone, I wept. Then I got up, stumbled to my room, and tucked myself into bed. Reaching over to my nightstand, I grabbed my journal and wrote what Kyle wouldn't allow me to say.

March 5, 1997
Kyle, I love you. I thank God for you. If I'm not with you much longer, we'll make the time we do have count. Don't give up on your faith. It's OK to be angry with God. But just remember, life without our Lord isn't worth living. But with faith in Jesus, we can touch the lives of others, we can know we will make a difference – no matter how long we live!

That's all I had written when the phone started ringing. Friends, who had heard the news, called to say they were praying for me.

My heart broke again later that evening when I stopped outside Kyle's closed bedroom door to say good night and overheard him talking on the phone.

"My mom can't go to the states," he said. "I'm afraid she's dying."

Such life-disrupting events force us to re-examine our lives. They make us stop and think about what is important. They cause us to readjust our priorities.

Although I never got to California that year to speak, I did send two questions to the women in the audience. One was, "If you found out tomorrow that your life was threatened, what would you change?" The other was, "What matters most to you, and are you taking the time to do it?"

That second question haunted me both before and after my surgery, even after I was miraculously handed a new lease on life. "Well, Georgia, I have good news," my doctor said as he stood at the end of the bed. "We were able to completely remove the tumor; you don't need any further treatments."

"Thank you, God!" I sighed with relief.

I still had some unfinished business. It was a dream God had tucked in my heart years earlier, during my recovery from the transplant. *Someday I want to write a book to help others restore their lives after loss, a book that will encourage them to move beyond existing or merely surviving to a brand new life.* It was time to turn that dream into reality.

Sydney Harris wrote, "Regret for the things we did can be tempered by time, it is regret for the things that we did not do that is inconsolable."

I needed to get writing, I didn't want to die with any "if onlys..."

Exercise

1) Examine the journal entry in this piece. Does it work for this kind of writing? Explain.
2) Do you keep a journal? What are the benefits? Are there disadvantages?
3) Georgia Shaffer includes the passion of life in her prose. Find three sentences that use emotion to tell her story. Recast those sentences in your own words.
4) Examine your journal if you keep one, what passages are the strongest? Which ones would speak to others? Explain.

Summary

Free writing is a technique that may help you probe the writing voice that you possess but can only coax out on special occasions. It works best when a writer allows herself to relax and write without regard to punctuation and the mechanics of the word slave. It is not a failsafe method, but it sometimes provides inventive combinations of words, images, even leads. Feature writing is about the skillful use of **creative writing** that relies on **word play, imperatives, question leads** and other openings that laugh out loud rather than sigh with relief. Among the ways to enhance your writing is the use of a journal and this chapter included the work of Georgia Shaffer who recommends this habit for writers.

Chapter 4

Developing the article and more
FeatureWriting.Net/Ideas

Chapter at-a-glance

- ➢ Selecting the right organization for your article
- ➢ Inserting observation into your article
- ➢ Understanding the story process

Writer William Least Heat-Moon tells a story in his *Blue Highways*[19] on the building of a wall. He joined a friend in New England and constructed a wall out of irregularly shaped rocks. Since the rocks were odd shapes, the men had to choose just the right one to put on top of another. The men began the project by surveying the inventory of rough fieldstones and selecting the best one to match the one before. In the end, the wall appears solid and Heat-Moon wonders if it could have been built any other way.

Moon suggests that the men **intuitively** knew what stone would be the best in the sequence. For writers, the sequence of information can't be based on a hunch; information must flow in a pattern that has some kind of order, even if it is transparent to the reader. The order may be chronological, but that is one of the weakest because the most important information

Building an article is a bit like building a wall.

---

[19] Heat-Moon, W. L. (1999). *Blue Highways: A journey into America.* New York: Little, Brown & Co.

may be halfway through the narrative, or even at the end, and writers want the most crucial points to be read first. A better approach is to make a decision based on the importance of the information.

Raw material

Writers collect facts, often using interviews, and shape that raw information into an easy-to-understand report. They work hard to make their words flow so the audience can grasp the ideas quickly. The process includes selecting the best raw material available – the best quotations, the best anecdotes, the best observations – and arranging it in a story that makes sense and reads well.

> **Tip:** When you know nothing of a subject on which you are about to write a feature article, read a children's book. Writers who pen long feature articles know the importance of speaking the argot of the experts. Before you talk to an expert on investing strategies for baby-boomers, read a children's book on stocks, bonds and OPM, a phrase some investors use to mean "other people's money." Children's books are designed to be easily understood, while giving the reader access to the fundamentals. This idea works for the big-league writers, and it will work for you and me, too.

Coherent reports begin by writing a lead that sums up the story, a second sentence that amplifies the first sentence with additional information and successive sentences that follow logically one after the other.

Fact arrangement

One of the best ways to organize a news story is to systematically arrange the information with the most important information first. By arranging the facts from most pertinent to least significant, your report helps the harried reader get the vital news first.

Imagine that you are a reporter assigned to find out about a couple who was about to be married on Valentine's Day on the 80th floor of the Empire State Building, à la *Sleepless in Seattle*.

Here are the facts.

FACT 1 Rose Marie Higby and Alan J. Ross, both of Langhorne, Pa., signed up to be wed on the 80th floor of the Empire State Building.

FACT 2 Thirty-four couples also signed up for weddings on the 80th floor.

FACT 3 Right before Higby and Ross were wed, a gust of wind blew the couple's marriage certificate off the 80th floor.

FACT 4 The 34th Street Partnership is a merchants' group that sponsors the "marriage marathon" at the Empire State Building.

FACT 5 Dan Sieger, spokesman for the merchants' group, said, "They (the couple) had been dating for 17 years, and they finally made the move." He also said, "They were mortified at first (when the certificate blew away). "We happened to have a Xerox of it downstairs and we were able to salvage the whole thing."

The strategy

The first task is to write a lead. Will you use a creative lead or a summary lead? Since the story is humorous with a happy ending, a creative lead is your best bet.

While it isn't given as one of the facts, the 1957 tear-jerker *An Affair to Remember* features a couple who pledge to meet on the 80th floor of the Empire State Building... if each decides the other is the one. This fact, part of the background that you might have to learn for yourself, might make a creative lead. If you wanted to refer to either *An Affair to Remember* or another movie, *Sleepless in Seattle*, you'd need to choose an element that relates to our Langhorne couple, too. In both movies, the lovers have plans for a meeting on the 80th floor, but somehow the plans are thwarted or confused, yet the conflict gets resolved. That bit of background, available by consulting a reference book on films or a telephone call to the reference librarian at the public library, might suggest:

> *The scene on the 80th floor of the Empire State Building had all the makings of a couple in love after the Sleepless in Seattle movie, plus added suspense when the marriage certificate they needed to be wed blew away.*
>
> *Not to worry. This story ends happily, too, when a photocopy was used to complete the wedding ceremony today on Valentine's Day.*

This creative lead, three sentences total, took longer than usual to get to the point of the story.

Perhaps you can suggest a quicker approach but be sure to get the place, the event and the surprise wind in the opening to snag your reader's interest.

> *What do a couple in love, the Empire State Building, Valentine's Day and a sudden gust of wind have in common?*

That's a question lead that gets all the elements in one sentence, but without a movie reference.

Here's one using the song title technique that is to be used very sparingly.

> *Gone With the Wind? Right action, wrong movie.*

The Associated Press led the story this way:

> *A couple who'd been together for 17 years planned to marry on Valentine's Day in the Empire State Building – only to have their marriage certificate blow out the 80th-floor window.*

Again, a loooooooong lead. No matter. Now we can tell the story. The next task is to arrange the facts by selecting the most important information and arranging it in the right order.

The leads tell the reader that a couple was to be **wed** but wind blew their marriage certificate away. The next pertinent bit of information is the **couple's identity**. Drop that fact into the story. Then offer a word of explanation in the form of a **quote**. This is similar to the paragraph below the story. Since we have a quotation from Sieger saying his group had a spare copy of the marriage certificate, the story could achieve a sense of completion by ending with that fact.

Here's a possible version of the story.

> *The scene on the 80th floor of the Empire State Building had all the makings of a couple in love after the Sleepless in Seattle movie, plus added suspense when the marriage certificate they needed to be wed blew away.*
>
> *Not to worry. This story ends happily, too, when a photocopy was used to complete the wedding ceremony today on Valentine's Day.* (**FACT 1-2**)
>
> *"They (the couple) had been dating for 17 years, and they finally made the move," said Dan Sieger, spokesman for the 34th Street Partnership, a merchants' group that sponsors the "marriage marathon" at the Empire State Building.* (**FACT 4-5**)
>
> *Right before Higby and Ross of Langhorne, Pa., were to be wed, a gust of wind blew the couple's marriage certificate off the 80th floor.* (**FACT 3**)
>
> *No problem. According to Sieger, "We happened to have a Xerox of it downstairs and we were able to salvage the whole thing."* (**FACT 5**)

What version works for you? Think about the various approaches and decide on how you want your article to read. The first step is to think about the content and what is the appropriate approach to take. Now you are ready to engage the writer's imagination to devote your special gifts to capturing this narrative with insight and panache.

Quotation as an organizing device

In developing an article, a writer must examine the facts to determine the proper order of the information for the maximum clarity and the most economical use of language. As stated earlier, the Valentine's Day story is an example of an article that presents the facts in order of most important information. One way to make this decision easier is to select **two quotations**. This idea works best when the two quotations are from the same person. Use the **first quotation** in **paragraph three** and the other quotation as the **last paragraph**.

Some considerations with the quotations

Quotations should be used for information that adds to the article; they shouldn't be used for facts and figures that can be better stated by the writer.

For instance, a quotation that says, "The party will begin at 5 p.m." is weak. You can state that kind of information, so why waste a valuable quotation on it. Save the quotations for the explanations, the answer to the " why" question.

Think of quotations as the sweet spot of the tennis racquet. It's in the center where the strings are most taut, and where the netting will give the ball the most power. Place the quotations that you use in sweet spots in your article to give them the most power. Select phrases from your subject that are picturesque and well-said. When a college dean of students once was interviewed by a leading newspaper on his opinion of a beleaguered college president, the dean said, "I would give him a D, not exactly a failure, but far from a success." The quotation works because it is clear but it draws on the culture of education, the all-important grade.

Often the reporter can condense a statement from a source, the person who is providing information. In these cases, the reporter can paraphrase the quotation. Paraphrasing means putting the quotation in your own words. It works because writers often can recast a turgid statement into a concise sentence. One magazine writer, speaking on the use of quotations, made this clumsy statement, "The only thing that I'd said for the use of quotations is that effective reporting is, part of it, at least, is to know what you're looking for before the interview." Yet, the idea is a good one: Writers must consider the article angle before starting the interview, but that journalist's quotation is gaseous.

71

Now look at this quote. "Go where the reporting leads you," said Jeffery L. Sheler, a contributing editor with *U.S. News and World Report*. "It's more than having a story in mind and going out quote-shopping."

Great quotation.

It plays on the metaphor that writing an article is like a trip to the grocery store where you pick up a little dairy, a little poultry and quart of ice cream. The act of gathering the information, commonly called **reporting**, is the combination of good planning and quick wits, not just two parts quotation, one part anecdote and a splash of humor.

In an article about nutrition labeling in a company cafeteria, the director of the cafeteria made the following question-and-answer response: "Can we do this? Yes. We will, with the help of staff, design and post signs, write signs, and make the changes by the deadline, and we'll make them."

The quotation contains good information. As a quotation, however, it is too unwieldy. The syntax is strained making the meaning difficult to understand. The writer can paraphrase the quotation in her own words:

> *By fall, signs labeling the nutritional content of food will be on display in the cafeteria, according to the director of dining services.*

In most cases, information must be attributed to give the reader some idea of the credibility of the source. In this case, the director of dining services is in the position to know about the labeling program. It's worth repeating that attribution is necessary. When it is missing, readers may wonder about the authority and source for information that stands alone.

Equal facts

In those rare cases when facts are of equal importance, the sequence is of no consequence. When writing an announcement of an event, for instance, the rooms where the function will be held may be considered to be equal in their relative importance.

> *Displays of old and rare newspapers will be shown Monday at 3 p.m. in hospital lounge and at 8 p.m. in the Hicks Humanity Center.*

Notice in that sentence, however, that the earlier time was mentioned first suggesting that even cases of equal facts, a sense of order is useful.

Veteran news-writing teacher George Hough represents the equal facts story this way:

FACT 1	Or	FACT 4
FACT 2		FACT 2
FACT 3		FACT 3
FACT 4		FACT 1

The **equal fact story** allows the writer to plunk the facts down in any order. Beware. This kind of story is best reserved for brief items of just a few sentences. While these items don't require much creativity, they should still follow the principles of good news writing – the concise use of a few well-chosen words. Strive for economy.

Suppose, for example, your organization asks you write an announcement about a celebrity appearing for a fund-raiser. The most important information concerns the celebrity's name and when and where he will appear.

Here are the elements:
Celebrity: Actor Davy Jones of *The Monkees*
When: June 13, 1996
Where: Talls Family Music Center
When: 2 to 4 p.m.

Other facts include that Jones will sign autographs, meet fans and talk about his acting career. To help your readers recall Jones' claim to fame, you add that Jones was part of the 1960s TV show *The Monkees* and he appeared in the 1995 movie *The Brady Bunch Movie*.

After the important information is inserted in the lead, these equal facts can be arranged randomly.

Here's one possibility.

Actor Davy Jones of 1960s TV hit The Monkees *will appear June 13 from 2 to 4 p.m. at Talls Family Music Center, Center Square.*
Jones appeared in the 1995 movie The Brady Bunch Movie. *He will meet fans and sign autographs at Talls.*

Anyone born after 1970 may not remember Jones or *The Monkees* and you might have to consult a reference book on entertainment to provide additional detail on the TV show, the music the band played, and the popularity of some of their songs.

The sample brief above takes a straightforward approach to the story, but an enterprising reporter can have some fun with the material by using a feature lead. As you develop as a writer, evaluate the story elements and decide if a light touch or somber touch is required.

Here's a light touch.

> *Hey, hey, he's still a Monkee, and he's still monkeying around.*
> *Today actor Davy Jones of the Monkees will monkey around at Talls Family Music Center, Center Square from 2 to 4 p.m.*

In this example, a line from the TV show theme song is used to build a lead. Be advised, these kinds of leads can be considered too cute and readers (and editors) may be turned-off, so use them with discretion.

> **Tip:** Contractions are good!
> He's still a Monkee. **Right.**
> He is still a Monkee. Wrong. Wooden.
> Often, the "be" and the "ing form of the verb can be deleted in briefs.
> He will monkey around. **Right.**
> He will be monkeying around. Wrong.
> The play will open tonight. **Right.**
> The play will be opening tonight. Wrong.
> The "be" can be used as the verb in the sentences where leanness is essential.
> The meeting will be Monday at 4 p.m.

For briefs, the acronym SOP will help. In this case, it doesn't mean "standard operating procedure." The acronym SOP can help a writer remember the order of a brief by putting the name of the speaker (S) first, followed by the organization (O) involved, then the place (P). SOP also stands for standard operating procedure and this mnemonic can be your SOP for this task.

Example: *Actor Davy Jones will speak to the Kiwanis Club at Talls Music Center Friday at 4 p.m.* (Use a.m. or p.m. for time.)

Exercise

Make up your own sentences using SOP.

I. _____

II. _____

III. _____

IV. _____

Choosing the right touch is part of the challenge in writing for mass media. Having some fun with Jones' *Monkees* lyric is appropriate for a feature article about a musician from the 1960s, but that kind of approach would be in poor taste for an article about crime, violence and tragedy. Hard news is concerned with the hard parts of life. Counselor Scott Peck begins his best-selling book, *The Road Less Traveled*[20], by telling his readers to learn that life is hard, and then they can respond well to the routine disappointments.

In news, however, hard refers to the more serious hardships of life – fires, car accidents, thefts and any event that is timely, that must be published or broadcast immediately or it loses its value as information. All crime is considered to be hard news. Social occasions such as weddings are considered soft news. In many cases soft news is read more readily than hard news, but the function of the information often determines the approach the writer should take when constructing the article.

Detecting the hard news edge

Consider the story of a three-year-old child who called 911 to help authorities extract her mother from the trunk of a car. Is that hard news or soft news?

It sounds as if it could be a fun story about a woman who accidentally locked herself in her trunk and her daughter saves the day.

Would it make any difference if an armed robber locked the woman in her trunk?

Yes, that behavior is a crime, making the story hard news. The tricky part is that the happy ending with a surprise hero, a toddler, gives the story an added dimension. It sounds as if it could be a feature article, soft news. **Soft news** is considered to be less **time-sensitive** than hard news. Furthermore, the approach used for soft news often has a richer narrative quality and allows the writer to break free of the economy of language reserved for hard news. In writing the story as a blend of hard and soft news, the writer must strike the right quality, a matter known as tone. Tone refers to the way the words are understood. Is the piece jocular, deadly serious, light-hearted or down-right hokey?

In the rescue story, considered a standard in mass media writing, the Associated Press treated the report the way a master of ceremony might use in bestowing an award. Here's the beginning.

> *Mary Graves has always thought her 3-year-old daughter was something special.*

---

[20] Peck, S. M. (2003). *The road less traveled.* New York: Simon & Schuster.

The toddler proved it by talking to a 911 operator and leading police to the car where an armed robber had locked her mother in the trunk.

"She's just really bright. I don't know how to explain it," Graves said Sunday night. "She has a photographic memory, and she's learning three different languages. She's a special little girl."

The report goes on to tell the story of the robber who reportedly locked Graves in the trunk but not before the mother pressed 911 and slipped her cellular telephone to the little girl. The girl was left in the car and the robber left.

Chronological development

Once the AP writer told the readers the end of a story – a toddler called authorities to help her mother escape from the locked trunk of a car – she went back and filled in the crucial details in chronological order.

Here's a way to practice this important writing technique. Think about yesterday. What were some of the highlights? Tell a story of one of those highlights, but instead of starting at the beginning and spinning the account in 1-2-3 fashion, tell the conclusion first, then go back and fill in the details.

Most of us are used to holding off on the dramatic conclusion, but in mass media writing, the audience usually wants to know the outcome first. The following example is a long anecdote that is notable for its lack of drama. However, it's the pedestrian quality that provides a bit of charm found in ordinary life.

Barbara Wojcik told me of her encounter at the swimming pool with a bright child very much like the one who used the cellular telephone. In the late 1990s, Taylor, a three-year-old spied a child in the baby pool. Toys surrounded the little girl and Taylor decided this tyke was a good prospect for friendship. However, when she started over to the girl, the little toy czar barked, "These are my toys. Stay away. Go back to your mother!"

Taylor stopped in her tracks, put a finger to her cheek and said, "Hmmmm. Let me think about this."

She really didn't know what to do next. Barbara sat about 10 feet away and noticed Taylor mumbling to herself and Barbara went over for a closer hear and discovered Taylor praying, "Jesus, help the little girl to be happy."

Anecdotal development

As suggested in the previous example, an **anecdote** is a **brief story**, but a story nonetheless, told in chronological fashion. How could it be told with the ending first. Take a minute and think about the approach you would use in developing this account, known as an anecdote or short story.

You need a way to sum up the story in a sentence. You ask yourself, "Is this hard news or soft news?" The subject isn't crime – it's politeness. It isn't tragedy, but it does have a sad note. In short, it's the kind of story that a proud mother might share with a friend, not the subject of an evening newscast; however, it still contains all the elements of a story that you can tell in mass media convention. This story has a clear ending, meaning that it must have a beginning, too. As you may recall from your literature days, short stories in fiction are defined as possessing a beginning, middle and end.

The end of the intercession-at-the-pool story is the prayer. As a writer, you could have asked, "But what happened next?" You could keep asking that question to peel the action back another layer, but let's stay with this version for the time being and work with the information we have.

The ending is a child praying. In searching for a feature opening, the writer wants a pithy statement that tells the conclusion but hints that more is involved.

Here are three openings that could be followed up with the same narrative.

Word association

Children who pray may not walk on water but they can sure rise above troubled currents.

That opening is OK, but it sounds a little moralistic. The tone should be light to avoid casting one child as the stark villain and the other as the angel. The idea is to use language associated with water to make the point. This idea is a good one but remember not to take it too far or your reader will be turned off.

An unadorned statement

Three-year-old Taylor Smith found that an afternoon prayer by the neighborhood pool was just the right response when she met another child who didn't want to share.

This version is similar to the AP story on the toddler and the telephone call. It merely tells us the conclusion and now we're ready to hear the details.

Word play

> *Some of us pay lip service to the idea of prayer in times of uncertainty. For three-year-old Taylor Smith, a prayer off the lips is as natural as the doggy paddle.*

This lead is a combination of the two approaches. It uses some mild word play "pay lip service" and "prayer off the lips" to suggest a playful tone.

The lead tries to suggest the context by mentioning the doggy paddle, a type of stroke that is used in swimming. Most readers will understand this association and the two sentences serve to set-up the story. Enough details are missing to pique the reader's curiosity. Provoking the reader to continue is among the most challenging of techniques and the most satisfying of results when it works.

Now you can insert the details. Let's go with that last lead and add some details.

> *Some of us pay lip service to the idea of prayer in times of uncertainty. For three-year-old Taylor Smith, a prayer off the lips is a natural as the doggy paddle.*
>
> *Taylor waded into the neighborhood pool the other day and spied a little girl about her age playing with toys. But when Taylor moved in closer for a chat, the little girl said, "These are my toys. Stay away. Go back to your mother!"*
>
> *Dazed, Taylor's mother, Barbara, saw the encounter and walked over to Taylor and could hear her toddler mumbling.*
>
> *"Jesus, help this little girl to be happy."*
>
> *The waters may have been troubled, but Taylor wasn't. She retrieved a toy whale and cup from her bag and began splashing with her oldest friend – Mom.*

Color

That anecdote has a few details not provided in the page before. As a writer, you might have to interview a source more than once to get the kind of detail called **color**. Sometimes the detail literally refers to the color of an object – the blue whale and red cup, for instance. In other cases, the **detail** refers to the person's facial expressions, the music playing in the background, the aroma of popcorn in the microwave, any sensation derived from your senses.

Among the best writers of color is Edna Buchanan of *Miami Herald* fame. In a feature article about Buchanan's work as a police reporter,

Calvin Trillin of *The New Yorker* said he liked the color of her writing, particularly in an article about Gary Robinson, an ex-con.[21] Buchanan reported that Robinson bullied his way to the counter at a Church's chicken restaurant only to be told that all the fried chicken had been sold and only nuggets were left. The man, drunk, slugged the woman at the counter and a fight ensued leaving the ex-con shot dead by a security guard. Buchanan began her piece with "Gary Robinson died hungry."

Buchanan has made a national reputation for writing about crime with the fascination of a person who wants to know what song played on the radio when the fight broke out, the kind of table cloth that a widow used in the dining room, the year, make and model of the luxury car where the gangster kept his golf clubs and all the other details that vary from story to story. These details make for compelling reading regarding the genre, but the pro knows when the detail adds and when the detail is irrelevant. As a writer you must use discernment to tell your audience the observations and sensations that add to the narrative. Add, don't distract.

The point for a short item such as the one about the little girl in the swimming pool is to keep it brief and snappy. By judiciously selecting the best words and reworking the prose to whittle it down to leanness form, the item will read well. In this case, we added an extra dimension, a modest moral. In most cases, a moral is inappropriate, and readers will find the lesson to be heavy-handed. However, if it works without calling undue attention to itself, then use it.

For those adventurous writers, try making a connection between a biblical account that mentions prayer and water. Can you think of any? Another angle is prayer and children. A writer could use a Bible concordance such as Strong's Exhaustive Concordance of the Bible[22] to find the precise biblical references to all these ideas. The word "children" takes up nearly five pages in that reference book. The potential danger to this approach is that a writer could lapse into a preachy tone and lose the sparkle.

The following short article uses the reportorial style of writing to tell the story of a public school and its practice of reading the Bible. Notice the use of numbers to add precision and the quotes to end the article. The last two paragraphs include an anecdote, a short story in the February 7, 1994 issue of *Christianity Today.*

---

[21] Trillin, C. (1986, February 17). Profiles. Covering the Cops. Reprinted from *The New Yorker* in a pamphlet, p. 1.

[22] Strong, J. (2001). *The new Strong's exhaustive concordance of the Bible.* Nashville: Nelson Reference.

Bible reading ends years after ban
By Michael Ray Smith

For nearly 40 years, students in Pennsylvania's Warrior Run School District began classes with Bible reading over the intercom system. In December, the practice stopped.

Since 1955, the 1,200-student district permitted public Bible reading and excused students who did not want to listen. Even though the U.S Supreme Court ruled in 1963 such Bible reading was "indirect coercive pressure," the recitation continued unabated until teacher Jay Nixon condemned it recently and the Silver Spring, Maryland-based Americans United for Separation of Church and State warned school officials that "your continuance with this practice will open the school district to a lawsuit and resulting attorney's fees."

Senior Janelle Smith read the last passage from Luke 1 in December. "It should have been 'Jesus wept,'" says school board president David Hunter. He has received dozens of letters of support and is optimistic. "Now we have to see what's possible within the law."

When you're stuck

Sometimes a writer just can't seem to get started. The lead is elusive, and, worse, the writing seems lame, weak and unimaginative. Here's a strategy used by Jeffery Sheler, the writer who is mentioned earlier in this chapter. When he is stuck for an opening, he **begins in the middle**, with the knowledge that he will return to the opening and hammer it out after he nails the middle. Once you begin writing feature articles on a regular basis, you, too, will develop some tricks that help you manage when you seem to be swimming in information. Sheler says that he can start in the middle because he has mastered the format of the typical article. Once you know the **formula**, you can deviate from it to write inventive feature articles that use refrains, regional dialects, literary devices, language that matches the topic, and more.

The formula

- The **lead**.
- A **quotation** from the primary source.
- A **background** paragraph, called the **nut graf** or nut paragraph, which provides the essential background and often the reason you are writing the article. The idea is the important information can be said in a nutshell.

- The body of the article, which features **competing voices** that challenge each other.
- **Anecdotes** and **quotations** arranged in some kind of organization as outlined in this chapter.
- A **conclusion** that often echoes ideas mentioned in the opening. Frequently, feature writers conclude a work by using a quotation from the first speaker, the primary source.

When stuck, Sheler found that he can ease his way into his magazine article by jumping to the middle, just below the nut graf, and develop the article's tension. Editors such as Marvin Olasky say that many articles have a kind of rhyme scheme that reflects the tension inherent in describing the point-counterpoint of many features. The scheme may be on the order of **A, B, A, B, B, A.** Each letter represents a point of view or a quotation, and the writer can alternate from one view to the other using transitions such as, "Not all archaeologists agree," or "The medical community is divided on the proper treatment." When you are hard-pressed to write, jump to this part of the article and work on it until the lead becomes apparent. Some writers even fashion the opening only after the rest of the article is complete. It's not a technique that will work for everyone, but it is a good one to keep in mind when you just can't get started.

Sheler often collects much of his information by telephone, and he types his sources' answers directly on the computer. This method can help a writer formulate an opening because the information is typed and easier to read than a notebook brimming with notes. To achieve this ease of reading, some writers type their notes. The **typed notes** make an **at-a-glance review** of notes very convenient. In addition, the theme of the article tends to emerge from the material when it can be examined easily. As you read your typed notes, highlight the rich quotations and underline the unusual anecdote.

Before long, the raw material of your article will stand out and you, the architect, only need to decide on the best way to design and construct the finished project. Get started. Write the draft, walk away from it, and then return for a second or third sweep. Soon, you will see the words take shape and a crude word building will be revealed. In time, the building will become sturdy. Don't give up. Too many people, who want "to have written" but never write, give up before they start. The task seems too daunting. Forget yourself. Remember, it's not about you. It's about the article. Then write with the conviction that your efforts may not be immortal, but what effort made by us is? All of it will pass away, so do your best, and be content knowing that you aren't yet the writer that you will be someday.

Feature stories as short stories

Writer Jon Franklin has a mysterious and thoughtful hypothesis. He says that feature writing for today is what **short stories** were to yesterday.[23] He calls it the **nonfiction short story**, but chides news reporters for focusing on the resolution, the end, without considering the complications. Journalists working in hard news, even feature writing, focus on the culminating event, the end of the drama, without exploring the events that led to the conclusion. To have a satisfying conclusion requires a thoughtful **beginning and middle**. As you develop your article, think about it as a part of the **human drama** where love, pain and death are part of life. Life is complicated and audiences want to witness the way a character resolves a problem. We all desire insight, coping skills, even easy lessons on the way life works.

Writers use devices to identify the action, often in pairs. Unemployment strikes a talented artist Lisa, **first card**. Lisa overcomes and makes her reputation, **second card**. See the pair? Unemployment, a defeat. Finds art, a success. In the process of the **struggle**, the **conflict**, Lisa shows tenacity as she fights back. It refines her and builds her character and others become inspired by her actions. The fight isn't without setbacks. Lisa tried and failed, tried again and learned from the mistakes. She learned about herself and about the world. As you write your feature article, remember to apply the narrative approach to tell us a story. You will feel more fulfilled and your audience will be more gratified. In the next section, you will read about Dr. Dennis E. Hensley who will provide practical ideas on ways to imbed the story in a feature article.

Dr. Dennis Hensley

Biography of Dennis Hensley

Dr. Dennis E. Hensley is a professor of English at Taylor University, Fort Wayne, Indiana, where he directs the professional writing major. His program is one of more than 300 around the nation that offer in-depth creative writing classes designed to get writers published. He is the author of six novels, 34 nonfiction books (including eight textbooks on

---

[23] Franklin, J. (1986). *Writing for story*. New York: New American Library.

writing), 150 short stories and more than 3,000 freelance articles including *Writer's Digest, The Writer, Modern Bride, Downbeat, The War Cry, Reader's Digest, The Detroit Free Press, The Indianapolis Star, The Cincinnati Enquirer* and others.

He has received many honors including The Dorothy Hamilton Memorial Writing Award and Indiana University's Award for Teaching Excellence, and he has served as Writer in Residence or "guest professor" at 47 colleges and universities. He was a sergeant in the U.S. Army in Vietnam in 1970-1971. He and his wife Rose have two grown children, Nathan and Jeanette.

Editor's note: Writer Judy Baker interviewed Dennis Hensley to learn his secrets for success in writing. Judy Baker is an award-winning freelance public relations counselor and writer with over 20 years of experience. She earned a Bachelor of Fine Arts degree from Old Dominion University in Norfolk, Va., and her master's degree in journalism from Regent University in Virginia Beach.

Judy Baker

Interview with Dennis Hensley

Q: How did you get started?

A: From the time I was a senior in high school, I knew I wanted to be a writer. Up to that point, I had been interested in studying law, but a teacher came into my life who changed all that. He opened books for me in a way no one had ever done before. I decided from that point on that I wanted to be a writer. The problem was that when you went to college and said you wanted to be a writer, it was interpreted as "Oh, you want to teach English." "No," I said. "I really want to be a writer – novels, short stories, that sort of thing." So, what I had to do was take straight English major courses and try to take as many of the courses that they called "creative writing" or "advanced expository writing."

I wasn't getting anywhere near the success I had hoped to find out of a college degree because while the teachers knew a lot about the esoteric value of literature, they didn't really know anything about the basics – like how do you land an agent, copyright laws and so on. So I was trying to learn that on my own by reading writing magazines, and books on writing and getting an awful lot of rejections. What I did sell were often small markets – like I started writing fiction when I was only 18 years old and I would sell to Sunday School take-home papers – we're talking a 1,200-word story at a half-penny a word, six bucks! It was exhilarating to say that I've sold fiction, but people would ask if I made a living at it and I would say, "I don't even make an existence at it."

It was an apprenticeship program. I look back at it now and realize that some of the editors who were taking time to edit my copy weren't paying me much in the way of money, but they were investing in my career and it was important for me to get that kind of feedback – something that I was missing in a college class.

By the time I got through college, I had done work on the college newspaper and that helped a great deal and had done all this other freelancing for Christian markets and small publications. I went in the service because I had met a literary agent and he looked at a manuscript of mine, even though he told me he didn't have time to take on any new clients, and it was the best and worst thing that happened to me simultaneously. He said, "You've got all the mechanical skills – you know how to use the semi-colon and all that – you just don't have anything to say."

He said, "So, what have you ever done? Have you ever been married?"
I said, "No."
"Have you ever traveled around the world?"
I said, "Not really."
"Have you ever been in the military?"
I said, "No."
"You ever bought a home or worked a full-time job?"
So, he went through all this stuff and I said no, no, no. Then he asked me why was I trying to tell people what life's all about if I've never done anything to find out myself.

And, really, he was right.

I was writing from that limited focus that I had from being only 18 to 20 years old. I didn't realize that I had to bring my own unique set of circumstances to what I wrote – and while there are only nine basic plots, it's how you approach it that requires imagination.

So, I took his advice and when I got out of college, I continued to work as a writer. I worked by day as a substitute teacher, and then I joined the military and that really changed my whole worldview. The second year I was in I went to Vietnam for 12 months and it changed my world perspective. The war lets you see people at their best and worst at the same time where little people become giants and giants become cowards.

My dad was in World War II and he asked me to keep a daily journal. He made me promise him I would keep a journal and he said that years later I would be glad that I had done it. Obviously, he was right. I thought I would never forget something that had happened but time does get away from you.

I kept a journal and I had time to do this activity because I'd worked 12 hours on and have 12 hours off. I had a lot of time to read. I read an awful lot of books then and talked to lots of interesting people. Back then during the draft, there were a lot of college students in the U.S. Army, so you could talk to really interesting people, which gave me a different perspective.

When I came back after being in the service, I used the G.I. Bill and went back to school and got a master's degree in English. But it was a different kind of life for me because I jumped into working on a master's degree in English, and I was reading Russian literature and the like but at the same time, I realized that I've got to be with other writers. Writers know about writing. So I started hanging out with writers and by that I mean journalists and novelists, people who really knew, and by hanging out, I mean I made contact with them by mail. I lined up jobs for myself with magazines and really found that you need to be around writers if you want to learn about writing.

So when I finished that and I went down to Ball State University in Indiana, I combined the two because I realized my life was going in two ways – there was going to be the pragmatic part – which I could write for a dollar – I could be a hired gun. But I also wanted to write novels and short stories and I wanted to take a literary approach to some of the journalism that I had done. So I got the best of both worlds. I started on a Ph.D. at Ball State University and began teaching part time there, too. But at night and on weekends, I worked as a newspaperman at the *Monthly Star*. Now that was a really great thing because nobody had time to be kind to you. They would just say things like this lead really stinks and they'd cross it out or they'd ask who really cares about what the burglar wore. What did he steal?

That experience is great if you have what I call the turtle shell hide – if you can shut up and take it, you can learn fast. It is the best training ground. In fact, I think I'd be a newspaperman today if it paid better. It was fun. I enjoyed hitting the beat. I'd go out and I'd do everything. I did interviews, covered civic theater and then I'd go back at 1 in the morning and write up the copy, and be out there again at 6 a.m. There is a real adrenaline rush when you're a newspaperman.

But I tried my hand at fiction, too. I wrote a novel, a mystery-romance novel, called *The Legacy of Lillian Parker*.[24] There's a character in that novel who is a POW in Vietnam, who after 10 years gets to come back home. He's a parallel of me in that he and I were born in the same city on the same day. We went in the U.S. Army at the same time; we went overseas at the same time.

Of course, then the character has to have a life of his own, and I was never a POW in Vietnam so that's where my journalism background came into play. I found Vietnam POWs at the VFW, the American Legion and so on and I put my interview skills to work. I asked what it was like, what did you say, what was your greatest worry, and how did you remain mentally tough. I just kept probing these guys all the time. I asked them to tell me about the other guys and what it was like and I actually wrote several profiles of these fascinating men and sold them to magazines, but the whole time this exercise was journalistic research that was to be put into fiction.

When I turned around and wrote a novel, *The Legacy of Lillian Parker*, I created POW scenes that rang true. That's where I really married the two, the skills of the one transferred to the other so people would say, "Now that may be fiction, but it has this verisimilitude, this semblance of truth that says this guy knows something about it."

Q: So you're saying that there really would have been no way you could have written this book without having employed your journalism skills?

A: I know people who try to do only fiction writing and they go off and try to do interviews and they don't have that savvy of knowing when somebody is conning you or when someone is leveling with you, and they don't know how to establish that rapport. All of the things that come with the practice of interviewing, plus I don't think they have the understanding of how much preparation you do for an interview. After I prepare well for an interview, the source often will say, "You found all that out about me?" Then they know that you're interested but they also know that you're going to get past the trivial stuff and let them talk about some deep material.

That's just one example of where knowing journalism came into play. Other times my skills as being a pretty fair researcher have really helped. I wrote a thriller medical novel, *The Gift*,[25] about a man who has some abilities other people don't have and knowing how to research diseases – going to the University of Michigan hospital and calling people at the

---

[24] Hensley, D. E. (1986). *The legacy of Lillian Parker*. Irvine, CA: Harvest House.

[25] Hensley, D. E. (1988). *The gift*. Irvine, CA: Harvest House.

Mayo Clinic. It's about knowing how to get information that I wanted from the Internet and from textbooks or contacting a doctor and nurse and a genetic researcher to make sure that I was using the right terms while not losing my reader. You know you can bury your reader in terms and then it becomes too hard for them to follow. So it's that balance of understanding how the newspaper person will write for the public and give them key information but in such a way that the lay person will say, "Oh, yeah, I'm following; I'm tracking on that."

Now the side of traditional journalism that we've always been taught is to use the inverted pyramid, but in fiction, that won't fly because you can't just throw a whole bunch of facts at people and expect them to bond with the character. They don't understand the plot and they don't really care. So there you have to use a different kind of technique and that's where studying literature really does help. And, oddly enough, that can transfer back the other way in good journalism.

Let's say that I'm writing my nonfiction book that came out in 1998, *Millennium Approaches*.[26] That's a nonfiction book about futurism. It's about what the 21st Century will be like. What I did there was to use my fiction writing and my literary writing to help so that I would able to say what I think medicine will be like in the 21st Century; however, rather than layer a bunch of statistics on top of each other, I used the narrative approach. When I did an interview and an expert said, "Okay, we're doing such and such research project," I'd stop them and make them tell a story. The source may say, "Our research shows that 27%," and I wrote it in as a narrative that caused readers to say, "That's fascinating."

By blending the literary with journalism, the result is good reading. I blended the two when I wrote *The Legacy of Lillian Parker* – pure journalism that helped me prepare for the novel. And that's what I call literary journalism – the idea that you can cross over back and forth and use those skills so that the reader is taught and fascinated at the same time.

Q: What is it that you want to happen to the audience on page 1 or online when the person reads the first sentence?

A: Obviously, you've got to have a great lead in modern journalism, but for me, when I'm writing fiction, I've got to do five basic tasks from the start.

1) Establish the setting
2) Because people not only want to know where they are, but
3) When they are.
4) You've got to make them bond with the main character; otherwise, why would I want to continue reading?

---

[26] Hensley, D. E. (1998). *Millennium approaches*. New York: Avon.

5) I have to establish what kind of story it's going to be – adventure, mystery, romance, whatever – I have to establish this format right away.

Q: All of this right from the beginning?

A: Yes. You've got to grab people's attention on the first page because when they go into the bookstore and pick up the book, they read the first few sentences to determine if it's going to pull them in, if it's readable. For example, in one of Jack London's short stories is this first line: *The Yukon, where to lose a glove is to lose a hand.* That is the greatest lead you can imagine because you're right there; you know where you are. You know what the tension of the story will be, you're going to freeze to death. It's all in one line, one line! That's a journalist telling you what it's really like because it puts you right there.

Q: But what about great novelists who have never spent a minute involved or engaged in journalism?

A: If you say a great novelist, then you will have to tell me who they are. There are so many who were journalists: Tom Wolfe, Truman Capote, Margaret Mitchell, Ernest Hemingway. If any of these writers had the ability to write, even Mark Twain and Damon Runyon, they were journalists. They understood how to write precisely. Now if you want to go the other way and talk about someone such as Ann Tyler, I'd say, "Okay." But I don't like her books.

Q: Is your view a little jaundiced?

A: No, I understand why people like her work because they are character-driven. I need a plot; she doesn't need a plot. I read her stuff about how people go through life and have these experiences and I think, "Okay, what's the point?" To other readers, that is the whole point. For me, I want to see how a character copes with life on a day-to-day basis. I want to see what shapes his or her life. I don't really need a crisis and an outcome. Writers such as Tyler don't need a background in journalism because they are just observing their community. It's a different kind of novel that appeals to a different kind of market and it's a very limited market.

John Grisham is a good writer not because he's a lawyer but because as a lawyer, he was a fact-researcher. He was digging into other people's lives, their backgrounds. See the power of a good researcher? Lawyers do the same kind of in-depth interviews that journalists do.

Q: So anyone who is by profession or by nature a curious person is going to be a better writer?

A: Yes, but let's not make the mistake saying lawyers are good writers! At the very start, you need to learn to research and, then, of course, you need to learn how to write.

Q: How has your faith impacted your writing, both as a news writer and as a fiction writer?

A: I am a writer who is a Christian. A Christian carpenter doesn't just build churches, right? I have never written anything that I would be embarrassed for someone in my Sunday School class or in my family to read or that I would worry about being held accountable for. I want it to be edifying and uplifting. I write for a living, but everything I write I think has a redeeming value to it. I don't think if you're a quality writer that you have to stoop to choosing either topics or styles or writing that are less than transferable to any audience. I've tried to hold certain standards to what I do. I don't use off-color language; I don't write graphic sex scenes and I don't write about gratuitous violence. As a reporter, sometimes that is what the story is, but I haven't set out to do that in my own writing.

I think, too, this decision has led me to be a point man for the secular world. In other words, I had a contract recently with Random House and prior to that it was Avon Books. Now these are top publishers in the secular world that will publish just about anything. When they approach me to do something, they know that there will be no off-color scenes and that it will be good, solid reporting. That's what they call a "Hensley book."

Q: You have deliberately built a reputation.

A: Yes, but that doesn't mean you don't fight over manuscripts. The editor may come back and ask me to spice it up by doing this or that, but the book belongs to the author. Publishing companies are in the business to make money, but the author may have to say no.

For instance, I wrote a book on time management for a secular publishing company, Bobbs-Merrill. The last chapter that I wrote was a testimonial to why I manage my time the way I do. I want quality time with my family, time in my community, time in my church and time for work. The publisher came back and said it sounded too religious and inspirational. I said but that's who I am and there needs to be a chapter in the book that explains why I, or anyone, should manage their time. They fought me about that and eventually I told them that I wasn't interested in doing more books with them unless I could have a voice in my work. They agreed to go with the time management book the way that I wanted it and, amazingly, they got marvelous feedback. People wrote me and told me how much they particularly liked the last chapter!

So, guess what? The second book that I wrote for them, *Uncommon Sense*,[27] they told me, "Go with your best judgment!" So, that's it. You earn your reputation one little challenge and response at a time.

---

[27] Hensley, D. E. (1984). *Uncommon Sense*. Chicago, Ill: Dearborn Trade.

Q: Why did you write some of your books under a pen name?

A: Holly Miller[28] and I have co-authored seven books. When we started doing this work together, we didn't want to write under a man's name and we didn't want to write under a woman's name, so we devised it this way. H O L is from her name, Holly. D E N is from Dennis. Together that equals HOLDEN. We say, "It's L E S of L I E to admit we're HOL and DEN to make Leslie Holden, the pen name. Research shows that women purchase 91% of romance novels, and they will not buy a romance novel unless a woman writes it.

My friend, Sally Stuart, writes westerns, but they won't let her write under her name. She uses George Dillon.

Q: Would there be an occasion that you wrote a book solo and used a pen name?

A: Yes. I wrote a book for Berkley under the name of Roberta Grimes because the average person who buys a mainstream novel is a woman between the ages of 38 and 46 years of age, a college graduate who expects the book to be written from a woman's perspective.

Q: What about *Memoirs of a Geisha*, written by a male author, Arthur S. Golden? [29]

A: But, you have to understand two things here. He presented himself as a man who has a master's degree in ancient oriental history, so he's a researcher and he was a man who was a journalist and had done a lot of writing before that. He went to Japan, studied about geishas, talked to geishas and learned all he could.

The reason that I spent so many years co-authoring novels with Holly Miller was because I didn't know how women thought and she taught me. She didn't know how men thought, so when I'd write a passage of dialogue, she'd say it was good dialogue, but it was not how a woman would express it. We taught each other as we went along. These days I can do my own dialogue for both men and women.

Q: Talk more about the concept of literary journalism and its worth today.

A: Print media has become polarized. In other words, either you're getting just the facts thrown at you or you're getting people who want incredible entertainment, such as the Harry Potter series. It's one extreme or the other. The literary journalist comes in and says, all right, I can give you the information, but I can make it very palatable. In an era prior to radio and television, that is what people wanted. They wanted their information, but in a very entertaining form. So when Jack London wrote

---

[28] A profile on writer Holly Miller appears in Chapter 7.

[29] Golden, A.S. (1999). *Memoirs of a geisha*. New York: Random House.

about the San Francisco earthquake in 1906, he put the reader right there. We're coming back to that kind of writing because we're such a visually-oriented society. Writers today know they have to give the facts, but in such a way that the reader stays with it. We have rediscovered literary journalism. You have to be a storyteller. That is the main thing. When you say a flood cascaded down Main Street causing $10 million worth of damage, no one is really going to pay any attention to that. But the minute you show a woman standing in her flooded basement, holding her child and everything is gone, then you have a story with which the reader can bond. If they don't bond with the story, they don't care.

As a professor of journalism and English and someone who runs a professional writing program, my focus for my students for the 21st century is going to be on pushing students both ways. I make my students take fiction writing and I make them take journalism. I tell them they've got to learn how to draw from the best of both. I tell them that if they learn to be a great interviewer, then they will be great novelists. Your dialogue will ring true and your settings will be visual. If you learn to be a good storyteller, your feature writing will come more alive. It worked for me and it will work for any feature writer.

A long way from home, a short story
By Dennis Hensley
Used with permission

George and Emma Rodgers got into their Ford Fairlane. Though the car was nearly 20 years old, it had not been used all that often. When it had, George – or "Pops" as he was affectionately called by the family – had made sure it was in excellent condition before leaving and on returning.

They set off for a short ride that day with the cool winds blowing in from the Pacific. Maybe they could find something that would make them feel less like strangers in a strange land.

George and Emma really had no need for a car. They had been living with their eldest son and his family for twelve years. They had watched their three grandchildren grow. The older two had married and were busy with children of their own.

The car was George and Emma's symbol of independence. Up until six months ago, the Rodgers family had lived in a small suburb of Columbus, Ohio. They had not always lived in Columbus. The entire family was originally from Pennsylvania. In fact, George and Emma had grown up in a small town in western Pennsylvania and had never been to the city of Pittsburgh. Then, suddenly, because of their age and

91

health, they found themselves being uprooted and moved to unfamiliar territory.

During the previous twelve years they had adjusted well to their new home. They had made friends in Columbus, become active in a local church, and had joined the senior citizen's club. All seemed to be going well for the Rodgers family... until the day their son came home and announced he had accepted a new job in southern California.

Of course, George and Emma were thrilled for their son. He was excited about the new opportunity, the challenges, and even where the job would take him and his family. What parents wouldn't have been happy? But George and Emma had already made one major adjustment late in life and had finally found their niche in that community. Beginning anew, now that they were in their seventies, seemed to be such an effort.

Their son wouldn't hear of leaving them behind. He reminded them that they had adjusted well to the Columbus area. Where they now were going wouldn't be that different. And, besides, look at the same weather they would enjoy year round.

When George and Emma first arrived in southern California they were fascinated. After two weeks, however, their fascination wore off, and they were ready to go back to Columbus.

It was true, they liked the mild climate. Leaving Ohio in February with six inches of snow on the ground and arriving in California with its palm trees and sunshine had lifted their spirits. But after the newness wore off, they took a good look around. It just wasn't home.

Many of the signs, billboards and advertisements were written in Spanish, Cantonese, and Vietnamese. Streets and residential areas all had foreign-sounding names that George and Emma could not pronounce. On both sides of their new home their neighbors spoke only foreign languages. No, it was just not "their" America.

Excursions with their son and his family proved dangerous and alien as well. The malls and stores were very different. The side streets looked like four lane highways. The residential speed they were used to, thirty-five, was now a fast forty-five. Cars were everywhere. George could not get over the number of cars – at all times of day and night.

But finally George and Emma had decided to take a ride on their own and try to turn negatives into positive. For the first 20 minutes, they experienced few problems. Some teenagers hung out of their car windows and yelled at the Rodgers' creeping car, and a couple of horns sounded, announcing the impatience of other drivers. But for the most part, the drive was fairly calm.

George was beginning to feel more confident and decided to venture a little farther than he had originally planned. Soon, however, he discovered he was lost. Had he realized he had inadvertently changed neighborhoods, there would have been no need for panic. But when he glanced at the street sign and saw that the familiar name had suddenly changed, he immediately thought the worst.

Frantically, George looked around seeking a place to pull over to read his map in order to discover some way of correcting his error. He always seemed to be in the wrong lane, however, and could not leave the main boulevard.

The farther he drove, the more panicked he felt. His speed slowed even more, and his sense of direction became confused as the road gradually began to turn.

"This is it! I've had it with southern California," George said. "I don't know what's so wonderful about it here. If I ever get us back to the house, we're going home."

"Home, dear?" Emma asked.

"Ohio," he replied.

Emma watched helplessly as her husband's confidence vanished. She tried to look ahead for something that could get them out of their predicament. But she had never driven in California. She was equally lost.

Ten more minutes passed before George saw a sign announcing a community park. He jerked at the wheel and maneuvered his car into the street. The "entrance" he chose, however, turned out to be an "exit." George didn't realize this until he had driven his car over the spikes. His hands were clasped to the wheel, but the car remained immobile as he felt the air whoosh from his front left tire.

Directly across from the park sat a Mercedes. The driver was a man in his mid-forties. He had left the office late and had only a half-hour to get to his next appointment. His car phone was out for repair and he had no way to get in touch with his client. He just hoped Mr. Decker would be understanding.

The man had been watching the traffic, praying for a break, when he had seen the old man purposely turn his car into the park exit. He shook his head in disbelief as he watched the car's tire sink, *Well,* he thought, *I guess I'm not the only one having problems today.*

He inched his car forward and made a break for it. He had just passed the park's exit when he knew he could not consciously leave this elderly couple stranded. He pulled over to the curb and put on the flashers.

Meanwhile, Emma had turned toward her husband, speechless. She watched as George curled and uncurled his fingers around the steering wheel. She was just about to ask what they should do when she looked up and saw the man approaching their car.

The man bent down and waited for the driver to roll down his window. "Well, mister, it looks like your day's going about the same as mine," he said with a smile.

George grunted and Emma's eyes grew wide.

The man laughed. "Why don't you two get out? You can sit on that bench in the shade. I'll just back the car up. No use changing the tire where it's sitting now."

Emma looked cautiously at her husband. As George started to open his car door, the man ran around to the other side of the car and assisted Emma.

"Name's Ted Snider, Ma'am," he said.

Emma tried to smile as Ted helped her out of the car. She waited for George before walking over to the bench.

Ted watched them sit down before he got back into the car and moved it back onto the main street. Then he quickly went about the business of jacking up the car and changing the flat.

George and Emma sat by, watching in surprise. Their car was soon fixed. They ambled over to the side of the road and George extracted his wallet.

"I really appreciate it more than I can tell you," George said. "I don't have much, but at least let me pay you for your time, young man."

"No. You keep your money, mister. I was glad to help out."

"But how ever can we repay you, Ted?" asked Emma.

"Do you believe in angels, ma'am?"

"When I saw you two," Ted said, "I couldn't get this verse out of my mind: 'Do not forget to entertain strangers, for by doing so some people have entertained angels without knowing it.' So, if you two are angels, then you can do me a favor by watching over my folks."

Emma chuckled. "We're not angels, Ted. But we'd be happy to watch over your parents. Where do they live?"

"Unfortunately, back in Cleveland. I was transferred out here last fall. I tried my best to get my folks to leave their home. I can't really blame them. California's still not really home for me either. We try to keep in touch, but it just isn't the same. Especially around holidays and all."

"Why don't you give us your address and your parents' address," said Emma. "I'd love to write and tell them how kind you've been.

Besides, we've recently moved from Ohio and I miss it terribly. I like to keep in touch with people from my neck of the woods."

Ted grinned as he took out a notebook and jotted down the addresses, then handed the paper to Emma.

As she took the paper from him, she patted his hand. "And you'll definitely be hearing from us," she said.

Ted smiled and waved as George and Emma drove down the road toward their home.

Emma turned toward her husband. "You know, Pops, I've been thinking. Being separated from the kids might be hard on us and them both."

"Yeah, Em," George replied, "I know what you mean. I guess we can learn to adjust to California. There has to be something out here that we're bound to like."

"There's Ted, our new friend," said Emma.

George smiled. "Not a bad start."

"Can you find our way back home?"

"I just did ... thanks to Ted."

Exercises

Re-read this short story.
1) Identify the beginning, middle and end of this article.
2) Can a feature article have a similar organization?
3) Count the number of times home is mentioned.
4) Can a feature article use a recurring device such as a repeated phrase or theme?

Re-read Dennis Hensley's biography.
1) What habit of successful living most impressed you about this writer?
2) What Hensley habit can you adopt to become a better writer?
3) What was Hensley's biggest mistake? What can you learn from it?
4) Does his writing career have a theme that you can adopt?
5) Did you notice how Dennis Hensley was able to sell portions of his work as articles yet work the information into a bigger work? How could that work for you?
6) Are there advantages to writing feature articles should a writer want to write fiction? Explain.

Rookies and prose:
Words to master

Because, since
Use "because" for a direct relationship with a cause and effect.
- *The senate president quit because the job was too demanding.*

Use "since" to suggest a sequence that follows logically.
- *He moved to Griffin, Ga., since he found a job there.*

Between, among
"Between" is used to introduce two items.
- *The contest was between Dole and Kemp.*

"Among" is used to introduce more than two items.
- *Among those interested in the nomination were Kemp, Dole and Buchanan.*

Fewer, less than
The rule for "fewer" and "less than" also involves the idea of numbers. Use "fewer" for items that can be counted.
- *The mass communication student possesses fewer marbles than the psychology major.*

Use "less than" for items that can't be counted.
- *However, the psychology student has less brains than the mass communication student.*

Cannon, canon
A cannon, two "n's," is a weapon, but a canon is a law, and is primarily used in association with churches.
- *The pastor and deacons admonished the congregation to uphold the canon of scripture.*

Developing the story: An example
Not long ago, a magazine asked me to write a feature article on U.S. Rep. Randy Forbes, R-4, who teaches an adult Sunday School class. The editor asked me to write a 1,000-word profile that examines this identity of an elected official's life – a congressman who regularly teaches Sunday School.

Time management as Swiss cheese

When writing any article, it is good to think of the overall task as a **series of tasks**. Some tasks require more effort than others and can be accomplished without heavy lifting. Think of the project as a wheel of cheese the size of a Volkswagen tire. You can begin nicking away at the job by **punching holes** in the cheese. Make Swiss cheese out of the wheel. By reducing the big task into discreet parts, you **manage your time**. Once you think about it, it is the most efficient use of your time because you end up breaking the task down one way or the other.

The holes represent the small tasks that you must accomplish to achieve your goal. Congressmen are often pressed from moment to moment so I knew I had to apprise his staff that I wanted to observe a Sunday School class session and follow it up with an interview. In this case, I punched a hole in the entire project by making the mandatory calls to Forbes's district office and then his Washington, D.C., office. The calls took nearly a week because the congressman's communication person had to check with Forbes and others to make sure no other activity would overlap. To hedge my approach, I punched another hole into the project by calling Forbes at home to make sure

> **Tip**: Avoid "due to" particularly when starting a sentence. It sounds stuffy. If you must start a sentence with this kind of reasoning, use "because."
> *Because of a death in the family, the shop will be closed for the next three days.*
>
> A better sentence, however, is: *The shop will be closed for the next three days following a death in the family.*
>
> **Tip**: Always use contractions of words suggesting negation. Use "don't" instead of "do not" and "can't" for "can not." The reason: In mass media writing, the "not" may be omitted accidentally as the reader reads, and the meaning would be distorted.
> Don't be like the writer of a sex manual that told her readers the wrong facts about ovulation because she left the crucial "not" out of the sentence.

he would be in town for the lesson. Writers can be a nuisance, but it's all part of the job to make sure the plan will work.

For the article, I knew I wanted anecdotes so I contacted the class president and asked him to ruminate on humorous stories. Feature writers love those anecdotes that are too funny, almost unbelievable. I gave him a couple of days to mull it over, knowing that some of us can't recite a funny story on the spot. It sometimes takes sleeping on it to produce a publishable quip. In this case, the anecdotes could be stronger.

Another source whom I thought would be helpful is a state house representative who is a member of the class. I met with him and jotted down notes. He gave me his **business card** and I quickly asked if I could get his **home telephone** number. I also asked him if I could double-check my information by calling him that day. By obtaining permission in advance, I bought myself **access** to the official after hours. During business hours, elected officials can be difficult to locate so the home number and email address can be a real boon to the labor of gathering information and checking it for accuracy.

On the day of the class, I checked the batteries in my pocket **tape recorder**. I wanted the tool as a backup for getting information during that compressed time following class when the congressman would answer my profile questions. In addition, I took a **35mm camera** with film and a digital camera. For the **digital camera**, I recharged the batteries and took an ample supply of floppy discs to make sure I'd get a good photograph. Next, I took a notebook and a couple of pens.

The congressman's office supplied background and a canned headshot and I located a **previously published article** on the congressman. With this background in hand, I made my way to the class, getting there well before the class began. The night before I called the class leader as a courtesy to let him know that I'd be at the class. I knew he wouldn't object; it's just a matter of courtesy. When I arrived at the class, I checked in and asked who would lead the class in announcements. Next, I went to that person and told him that I'd like to take some photographs and would he mind alerting the class. That leader took a light-hearted approach to the announcement and **put everyone at ease**.

Once the congressman began his lesson, the only real distraction was when I stood on a chair to get a better angle. Knowing how intrusive writers can be, I took the photographs of Forbes at the podium and then retreated to the back of the horseshoe-shaped room to become a **fly on the wall.**

I listened to the presentation, did my follow-up interview and later that day, I typed up my notes that I retyped for myself to help me as I developed the article. Here's the article that the publication accepted, 388 words, from about three days of work.

Congressman expresses faith on the job
By Michael Ray Smith

CHESAPEAKE, Va.-Midway through the Sunday School class, U. S. Rep. Randy Forbes spread his arms wide and asked the class of nearly 50 adults: "Who here worries?" All but two hands went up.

"Come on. Put your hands up," urged the two-term congressman, a playful smile creeping across his face—and then he asked those who said they don't worry to give the remedy. The class spent the rest of the hour reviewing exhortations from the Sermon on the Mount as a strategy for beating the anxiety of finances, family and a world fraught with peril.

Mr. Forbes is known at his Great Bridge Baptist Church in Southeastern Virginia first as a Sunday School teacher – he's been doing it for 15 years – and then as an elected official. The class of 162 members can be too impersonal for some, leading to a modest but regular exodus of people who yearn for an ordinary teacher, yet the Republican congressman maintains a loyal following.

An attorney, Mr. Forbes gained election to the state house of representatives in 1989 and then to the state senate in 1997. A special election in 2001 put him in the House, and he was elected to a second-term unopposed in 2002. He is one of four chief sponsors of HR 1897, the Unborn Victims of Violence Act of 2003. If enacted, this bill would make federal law the killing of a mother and her unborn child two deaths, not one. It is expected to come to a vote in the House sometime this summer.

For Ira M. Steingold, secretary of the Democratic committee in Suffolk, a part of the Forbes district, this law is a way for the GOP to expand its voter base: "It is a ruse to treat a fetus as a child." But Mr. Forbes seems to have a ruse-free voting record: it's 100% conservative, according to the American Conservative Union, which gave only 59 of the 435 members of Congress what it considers to be perfect scores.

Mr. Forbes received that rating on issues such as support for the partial birth abortion ban and tax-exemption for religious organizations that participate in politics as long as it's not their primary mission. Unsurprisingly, Americans for Democratic Action, the nation's oldest independent liberal political organization, gave Forbes a zero on his 2002 voting record.

Exercises

1) What kind of lead is used here?
2) Find an example of a transition. Does it work for you or not? Explain.

Summary

Building an article is a bit like **fashioning a house**. It can be a summer residence with a bit of paint and thatch, or it can be the manor house with canopies and turrets. Writers learn to arrange facts in some kind of order, from most important to least important, with attention to logic or some other system. For instance, quotations can be used to provide necessary information while providing needed transitions. Other strategies for arranging the article include a **chronological development** or an **anecdotal pattern**. Throughout the development of an article, good writers explore the value of **observation**, known as **color**.

In a jam, when the natural organization for the piece just won't reveal itself, some writers have learned to resort to writing the end first, then the beginning, or they use a standard formula such as "lead, quotation and then background." Ideas on the writing process are included in a long interview with writer Dennis Hensley who talked about the benefit of understanding **fictional techniques** in writing non-fiction. It ended with some suggestions on time management and two articles to illustrate the ways an article can be conceived and executed.

Chapter 5

Interviews that work
FeatureWriting.Net/CallMe

Chapter at-a-glance

➢ Preparing for interviews
➢ Developing questions for interviews
➢ Using silences and other techniques in the interview

Writers have two jobs. They gather raw information and then tell a story. Simple, right? It can be manageable, but all creative work takes effort. Writers have lots of ways to get information including research and interviews. Research includes searching electronic databases, pouring over documents, looking at public records and so on. However, the better feature articles demand the voice of sources, **official sources** such as paid spokesmen and **unofficial sources** such as ordinary people. These voices will give the article a sense of verisimilitude. It will sound real because it is real. It's the difference between writing: "The mayor said voting is important" and telling someone, "His exact words were, 'Vote for me or expect a visit from the police.'"

Waiting for a call back from a source can leave a writer exhausted. Solution? Call a second or third time. Polite persistence will pay off.

Don't impress your new friend

Interviews can be the most enjoyable part of the story-telling process. The writer will make a new friend, but it's important to realize that the goal is to gather information. The temptation is to impress the person with background about you, but that's not the point. The point is to collect information from the source. She's the main event, and you are the hired help with a unique role to get the story and get it right.

Some writers get lazy and use quotations from other writers. Even worse are writers who make up quotations from imaginary sources. The best writers arrange interviews and do their own questioning. The process can be fun, but only if the writer works hard to prepare well and handle herself with a sense of professionalism.

This chapter will provide a series of **steps** for making the most of the interview. It includes **preparing before the interview, strategies during the interview** and **ideas on concluding the interview** and **following up**. In addition, this chapter will provide some ideas on conducting those interviews where no planning is possible and some of the problems associated with sources who want to talk, but ask you to shield them in your published work. As a convenience in this chapter, I usually call the interviewer *the writer*, the interviewee *the source*, and the project *the article*.

The interview goal

Among the most basic questions an interviewer must ask herself is the reason she chose the source. Is the article a **profile piece**, an article that highlights the subject's achievements and philosophy? Or will the interview be **in depth** and probe the source's life, philosophy, victories and defeats? Or, is this interview part of a **series** of interviews that the writer is conducting to ventilate a topic? You decide and plan accordingly.

Think of an interview as a **directed conversation** with the writer in control. The writer will guide the source through a series of questions, some open-ended and some closed-ended. As the master of the "interview universe," you have the power to steer the conversation into the directions that are most relevant for the article that you envision. When your source gets off topic, say, "That's intriguing, and I'd like to pursue that topic in a few minutes. For now, I'd like to know about..." Make a note to yourself to ask about the stray topic and broach it at the end of the interview.

Control within flexibility

Be advised. At times the source will interject a thought that you haven't considered, and you must be sensitive to the possibility of a new topic. One freelance writer tended to reject those little stories all of us tend to use when illustrating a point. The writer thought these anecdotes interrupted the flow of fact stacked upon fact. Years later, he learned the power and appeal of a little story, and the role of a source in the collaborative effort to create an article of merit.

While it is good to think of your source as the key to the effort, don't allow her to bully you. Some sources feel entitled to **interview the interviewer**. They may demand to know your political identity, your marital status, or the size of your bowling shoe. Resist the urge to be combative; rather tell the source enough information to get on with the business at hand. Should the source persist and demand to know personal information about you, gently suggest that her story is of more interest, and, if time permits, perhaps you can share some of your background.

This give-a-little to get-a-little approach is the basis of a conversation, and a writer must sense that good manners dictate that some exchange is necessary, but how much? As a religion editor, I often found sources questioning me about major and minor theological issues. Often, they were afraid that I may distort their views by virtue of my existing convictions. Try to put your source at ease by assuring her that your goal is to be accurate. Or, in very awkward moments, tell the source that you would love to share more personal information about yourself, but you can't because of doctor's orders. The statement makes no sense, but it has the power of authority, and it may throw the person off the scent. Be sure to ask your physician if you can use that line! You may be amazed how well this harmless rebuttal works. Say it whimsically with laughter in your eyes, and your source will get the hint that the story is about her, not you.

If all else fails, you can always answer a question by posing a question: "Why do you ask? Is that a problem? Are you concerned?" Again, remind your source that your goal is to write about her with gusto. Sometimes all a source wants is some reassurance. Give her as much reassurance as you can, but avoid deception. If your article is about the person's criminal past, be honest. Say, "I plan to ask you some tough questions, but I want to give you a chance to give your side."

Do your homework

To get to the meaty questions about philosophy, toil, hardship and success, the routine questions must be satisfied. Questions about age, education and work history can be avoided by doing **research before the interview**. The World Wide Web is one source of information about a person and the topic with which she is associated. Electronic databases such as **Lexis-Nexis** and others mentioned in Chapter 8, *Using the Internet*, will allow you to search newspapers and magazines for articles already published on the person and topic.

If that fails, contact the source, and ask her to recommend articles that may have been published on her. Ask about articles on the topic that are associated with your source. Often the source can direct you to "*the article*" that you can use to develop your article. Failing that, obtain a copy of the person's résumé or vita. Always **check** and **double-check** the information. Ask the source if anything has changed in the résumé, or if the previously published articles contained errors. I make it a habit of checking facts before the article goes to print. I've never had a source refuse a request to double-check my information.

Make a list

From your research, you can develop a series of questions. Your goal is to write an article that reveals the source in a fresh way, so think of questions that **build on what is already known**. It's a good practice to talk to the source's friends and co-workers as part of the interview preparation. Using the previously published articles, interviews with others, the vita or résumé, you can develop a series of questions that will help you in the interview. Have a direction to pursue, but be ready to change directions if the source offers new information that is compelling.

Some writers use three-by-five cards like private investigator Kinsey Millhone in Sue Grafton's novels. The P.I. uses index cards to list her facts as she explores the case for suspects. You can use these cards to list your questions. Arrange them in order from easy to more difficult. It is good to memorize them, and be ready to jump ahead depending on the flow of the interview.

Above all, **listen well**. Listen for facts, and listen for feeling. It's called **active listening**. A person who sighs as she tells you a fact may be saying she is sad, hurt, broken or philosophical. Stop. Say, "You seem to be sad. Are you? Why?" This active listening technique works well, but it can slow down the rhythm of the interview if you are after just the facts, not the emotions. Use judgment. The technique works, but it is best to keep it in reserve for special occasions. Imagine the emotions that may erupt if you insist on identifying the affect of the source each time she speaks. Be careful, and don't use this advanced technique with people who are too young or too immature to know that they don't have to answer your questions. Sources are allowed to decline to comment.

One writer interviewed a poet about her literary work. The writer dutifully asked about the woman's career including her first poem. In the process, the woman mentioned that she used her poetry as therapy with her cancer. The writer wrote down the remark and went on with her prepared questions. By not listening, the writer missed an opportunity to mine that intriguing area of cancer therapy – poetry! We must listen.

The beauty of the writing process is the challenge to think on the spot, to listen for that rare insight, to see the color that others walk by. It's the joy of writing. It's the gift of storytelling. To do it well, prepare hard with good questions, but listen well to hear the heartbeat of your source. At times, an interview will be a couple of questions that provide basic information; at other times, the interview will be an elaborate exchange where you may feel like a psychiatrist, parent or confessor. Be responsible with this role. You are empowered to collect information for your audience. Don't waste anyone's time by probing into issues that are irrelevant, but be ready to ask the tough questions with all the skill you can possess.

Formulating questions and recording answers

The better interviewers ask sources to provide explanations. At times the writer will ask routine information such as her work title, but the better questions, the ones that excite the source, **get at her opinions** and the rationale for them.

Your goal is to help the source relax and speak freely. It's a kind of dance, a kata, where the interviewer starts slow, gaining the confidence of the source, and then moving into more difficult questions. It requires taking notes, but the goal is to be unobtrusive about the note-taking to keep the source relaxed. Pocket tape recorders are fine, but mechanical instruments can fail; note pads won't.

When using a **recording device**, allow the source to know that you are recording. You can reassure her by explaining that it will help with accuracy. It's better to keep the recorder out of sight once the source has agreed to the interview. When tapes are running, people tend to measure their words and the rhythm of real speech is lost. If the source doesn't want the interview recorded, don't fight with her. Try to explain that the recording is meant to supplement your notes. If she still refuses, resort to the old-fashioned technique and write fast.

Most writers develop some kind of **note hand** where they get the subject and verb and some of the other main words. To get it right, take time immediately following the interview to insert all the words that you can in your notes, then type the notes. The writing of the story will go so much more smoothly this way. If possible, try crafting an article as soon after the interview as possible. Again the article will go much better if written while the information is fresh.

New writers may not be aware of the **impressions** that can be banked following an interview. Your story will be better if you include more than the source's words. How did the source hold her head when she recounted the tragic fall off the ladder? Watch her hands. Listen for background noises, including traffic and music. When appropriate, ask the source to explain why she wagged her finger at you during her answer. How do these gestures link to the words? It is best for you to write down these gestures as the person is talking.

When you can't listen, write, watch and think all at the same time, make sure you pause following the interview to fill in as much of the information as possible. One freelance writer admitted, "This is my weakest area, I'm so busy doing all the other things that I fail to listen sometimes and miss what's being said. I really have to concentrate. I rely on my tape recorder to bail me out."

You may not need it, but it gives you a sense of authorial power to know the carpet was a misty green color, that the cherry bookshelves have five shelves, and that the potpourri scent was apple spice. Irrelevant? Maybe. Only you, the writer, know how you will craft this article, and it is easier to have all the raw materials ready to go, rather than make a return visit just for one or two items.

Complicated material

Above all, make sure you understand the topic. That's rule one in interviewing, according to veteran newsman-turned-academic Merlin R. Mann. He says that if you don't understand, you can't explain it to the reader.

An environmental writer interviewed an entrepreneur about a maverick energy program that recycled, recycled oil. Got that? She didn't. No one could understand the concept of recycling oil that was already recycled. Consequently, the article sagged miserably.

When someone explains a complicated process, you must go over the explanation until you **understand it**. Review your notes. Ask for definitions and metaphors that may make it easier for you to convey the information to your audience. Have the source draw you a picture, then think about using a picture with your article to aid in comprehension. Some educators say we think in pictures, so it makes sense to reduce thorny explanations to a visual representation.

Writers use many approaches to get information and keep sources talking. When a writer doesn't understand, it is best to say so. Naturally, some sources will lose confidence in the writer who appears weak-minded. However, better writers know how to turn this weakness into a strength by playing dumb. Many times a source will go overboard trying to help the dim-witted writer. Like the character Peter Falk played in the TV show *Colombo*, by the enormity of his courtesy, the police detective eased his sources into talking freely just by asking the same question in a slightly different way, always with a smile and a nod.

When using this technique, try saying a few simple comments to keep the source going. A well placed, "No, really?" may help. Even a non-committal "Hmmmm" sometimes works. These comments work more like interview filler than questions, but the effect is the same. It propels the interview forward. Also called the **non-question question**[30], this technique helps the interviewer sidestep those awful *how did you feel* questions. Instead of asking survivors about the death of family members in a house fire, the sensitive interviewer could ask what the person will miss most about his family and the happiest memory.

Silence

Another technique that will serve you well when the topic is simple or complex is the use of **silence**. Ask a question and be quiet. Mentally count to 10. The pause will seem very long and unnatural. Stare at your source and wait. Just wait. Is there anything harder for a writer? To yourself, count "One, two, three..." Finally, your source will repeat herself, or, more likely, add information – information that you may have not received if you hadn't waited. This technique, like the active-listening technique, isn't to be used all the time. Use it judiciously with some thought.

If you ask a question for factual information, but the source is too sterile, try it. You may ask, "Why did you leave the job?" The source may say, "I got a better job," and you think to yourself, "There's more to this situation," and you begin counting to yourself. If she hasn't said anything else at 30, you may have to pose the question again or move on. Remember, the interview is like a dance. You may be the lead, but your partner can limbo when you least expect it.

Appointments

Ideally, you prepare for the interview with research, interviews with secondary sources and some time to think about the questions you want to pose. Somewhere in this process, you will contact the source, and **request an interview**. Sources agree to interviews for many reasons, some noble and some vain. Some sources are public-minded and want to educate others. Others see the interview as an opportunity to promote a cause. Still others want to promote themselves.

In most cases, you will have to make an appointment and meet at the source's convenience. In some cases, the source is as anxious to talk to you as you are to interview her. Work it out, but try to meet the source in her office, or better yet, her home. Why? You can learn about the source

---

[30] Tompkins, A. (2002, Fall). The art of the interview. *Poynter Report.* pp. 21-22.

and the topic by observing her in her surroundings. Be sure to be a little early. If you're late, call and explain.

Dress for the interview. If the source is a banker, dress for the occasion. If the source is a landscaper, dress for the part. Arrive at the interview with enough time to look around the office, home or meeting place. An office or home is better than a restaurant or other public place because of the personal touch. A person tends to extend her personality in the decoration of an office or home. **Observe** and **take notes** on the wall hangings, the awards, and the type of furniture, rug and tools of the work such as calculators, lighting, tables and computers.

As you begin the interview, introduce yourself, state the purpose, take a deep breath and relax. Begin the interview, but monitor yourself. Let the source speak. Avoid long preambles to questions. Just **ask the question**. Too often press conferences degenerate into monologues that put the klieg light on the interviewer. No good.

Instead of saying. "You were rather incensed when people protested at your film school's opening night because of the content of the movies. Even though you won't go into detail or tell us who was involved, could you tell us about what you plan to do?" Too complicated. The first part is an opinion; the next part is an interpretation that may be wrong. The final part of the question works: "What do you plan to do in light of the controversy?" Boom. The question explodes, and the source is free to answer it her way. That simple unadorned question gets to the point with no fanfare. Simplicity is the essence of good interviewing.

For the quick quotation or fact, the telephone is fine. For long-distance interviews, email is quite handy, but the interview in the subject's home or office is ideal. Face-to-face conversations allow for better rapport. You can see and hear the person interact with others, sense the pace of the work place, and drink in the ambience of the décor. If the telephone is the only means to contact your source, you can still obtain that kind of valuable information. To duplicate this color-collection, the gathering of information from the scene, ask your source to describe what she sees, hears, smells and so on. If you think it is necessary, you may contact the source's secretary to verify the information. Email also works well for this technique. The problem, of course, is that you can't verify the information, leaving you at the mercy of your source's ability to observe and report.

Whether by telephone, email or in person, many interviews call for quick responses. You need information, like pieces in a mosaic. When rushed, skip discussions about the ivy in the potted plant and get to business, but make a game of taking a mental snapshot of the setting. It may pay article dividends later. Editor Jill Darling suggests that writers take a photograph of the scene to make sure the detail is accurate.

The notebook method

Bob Dubill, once senior editor of *USA Today*, tells the next generation of writers to keep a series of **notebooks**. One notebook is for the story that you are writing for deadline. The second notebook is a kind of Rolodex for telephone numbers, email addresses and information on the source such as the circumstances on which you met. Keep this information to help you with future feature articles. The third notebook is for possible stories based on the leftovers from today's assignment. The observations from the office could be socked away in this notebook. These days a Personal Data Assistant can help you record all these ideas in a portable unit, but some of us do prefer the old paper-and-pen notebook. It is more tactile, and, in some cases, easier to use in retrieval.

Difficult interviews

As in the feature-oriented interview, the best approach is to find out about the person to be interviewed. Check with the editor in advance to discern the emphasis, the angle that will be used for the article. As a rule, regular contact with your editor will enhance your ability to sell the article. Practicing this kind of interaction from the article suggestion to the article implementation in a joint effort is commonly called **collaborative editing**.

In rare cases, you may receive an assignment where you have no time to prepare.

> **Tip:** Dubill had other ideas you may want to consider. You may do only one interview a week, but you experience life every day and he suggests that all writers **keep a diary**. In it, writers can record the events and impressions that are memorable, but with a twist. Add a headline, a title, to the passage. It will make it easier for you to recall the time, and others will appreciate the summation. Among the benefits of the diary, Dubill says, is that it is a record of your unique life for your family to enjoy for generations to come.

A candidate comes to town and you are assigned to meet her within a few minutes. In those cases, you have to be quick of wit. If possible, obtain a handout or press release in the moments before the interview begins. If no time permits, think about the 5 W's and proceed accordingly. Ask the candidate what the most salient issues are facing the electorate. If it is an entertainer, ask her about the most pressing issues facing her or the act. If it is someone representing a *cause celèbre*, ask her to state the case and what she would like to see happen. If all else fails, say, "Why are you here?" and "What is the most important issue, idea, goal that you want our audience to know today?" That blanket question just about covers it all, don't you think?

In any interview, it is best to schedule an appointment with the source. However, many times secretaries and personal assistants screen contacts with sources making it difficult for you to use the telephone to pose a question, let alone make an appointment. For this reason, it is important for writers to be as personable as possible, not duplicitous, just cordial in making requests. When the contact will be regular, it is worth your while to get to know these important gatekeepers. You may feel as if you are selling yourself or selling the interview. It's all part of writing. Explain the purpose and hope for the best. If the source persists in dismissing your overtures, you may have to consider the ambush interview. Watergate investigative reporters Bob Woodward and Carl Bernstein used **ambush interviews** for sources who refused to be interviewed. This approach is a last resort, and to be attempted only with the approval of an editor.

In this interview, the writer meets the source when she is not expecting company. The writer may find the source on the way to work, taking a walk or doing some shopping. As much as possible, be polite and explain that you have tried to schedule an interview without success. Be sure to identify yourself and quickly pose the question. Emphasize that you are trying to be accurate and you want her comments. If she refuses, explain that you plan to tell your audience that the source refused to comment. Say, "Unless you give a more complete answer, I'll have to use your no-comment." As stated earlier, no one has to talk to the press, and that number includes writers, authors and freelancers. However, by telling the source of your intent to inform the audience that you attempted to get a remark, the source knows it may be in her best interest to say something of value. This approach can be heavy-handed, even mean-spirited. The goal is to get the information that is relevant for the article. That's all. If you are uneasy about the ambush interview, tell your editor, and she may have some ideas on how to proceed short of confronting a source without her foreknowledge.

As with any interview, save **embarrassing questions**, the bomb question, for last. In the ambush interview, you may only get one question, the bombshell. However, a series of innocuous questions like the kind TV attorney Matlock uses before he levels his witness helps build to a point. A feature allows a writer to be more leisurely. Hard news sometimes requires tough questions. Regardless of the article, all writers must be ready to ask questions relevant to the assignment.

Questions and approach

Your preparation for an interview will lead you to a variety of questions. In some cases, you may want specific information. If you read that the person weeps after reading Benjamin Franklin's *The Way to Wealth*[31] you may want to know what part in the 30 pages led to tears. That is a closed-ended question that typically elicits a short response. Open-ended questions are more fun and can be as simple as "Talk about blank," or can be more complicated such as "When you skydive through a cloud, what goes through your mind?" Mix them up. In an interview where you are fishing for information, but you don't know what you may catch, open-ended questions work well. However, for a feature article about the weird trend where people allow themselves to be shot to produce a scar, you may want to know about fibroblasts, connective tissue cells, and their formation. See? Short answer responses are meant to give the audience specific, usually clinical information. Open-ended questions tend to get opinions, while closed-ended tend to get more factual responses, but the reverse can be true, too.

As the interview unfolds, make eye contact as much as possible and try to be unobtrusive about taking notes. Beginning writers will interrupt the source to make sure the quotation is correct. A better method is to take as good of notes as possible and telephone the source later to check the facts in a quotation. You don't have to read the quote word for word, but make sure you have the meaning correct. In keeping with the metaphor of an interview as a dance, consider the problems of the start-and-stop-conversation. Like a dance, too much attention to words, like too much attention to the steps, will spoil the rhythm of the question-and-answer flow.

If possible, sit forward slightly in the chair. Avoid eating anything. (And that goes for your chewing gum!) Make the source your primary focus. Listen. Listen. Listen. As stated earlier in this chapter, listen to the words, but listen with your eyes, too. How did the sentence sound? Happy? Sad? Occasionally, comment on the speaker's words with a statement such as, "That sounds as if it makes you very happy" or "You sound as if you regret that remark." Then stop. Let the source talk. She may change the subject or press on into more detail. People tend to talk more candidly when they receive encouragement such as head nods.

Some writers admit to feeling self-conscious during the interview. One writer confessed, "I'm often more aware of how I'm being perceived by the source and others on the scene, that I'm not doing what I need to do

---

[31] Franklin, B. (1986). *The way to wealth*. Bedford, MA: Applewood Books.

with much finesse." As a writer, work to blend into the background. In some ways, you are a talking prop who plays a supporting role to the star, the source. Remember that the interview is about the other person. When you concentrate on the job at hand, the tendency to be self-absorbed will fade.

When interest seems to lag, be ready to ask an **off-the-wall question** such as "Did you ever call the White House?" or "When's the last time you cried?" or "What do you want your epitaph to read?" Sometimes the best information from the interview comes out as you are about to leave. Be ready to change directions and do the interview that you had not planned. Stick with the questions that you formulated until better material comes along, then jettison the old questions and go free style.

As the interview winds up, be sure to ask the mop-up question. Say, "Is there anything I didn't ask that you'd like to tell me?" Another question along that line is: "What's the most important idea you shared with me today?" Sometimes sources miss the point entirely and you can help her stay on track. Try, "I just have to ask you" and ask the question.

Odd occurrences happen during the **fare-thee-well stage** of the interview. Often, the source will say something brilliant. Be ready. Make your way to leave, but be alert to that last bit of information.

As you leave, be sure to **verify a contact number** and **email address**. Naturally, you should end on time. If you said the interview will conclude at 5 p.m., stop. However, if you are unsure of some of the information, ask if you can call back later and check the information. Verification may be the final part of the interview, but it is vital. Keep asking, "Is this correct?" Add, "Did I understand you correctly?" and "Did I hear you right?" Take time to think. Pause. Review in your mind the article that you envision. What did you leave out?

Off the record and background

As you talk to your source, she may become self-conscious and tell you, "**off the record**," and plunge ahead with some kind of detail. Off the record is the idea that the information shared in an interview is not for publication. Work to keep your source on the record. While the information provided may help you understand a complicated situation, it will do no good in explaining it to your audience if you agree not to include the controversial information in the finished article. It's better to stop the source and question her on wanting to avoid using the information in an article. Often, the source wants to be polite and avoid unduly embarrassing a third party.

Most people rarely meet reporters, so you may have to explain to your source that she can't just say the magic words, "off the record," and continue talking without impunity. Once a reporter or writer identifies herself and tells a source that she is collecting information for an article, the source is on the record. To go off the record, the reporter or writer must agree to listen to the information with the understanding it will not be used in the article. How likely is that? When a source becomes uneasy and asks to talk off the record, stop her and say that it is confusing when sources go off the record. Explain that as a writer, you plan to interview others and someone will share the information that is questionable at the moment. By not agreeing to off the record, the writer can say with honesty that no agreement was violated in obtaining information. However, if a reporter agrees to go off the record, she should negotiate. Be sure to ask when the source is back on the record.

Writers who go off the record usually make a point of putting their pens down or turning off the tape recorder. Should you continue to collect notes, be sure to make a mark in your copy indicating that those words should not be reported. See? It gets difficult to keep straight. Most writers use humor or some other disarming technique to keep the source on the record. Nonetheless, once a deal is struck, a writer must abide by it.

Background and **deep background** are other ways for a writer to use the information with the understanding it will not be linked to the source. Vague identification such as "a government source" can be used, but most editors will question the lack of specific identification. Too many inexperienced writers have avoided the hard work of getting a proper source, relying on other writers or, in rare cases, their own imaginations to supply the missing information. It's dangerous because the information may be absolutely incorrect, and the practice is absolutely wrong.

From time to time, a source will want to provide information and say it is not for attribution. At the very least, the source doesn't want her name used in the article or reference made to her in association with the information.

Privacy

A rule of thumb sometimes used is that the misconduct must demonstrably affect a public person's performance of his job before it should be reported. Publishing the name of a rape victim might well discourage other women from coming forward and pursuing sex crime cases in court. Newspapers and magazines continue to grapple with this issue, and it is one of the more vexing dilemmas facing writers.

Protecting a person sounds noble, but too many writers are quick to allow a source to remain unidentified. The novice writer sometimes calls these sources anonymous, which is incorrect. If the person were anonymous, no one would know the person's identity. A better description is to say the person asked to be unidentified, presumably to protect herself from incrimination. The rule is to name all the people with whom you interact to allow your audience to know that a real person contributed to the article. Made up stories happen as witnessed by Janet Cooke's infamous "Jimmy's World" piece that won the 1981 Pulitzer Prize for feature writing, only it was fiction. In the article for *The Washington Post*, she created an eight-year-old boy named Jimmy, calling him a third-generation heroin addict. *The Post* returned the Pulitzer and fired Cooke. She violated the idea of accuracy in her article, a non-negotiable principle.

Seven steps to the interview
1) Prepare questions in advance.
2) Consider a mix of open-ended (general) questions and closed-ended (specific) questions.
3) Avoid complicated questions.
4) Use silence.
5) Try to interview the person in person in her surroundings.
6) Listen for emotions.
7) Ask a clean-up or mop-up question such as, "Is there anything important about this subject that I haven't asked you about?"

Exercise

Identify the following questions as either open-ended (O) or closed-ended (C).
1) How old are you?
2) What was it like to jump off the house?
3) What do you want your tombstone to read?
4) What makes you cry?
5) When is the last time you cried?
6) Who is your hero?

Read the following article. Identify the quotations and write the questions that provoked those answers.

Holy Land tourism plunges:[32]
Visits to Israel fall 45 percent as violence escalates
By Michael Ray Smith

JERUSALEM – In the mid-1980s, visiting Israel around Easter Sunday was like shopping in a farmer's market at rush hour. "We'd wait three hours at some sites to get in," says Vincent Cioffi of Emmaus Tours in Margate, Florida.

In a typical year, Cioffi takes 2,000 people to the Holy Land. Recent months have been anything but typical. Only 41 people participated in Cioffi's $700 promotional package tour of Israel in January. Cioffi says that is roughly an 80 percent drop from the usual January business.

"I have no Easter tours," says Cioffi, a 20-year veteran of the tourism business. "This year is worse than last year."

Since the outbreak of violence in September 2000, more than 300 Israelis and more then 1,000 Palestinians have died in Israel, the West Bank, and Gaza. Tourism, one of Israel's largest industries, declined 45 percent last year compared to 2000. Overall, the number of visitors to Israel has plunged from 2.2 million in 2000 to 1.2 million last year.

North American Christians, one of Israel's most important markets, appear to be in no hurry to return. About 485,000 Americans, most of them Christians, visited Israel in 2000. Only 253,000 made the trek in 2001. Educational Opportunities Tours of Lakeland, Florida, one of the largest Christian tour operations in the United States, transported about 5,000 people to the Holy Land in 2001. According to Susan Andrus, director of marketing, its best year was 1996, when it took 14,000 Americans to Israel.

Andrus believes it is still possible to travel safely in Israel. Speaking of her 3-year-old daughter, she said, "I would take her to the Holy Land in a heartbeat. I know it is safe, and it's important to support the Christian community there."

Some tourism officials blame the news media for the perception that travel to Israel is unsafe. But the U.S. State Department issued a travel warning in December. "Ongoing violence has caused numerous civilian deaths and injuries, including to some American tourists," the department warned. "The potential for further terrorist acts remains

---

[32] Smith, M. (2002, April 1). Holy Land tourism plunges, Visits to Israel fall 45 percent as violence escalates. *Christianity Today*. 46(4), 34.

high. The situation in Gaza and the West Bank remains extremely volatile with continuing confrontations and clashes."

This year, the Israeli Ministry of Tourism is sharpening its marketing efforts toward American Christians. "For many years, American Christians have been among our best friends and greatest supporters of the State of Israel and of tourism to Israel," said Mina Ganem of the Israeli Tourist Office. "We really appreciate it. We are calling upon all of those who have encouraged tourism in the past to work with us to bring as many American Christians to Israel as possible, despite the headlines."

The convention business has also slackened. The Evangelical Press Association agreed to hold its April 2002 convention in Israel, but organizers switched the venue to Colorado Springs as violence escalated. Nevertheless, the International Christian Embassy Jerusalem, a Christian Zionist group, held its annual celebration of the Feast of Tabernacles in Jerusalem in October, attracting overseas Christians.

Following a time-tested strategy, Israeli tourism leaders are showcasing visits by high-profile Christians. "We believe that as this community sees Christian leaders they respect go and return with a good report, that will stimulate others to travel as well," says Butch Maltby, a Colorado Springs consultant who works with the Israelis.

"For example, author Kay Arthur faithfully brings hundreds of Christians to Israel each year," he said. "She has told us that many of the people on those tours have thanked her for the opportunity to travel and for her bravery to defy the majority."

Arthur's Precept Ministries is still inviting participants to an April tour of Jerusalem, Galilee, and surrounding areas. Others in the Middle East are turning to additional markets to boost tourism. Resourceful Arab Christians are looking beyond the United States in search of fellow believers willing to visit. Habib Khoury, co-owner of Shepherds Tours & Travel Co. Ltd., says he is working with a Christian group from Uganda for an Easter tour. A passionate Christian, Khoury urged more Christians to travel to the Middle East.

"Christians of the Holy Land can be Palestinians, and we are suffering the same as our Palestinian Muslim brothers," Khoury says. "Occupation does not differentiate between Christian and Muslim, and a pilgrimage to the Holy Land at this time is very important."

Biography of Jeffery L. Sheler

Writer Jeffery L. Sheler covered religion for *U.S. News & World Report.* He joined the magazine as Detroit bureau chief in 1979. In 1980, he was appointed associate editor in Washington, D.C., covering labor. In 1983, he was assigned to the magazine's Capitol Hill staff and was named chief congressional correspondent in 1985. In 1986, he was promoted to senior editor, reporting and writing on national and international affairs. Since becoming a religion writer in 1989, he has dramatically expanded the magazine's religion coverage

Jeffery L. Sheler

and has written more than 30 cover stories on major religious topics. He has written extensively on biblical archaeology, the Dead Sea Scrolls, and the "quest for the historical Jesus." He was promoted to senior writer in July 1992. These days he is a contributing editor to *U.S. News & World Report.*

Sheler is the author of *Is the Bible True? How Modern Debates and Discoveries Affirm the Essence of the Scriptures* (HarperSanFrancisco /Zondervan, 1999), which was named one of the top 10 religion books of the year 2000 by *Christianity Today* magazine. He is an occasional correspondent on the weekly PBS public affairs program *Religion & Ethics News Weekly,* is a frequent guest on national radio broadcasts, and has appeared on network television programs including CNN*'s Crossfire* and *John McLaughlin One On One.*

In 1992, Sheler received second place honors in the Religion Newswriters Association's annual John M. Templeton Religion Reporting Award competition. He also was named the first William Randolph Hearst Visiting Professor of Journalism at the University of Maryland in College Park.

A native of Grand Rapids, Mich., Sheler attended Olivet Nazarene College (now University), Kankakee, Ill., before earning a bachelor of arts degree in journalism at Michigan State University where he graduated with honors in 1971. In 1994, he received a Master of Arts in Liberal Studies with a concentration in religion at Georgetown University.

Upon graduation from Michigan State, Sheler joined United Press International in Chicago. A year later he was assigned to the statehouse bureau in Springfield, Ill., where he covered the state senate, education and Illinois politics. In 1975, he was appointed western Michigan correspondent, based in Grand Rapids, and in 1977 became UPI's automotive writer, based in Detroit.

Sheler serves on the governing boards of the Religion Newswriters Association and the Religion Newswriters Foundation, and is a member of Theta Alpha Kappa, the national honor society of religious studies/theology, and of St. John's Episcopal Church in Portsmouth, Virginia. He is married to the former Doreen G. Elias, a public school teacher. They have two married daughters.

Author's note: The following are notes from an interview with writer Jeffery L. Sheler. Following the interview, I typed my notes, which included my impressions as well as quotations, observations, and irrelevant color that just helps me revisit the moment. Notes are not the same as an article. They can be written in chronological order (as these are), as a series of quotations, as a series of questions and answers (called Q-and-A), as a series of anecdotes or other ways. The goal is to type your notes to make it easier for you to select the good ore from the fool's gold. The notes explore Jeffery L. Sheler's article, A Discovery and a Debate. The opening of the article follows the interview. The entire article may be obtained from LexisNexis. See chapter 10, SHOP talk for writers, on accessing that database.

Interview with Jeffery L. Sheler

Jeffery and I met about five years ago when he worked for *U.S. News & World Report* in Washington, D.C. (In an article, I'd refer to a source by his last name. For these notes, I'll use his first name throughout). In 2001, he moved to Old Town Portsmouth, Va., and I met him at his three-story house, built in 1832, near St. John's Episcopal Church off Washington Street.

A set of stairs leads to his front door, perched on the second floor and opens to the foyer and the living room where we conducted the interview. Five-inch boards make up the wooden floor, original to this historic home. A fireplace dominates one of the walls in the room, flanked by a couch and a loveseat. A glass coffee table features books including *Soul Survivor* by Philip Yancey and a floral centerpiece. On the bookshelf is Billy Graham's *Just As I Am* and tucked away, very discreetly, are two copies of Jeffery's recent book, *Is the Bible True? How Modern Debates and Discoveries Affirm the Essence of the Scriptures* published in 1999 by HarperSanFrancisco/Zondervan. Many writers keep a copy of their book in a prominent place, a trophy of sorts; Jeffery is not that kind of person. He's quietly confident – polite, helpful and knowledgeable.

On the chilly day we met, Jeffery wore a deep blue Oxford shirt with the name Milligan College over the breast pocket. We talked about the shirt because my daughter is a student at this school in Eastern Tennessee, and we both happened to be speaking on campus the same day in fall 2000. Jeffery was there to present a Feldstead lecture on the business of working as a journalist who possesses a sense of faith. I was at Milligan representing a university and spoke to a class of writers.

After we talked about Milligan and the day we both met for breakfast with some other colleagues in Johnson City, Tenn., we began to move into the formal interview. When he spoke, his manner was kind but energetic. At times, he raked his hair off his forehead, and I became aware of his wristwatch with a brown band. At other times, he rubbed his little finger, and we talked, one writer to another. I mention some of these observations to help myself see the scene, to keep it as fresh as possible so when I re-read these notes, they will have a three-dimensional feel to them. I used a pocket tape-recorder, but I didn't transcript that tape. Instead I referred to snippets here and there to check myself.

As I arranged my notes and camera, Jeffery made some hot tea. My seat on the couch seemed too far from Jeffery's chair, so I asked if I could move a wooden rocking chair a little closer to his chair, and I made camp, using the coffee table as a desk.

Once we were settled and had some tea, I began with some general questions about his new life in Portsmouth, 200 miles from Washington, D.C. He explained that he and his wife often traveled to the Tidewater area to be closer to family. While Jeffery continues to go to the office up to three times a month, he found he could do his reporting from home, an option many new writers won't have until they have proven their mettle. Working from home is a tradeoff. The writer misses out on the hallway banter and can't lobby for an article that is in jeopardy when the space crunch gets heated. Nonetheless, some publications are finding that they can enrich their bottom lines by leasing the pricey city real estate and allowing writers to telecommute.

After discussing the time demands of a magazine writer, we talked about Jeffery's book and his approach to it. "I thought 75% of it was done before I began," Jeffery recalled. "But I underestimated the work, and not just the writing. I couldn't write a paragraph without pulling a book off the shelf and checking on something. It was a slow process."

With a strong track record with his magazine, Jeffery created an informal sabbatical for himself and took some extended time off to complete the book project. His editor considered the project a win for the magazine, so it made sense to encourage the effort.

"Writing is not easy for me," Jeffery said. "Some people say, 'I love to write,' or 'Writing is my life.' I say, 'I hate to write, but I love to have written.'"

Like many of us, Jeffery enjoys the researching and the reporting, the gathering of information, but he confessed he could just as easily wash a car, a less demanding, instantly gratifying experience.

Jeffery is a meticulous writer, who spends his days working sentences, or as one novelist said, "turning sentences around."

"I spend far too much time on one paragraph," he said, adding that he has spent a half-day working and reworking an opening to an article. When in a bind, Jeffery sometimes moves to the body of his article and builds the piece, and returns to the beginning later.

When I interview a subject, I like the dialogue to flow like a conversation. I have destinations in mind, but I enjoy chasing a cognitive thread when one presents itself. As Jeffery talked about the newsroom, I asked him if his personal faith is a sore spot for a religion writer. Religion writers cover religion and don't necessarily possess a personal faith, although many do.

"I don't go around preaching," Jeffery said. "It's not my style." Jeffery added that he doesn't aspire to be an evangelist but his faith is important to him, and he considers the work a calling.

The newsroom culture expects writers to give the appearance that they are not lobbying for one cause over another. In magazine offices where the editorial policy is adversarial, it's considered good form to be an advocate, but mainstream newsrooms work to retain the impression that the writers, like well-trained social scientists, will let the story be revealed by the facts. Naturally, this position is the subject of much debate, but it is a traditional view with much support.

The following is a question-and-answer piece on Jeffery L. Sheler's feature article, *A Discovery and a Debate*. The first couple of sentences follow this interview. Try to locate the entire article on the web.

Q: How did you select the sources for this article?

A: Some writers use a Rolodex of names of people that they can quote. This method is acceptable unless you find that the same voices are quoted over and over again. With some articles, a source will call and give me a heads-up on a coming issue, which is what Hershel Shanks, editor of *Biblical Archaeology Review*, did. Hershel Shanks called with the news that his publication was running a piece on the ossuary.

Q: Here's a case of the press not only reading the press, but the press promoting each other in the press. It is a win-win situation. Hershel Shanks received some promotional value for his periodical and validation from the mainstream press, while the magazine received additional access on an important topic. So, Hershel Shanks provided the germ of the idea, how did you decide on the other sources quoted in the article?

A: As a religion writer, I receive up to eight books per week along with a profusion of news releases, most of which are electronic. Book writers often are keen to be quoted in an article, to raise their talk quotient, to promote their book and to educate an audience, so they make well-informed sources for stories. The subject of James was the topic in a book I received the week I was working on this story, so I contacted that writer on the ossuary.

In addition, I try to select sources that aren't easily pigeonholed. For example, John Meier, New Testament professor at the University of Notre Dame. John Meier provided a Catholic voice in the ossuary piece, and he provided an opinion that challenges some of the mainstream thinking of the Church.

Q: How do you interview these people, most of whom live hundreds of miles from you?

A: I call most of my sources on the telephone because real-time conversations allow for follow-up questions and a chance to get examples when appropriate. Once I finish the interview, I review my typed notes and clean them up immediately. Words that will challenge any decoding can be easily spotted if the writer takes a moment to re-read the passage.

Time and distance make meeting sources in person difficult except for the longer, in-depth profile pieces, so the face-to-face interview is harder to do with every story. As for email interview, however, I conduct them from time to time for those fast-talking speakers who are nearly impossible to track word for word. The disadvantage of the email interview is that the interviewer can't do the follow-up on the fly as is possible in a live interview.

Jeffery L. Sheler's tips for writers

- Have a game plan. Know the direction that you want to explore in your article before you start the interview. Start with a thesis, *but do not hesitate to adjust – or abandon – the thesis as your reporting unfolds.*
- Prepare questions in advance. Have them in front of you as you conduct the interview. A writer can depart from the prepared questions, but the prepared questions allow you to maintain a concrete game plan.
- As you conceptualize the story, think about the parts you will need. For instance, in a personal interview of Bishop Wilton Gregory, Jeffery knew he wanted to begin with an anecdotal lead. As he walked into a church to hear Bishop

Gregory at Mass, Jeffery was on the lookout for an anecdote that would work for his article.

- Review your notes immediately following an interview. Underline the items that are key. Make additional notes in the margin to remind you of germane facts, ideas, color or quotations.
- Keep an enterprise file of future ideas. Keep a few handy for dry spells.

Here are a couple of sentences from the opening of the article written by Jeffery L. Sheler.

Ancient writers remembered him as "James the Just," leader of the early Christian church in Jerusalem and, according to the New Testament, "the brother of the Lord."[33] Yet in Christian tradition, he has been a rather neglected figure, taking a back seat to such luminaries as the Apostles Peter – regarded by Roman Catholics as the first pope – and Paul, the great missionary and writer of much of the New Testament. Last week, however, James became the focus of new attention with the dramatic announcement of the discovery of a burial box inscribed "James, son of Joseph, brother of Jesus."

Exercises

1) Review the information on Jeffery L. Sheler.
   Make a list of five closed-ended short-answer questions for him.
   Make a list of five open-ended questions for him.
2) Review the beginning of his article. Rewrite the first two lines in 50 words or less. Now review the article and consider ways to make it twice as long. Make a list of questions that you could ask to expand the article.

Summary

To tell how to write a feature article without talking about interviewing is to tell the story of James Bond without mentioning gadgets. Yet, interviewing may not come naturally to all of us. We have to **plan ahead**, prepare ourselves with background and **write out questions** that we may

---

[33] Sheler, J. L. (2002, November 4). A Discovery and a debate. *U.S. News & World Report*, p. 50.

or may not use in the course of a conversation of which we are supreme commander. Writers must be sensitive to explosive comments that may go off with a whisper and wise enough to **listen with mind and heart**. In the process, we scribble, record and observe – a carnival of activity that we hope to present as a dignified visit to court. The best interviewers know the value of **silence** and the use of a series of notebooks to plan for the next article and the sense of making meaning in life. The interviewing process can be enjoyable or hostile, and interviewers must think of ways to navigate all the reactions that may be uncomfortable at the time but so valuable when we begin to write. Interviewers must be aware of the rules of this "contact sport" by knowing when to go off the record and the reasons not to be led in that direction. This chapter included an interview with writer Jeffery L. Sheler and his ideas on interviewing, chief of which is to plan, plan, plan.

Chapter 6

Sell it first, sell yourself
FeatureWriting.Net/SellItFirst

Chapter at-a-glance

➤ Finding the assignment
➤ Attending writers' conferences
➤ Participating in writers' groups

Veteran writer Norm Rohrer has a saying that should be the motto for writers: "Sell it first, then write it." This idea may sound odd, but it's the best strategy for success in penning a news article, feature story, inspiration piece or any other work you hope to have published.

Publications have personalities, just like people. Your news story on a student who took a train, taxi, airplane and boat to return to school during the worst blizzard in United States history may sound as if any publication would want it, but that may not be the case. A periodical published by American Automobile Association may find the idea suitable for its purposes, but the Valley Entertainment Guide may have no use for this piece. So what's a gifted writer such as you supposed to do?

Sell it first, and then write it.

Before conducting the interview, getting the quotations, verifying the facts, experienced writers know to contact the editor of the publication for which they are interested in working and earning a freelancer's paycheck.

Do your research before you sell your article.

Sometimes an article presents itself, and a writer takes her chances that someone will want an interview with a luminary who is in town to give a speech, or a young woman who rescued a child from a fire, or a plethora of other ideas. Most likely, however, the periodical for which you want to write has a publishing schedule and topics of its own. For this reason, you must **think of a feature story idea and *then* approach the editor.** The last chapter in this book lists a number of timeless ideas, but part of your job is to start today to scout for feature stories. In the words of journalism professor William Ruehlmann, stalk the feature story by following the advice of philosopher Henry James: "Be one on whom nothing is lost."[34]

By reviewing the ideas in this book and reading the magazines you love (and forcing yourself to read those you dislike), you will develop a sense for the feature article. Soon your vision will radiate with unlimited possibilities, and your idea notebook will burst with ideas. Resist the urge to write these articles without an assignment. Find the article a home, and then work with abandon. Here's a sales plan in 1-2-3 order.

Steps to selling an article the old-fashioned way

1) Write a short letter suggesting the idea and include the crucial information that you possess access to the valuable source. Access is crucial. Suggest a word length, deadline and a working headline or title. This letter is known as a **query letter**. You can end your missive by requesting the publication's writer's guidelines, their letter to you on the publication's personality highlights.

2) Enclose a self-addressed, stamped envelope, commonly called the **SASE.** It's expensive to correspond with writers. This touch will alert the editor to your maturity as a writer, even if it's your first attempt.

3) Include a one-page **résumé** highlighting your writing victories or other information that suggests you are a professional.

Or you can try the 21st century approach and use some of the tools mentioned below.

You may be wondering where a writer gets the address of a publication or, equally important, the editor's name. Periodicals feature this information toward the front of the issue; however, most libraries possess the *Writer's Market*, a valuable reference book that lists the names of publications across the United States. In addition to the editor's name, the listing includes the magazine's address along with its editorial needs and other pertinent information. The *Writer's Market* is an excellent research tool, and you may want to request it as a Christmas present.

---

[34] Ruehlmann, W. (1977). *Stalking the feature story*. New York: Random House, p. 28.

For the inspirational market, Sally E. Stuart's *Christian Writers' Market Guide*, published by Harold Shaw, is considered the best source for contact information. Periodicals for writers are helpful, too, and many are online. Also see Chapter 8, *Using the Internet,* for valuable sites for writers. Magazines such as *The Writer, Writer's Digest, The Christian Communicator, Editor & Publisher, Columbia Journalism Review* and many others will help you keep abreast on who is doing what in publishing. Organizations from the National Association of Black Journalists to the Religion Newswriters Association to the Society of Professional Journalists are just a few writer organizations that can help you succeed in your feature-writing career. Consider joining some of these groups, which entitles you to receive a newsletter, and gain access to member benefits such as exclusive job opportunities.

When you locate a publication for which you'd like to write, pay careful attention to the guidelines and the contact information. More and more periodicals accept e-mail queries, which streamlines the process and gives writers quicker feedback, but some still prefer snail mail. It is acceptable to call an editor after having sent your query and waiting a couple of weeks after the publication's typical response time.

When you correspond, be sure to alert the editor of your ability to provide photographs and other art. Editors are always in need of illustrations and photographs to accompany articles. If you can take photographs or prepare computer images, include that information in your letter. Make sure your letter is word perfect with no typographical errors, known derisively as **typos**. Allow between four and six weeks for the editor to respond. These people are very busy, but they need content and they need writers such as you to fill their pages day after day, week after week, and month after month.

That's fine, you may be thinking, but what about timely articles that have a short shelf life. In these cases, editors are glad to take a telephone call. A daily newspaper, for instance, wants the information now and will talk to writers about getting the story to them fast[35]. The same rule still applies – sell it first, then write it. Obviously, a writer in search of a sale must have some information to share with the editor or the conversation will be short indeed, but avoid conducting a windy interview with a source before the sale is made. Get enough facts to make the call and sell the story.

---

[35] John McCandlish Phillips wrote for *The New York Times* from 1952 through 1973 and said that getting the story often included being at the right place according to his Aug. 17, 2001, speech to the World Journalism Institute.

While this process sounds as if only writing hacks deign to do it, it's not just them. Having made that point, let me urge you not to argue with an editor. They say no sometimes, often, in fact. Don't be discouraged. There are hundreds of publications and what one rejects this morning, another may thank Heaven for this afternoon. When an editor does reject your idea, take a minute to determine if the idea is just not interesting. Once you have confirmed the legitimacy of your instincts, try again. As Churchill once said, "Never give up. Never."

Keep in mind that most publications are planned in advance, so the prospect that your idea will fit exactly into the editor's plans is unlikely. For this reason, don't be unduly offended if one editor passes on your idea. If nothing else, you made a valuable contact for the future. Ask the editor to keep you in mind for assignments and contact another publication with the same idea. However, if the first editor raises a question that you couldn't answer, find that answer before moving on to your next target. That way you're prepared if the second or third editor raises the original point.

Keep your **story idea antennae** up at all times, and your possibility well will never be dry. Larry Hicks is a prize-winning columnist in York, Pa., and he worried that he would run out of ideas when he began his columns in the early 1990s. Now his files are backed up with ideas because he's always on the prowl for material. "Seek and ye shall find," says the book of wisdom. Larry's story can be your story, too. Read newspapers, watch TV, talk to friends and always keep some paper and pen handy to jot down the next idea you can develop into a story for that next byline and paycheck.

Depending on the publication, cold calling (calling an editor out of the blue) may be an option, but be advised, don't expect a hero's welcome. The editor will be busy on some project when you telephone. This call means she will have to stop her progress and think about your idea. While it's her business to be on the lookout for new ideas, the interruption may not put the editor in the mental and psychological state that you want to get the best reception for your award-winning story. Use the U.S. postal service or try a well-written email, and you can excite the editor from the safety of your letter.

Build goodwill with the editor by proving that you studied her publication. Seasoned writers say to make sure and study it beforehand. Get a **sample copy**. Often it is free for the asking along with writer guidelines. Often, guidelines are available online. Monitor the topics and the advertising of the publication or the online service. Read between the lines to sense the bias and prejudice of the editor. It is best to create a grid and take notes on each article. How many sources are used? How many anecdotes are mentioned? Are articles top-heavy with statistics such as numbers, or is the magazine or online service built around long narratives with personal references? The grid will help you understand the slant used by the publication, but you'll have to do the interpretation and your findings will be subjective. Nonetheless, this approach will help you gain an edge on sensing the content that is most likely to be used.

Road trips

Among the best advice I ever received on selling articles is to **befriend editors**. Make a point of introducing yourself to editors when you are on the road, or when you attend a conference. Explain your interests, and offer to keep in touch with ideas. Enterprising writers make initial contact with editors by telephone or email and request a 10-minute session the next time they are in town. Most editors know the writer will be coming with an agenda. That's OK. Editors need writers as much as writers need editors.

You may want to try a **fact-finding, get-acquainted trip** to a number of publications. An inexpensive trip may be planned by restricting your meals to sandwiches in the cooler and overnight stays at inexpensive hotels. Web sites such as Travelocity.com will allow a guest to submit a bid for a room. I have stayed at a Washington-area Hilton for $60 per night using this kind of service.

When you arrive for your get-acquainted chat, keep to the time schedule. The editor can always extend it, but be sensitive to her time. Editors are always facing a deadline. It's OK to leave a résumé or one of your articles that you recently published. It's very likely that the editor will ask if you have any feature article ideas. Be ready with a list of five ideas that target her audience. Practice pitching the idea in one well-crafted sentence. Practice saying the line with grace and speed. Your new friend will be impressed. Monitor your time, and then offer to take your leave. Ask permission to stay in touch. Assuming that you don't drag mud into the office, the editor is very likely to encourage you to submit future ideas.

If all else fails, ask the editor if she can give you one piece of advice on succeeding in writing. This approach may sound demanding, even too self-serving. It isn't for everyone, but it may work for the new writer with lava coursing her veins who is in need of a place to erupt in print or online. Published authors sometime quip. "Writing is easy; you just open a vein and bleed." For new writers, you can open a vein and let the fire saturate the paper. The words may be too hot to handle, but at least you got it out of your system! Getting to know editors on a personal level will help you use your eruptions for the byline and the paycheck.

Submitting the article

Editors can be very forgiving to writers on the **format** of the submission, but why risk it? It's very likely that the periodical will want you to send the manuscript electronically using a software program such as Microsoft Word. Identify the document with a name such as "tires.doc" when writing about trends in tire swings. Double space your piece and use a 12-point size font in Times or something similar. Include your name, address, telephone number, email address on top, left side of the article. The top right-hand side of the document is a good place to include the rights you are selling, word length, social security number, copyright symbol, year and your name. It should look similar to the following example.

Jill Darling 123 Any Street Anytown, PA 12345 JillDarling@ISPaddress.com	**One-time Rights** 550 words SS# 000-00-0000 © 2005 Jill Darling

Pennsylvania Magazine

Mountains Set the Stage for "Endless" Festivities in Forksville

The right side of the top of your title page is the area where most writers tell the publication they are selling first rights, which means that the publication will be the first to use the piece. After it is published once, the writer can sell it again using one-time rights. In both cases, there is one-time usage.

These days some publications are asking writers to sign a **work-for-hire contract**, which allows the publication to retain exclusive rights, including the right to publish the article on the Internet. This phrase means that the writer gives up copyright privileges. Most writers avoid those kinds of contracts when marketing their own freelance articles because the work cannot be resold (since the writer doesn't own it). With first-rights and one-time rights, the writer is free to sell the article, once it is published, to another publication as long as the audiences don't overlap. (More information on your rights follows this section, but let's stay with the typical format for the look of your article.)

About halfway down the page, insert the suggested headline or title for your work and your byline. Allow some white space and begin your article. If you plan to submit it by paper, it's a good idea to format the manuscript to have a running head that includes a keyword from the headline or title and your name and page number. Some publications maintain a tradition of listing the total number of sheets of paper in the upper right-hand corner. For each successive page, the writer would list the order. So, "2/4" means "second of four pages." It's a technique that allows an editor to be sure that all the pages are intact. Another old convention is to add "30" to the end of the article to alert the editor that the article concluded. Numbers like these were the rage during the 1970s, the heyday of Citizen Band radios with sayings such as "10-4, good buddy." The number "30" is the radio version of good-bye, or this is the end of the transmission.

Your rights

A word about **copyright**. No one can copyright an idea, but your creative work can be copyrighted. Copyright protects a writer's right to copy the work, to use a portion of it elsewhere and make money on it. New writers tend to worry needlessly about copyright. The work is copyrighted once it is published, but if you feel uneasy about someone purloining your unpublished intellectual property, write something such as "©2005. Your name. All Rights Reserved," or just "copyright," and try to use the copyright symbol from your keyboard or handwrite it on the work. For $30, the U.S. Copyright Office will register unpublished works, which ensure you protection in the unlikely event of a copyright infringement suit.

Writers may sell many different rights. As stated earlier, when a writer sells a publication the right to be the first publication to use the material, those rights are called **First North American Serial Rights.** Once the publication in North America publishes your article, all the rights to it revert back to the writer. In general, First North American Serial Rights is sometimes called **First Rights**, but you could sell first rights for an electronic service. In addition, writers sell one-time rights, which isn't the same as First North American Serial Rights. **One-time rights** means a publication can print the article once. **Reprint Rights** means that your article has appeared somewhere else and now you are selling the right to reprint it. **First Electronic Rights** or **First World Electronic Rights** is the right to be the first to publish the piece to electronic media. Writers are cautious of selling this right because it is so broad.

A **work-made-for-hire** (WMFH) contract gives exclusive rights, including the copyright to the publisher. Complete ownership of the work is transferred to the publisher, and if the publisher so chooses, the writer may not even be considered the author of the work anymore. A WMFH can't be resold because the writer no longer owns it and can't resell it. As stated earlier, many freelance writers are refusing to sign WMFH contracts because of this odious practice. For in-depth information on rights, visit www.writing-world.com. Moira Allen, the owner of this commercial site, publishes articles on rights and copyright information and other aspects of writing.

Taxes and expenses

As a writer, your **expenses** can be taken off your taxes along with any other expenses associated with your work. The federal government allows a writer, or anyone who is self-employed, to deduct expenses. Desks, computers, paper and other supplies may be deducted, but it is wise to work with a certified public accountant or licensed tax preparer. For instance, your computer must be dedicated to your work as a writer and may not be used for other purposes if you are seeking a deduction. Offices can be a problem unless this space is used strictly for writing. Computers, Internet connections and software are legitimate expenses for the serious writer.

Habits that lead to sales

Write every day whether you feel like it or not. Keep a journal and that idea notebook. Write to editors and writers that you admire and share your ideas. Take them to lunch if you can. Attend their workshops and writers' seminars. Most importantly, be sure to read their publication. Nothing is as embarrassing as contacting an editor about a story idea that the publication ran just two issues before.

Enroll in a class at your nearby college, and ask the academics about their contacts. Most of all, write. Write. Write. Write as if your legacy would be a book.

Think of the influence that Oxford don C.S. Lewis continues to have today, years after his death in November 1963. His *Mere Christianity*,[36] that went into 50 editions, is as powerful as when it was first written in 1943. Imagine speaking to us beyond the grave through a book with great lines such as these: "I must keep alive in myself the desire for my true country, which I shall not find till after death: I must never let it get snowed under or turned aside: I must make it the main object of life to press on to that other country and to help others to do the same."

Right, he is.

---

[36] Lewis, C. S. (2001). *Mere Christianity*. New York: HarperCollins Publishers

Mentors

Most artists go through a time of **apprenticeship**. It's no different for writers. Some hit their stride in a matter of months; for others, it may take up to five years of regular writing under the watchful eye of a good editor. For many of us, editors come and go, weakening our learning curve. One remedy is to seek **your own editor**, who will stay with you for a lifetime. Your goal is to find a trusted friend, a more mature writer, and ask her to peruse your copy from time to time. Reward her with lunches, books, or a magazine subscription. Let her know that her feedback, although jarring at times, will help you excel as a wordsmith. This person can serve as your mentor, and all of us need one.

The better writers will seek out a variety of **mentors**, and create an informal group of voices. Perhaps, it's best not to go to the same well over and over, and this circle of readers may serve as an intermediate step between writing of the article and the publication of it. Or, your mentor may help you by reading your published work and offering ideas on improving it. Keep a notebook on yourself and your craft. Study the original and the edited version. What is different? Sometimes, your mentor will suggest that you gather more information, talk to additional sources, or add direct observation into your article. At other times, the article may need a different organization pattern, or the tone may be off. The target moves, and you must be ready to move with it.

Remember the Woody Allen 1977 film, *Annie Hall,* about a nervous romance? It began as a murder mystery film, but in post-production the relationship between the two characters emerged as central to the movie, and it was pared down and re-edited as a romantic comedy.

Your writing can be like that. You collect the **raw material**, the quotations, the background, the facts and statistics, the anecdotes and color and build a feature article on anti-terrorism strategies in public schools. However, your mentor may see the information differently and suggest that you refashion the piece to explore the increasing demands on schoolteachers to assume yet another role in our society. The best attitude for writing is to remain teachable. It's not about education or number of articles published; it's about the audience. What works? Once you've penned your work of art, you may not have the distance to see the article differently than the draft that you submitted. For this reason, consider showing your mentor your article.

In some cases, writers **share articles** with each other. Writers who share mutual respect for each other can weigh in knowing that the criticism will be received with gratitude, not surliness. All of us know the chagrin that accompanies an article weak in spots, or worse, that contains odd spelling and awkward grammar. It hurts to see this creative work

133

castigated with the silent and eternal edits, hemorrhaging with red ink. Yet the hurt heals because each time you study a mistake, you learn. Each time you learn, you grow as a writer, and this maturity finds its way into another article, then another, and soon you will be sharing ideas with your fellow writers. Embrace the process. You may not want to celebrate, but see the experience as yet another opportunity to become the writer you are destined to be. Mentors can be the subterranean route to getting published. In a way, you are selling the article first to a mentor, and then to an editor.

Writing groups

Many writers find that mentoring can go on in a series of directions simultaneously. Like the salons of yesteryear, writers can gather for a monthly meeting and explore the good, the bad and ugly of each other's work. The process worked for C.S. Lewis and his Inklings in Oxford, and it will work for you. Many universities sponsor **writing groups,** and some have web sites that promote meetings and special speakers. The best writers' groups make a commitment to each other to read a colleague's work in advance of a meeting. Members show up with the copy marked, ready to share constructive criticism with a fellow writer.

This technique, like mentoring, is a step within the sell-it-first model. Some writers skip it altogether. Others feel drawn to kindred spirits and yearn for a time to commiserate and celebrate the often turbulent life of a feature writer. Find what works best for you, and repeat a line from the British Royal Navy's Lt. Horatio Hornblower of the C.S. Forester novels. Hornblower charged his crew, "Put your back into it!"

Author's note: Cecil "Cec" Murphey organized a writer's group in 1971. Any writer that remained in the group for five years published. He's a writer who knows what works and works well. Every year he speaks to hundreds of writers on ideas for breaking into print. Following Cecil's biography is a question-and-answer interview and then an article he wrote that gives promising writers ideas on breaking into print by avoiding a tendency to be shy. As a prolific author, Cecil adopts a role in the article that most of us can't. He is the resident expert, so he doesn't have to use the authority of a source. He is the authority and can offer suggestions in a how-to type article. You should only attempt this technique when you are well-qualified to offer ideas that you know are valid because of your expertise.

Biography of Cecil "Cec" Murphey

Cecil "Cec" Murphey is an award-winning and widely published writer. He is the author or co-author of 90 books, in such wide-ranging fields as health and fitness, motivation, travel and inspiration. He has ghostwritten autobiographies for a number of celebrities, including singer B.J. Thomas, Franklin Graham, pianist Dino Karsanakas, Chick-fil-A founder S. Truett Cathy, ultra-marathon runner Stan Cottrell, and Dr. Ben Carson of Johns Hopkins Hospital. Cecil Murphey, who resides in the Atlanta area, is a three-time winner of

Cecil "Cec" Murphey

the Author of the Year Award by the Dixie Council of authors and Journalists. He is also a winner of the Golden Medallion Award.

One of Cecil's best-selling books, *Gifted Hands*, which he co-wrote with Dr. Ben Carson, has now sold more than a million copies. The companion volume, *Think Big,* has sold more than 700,000 copies.

Interview with Cecil Murphey

Q: You once said that when you became committed to becoming a writer, you read about 25 books on writing in a matter of three months. What's the most outstanding lesson that you learned from all that reading?

A: When I chose to leave the pastorate after 14 years and become a full-time writer, I prepared as much as possible. Not only was I selling regularly and lining up projects, I talked to successful entrepreneurs and then read articles and books by and about them. I discovered an interesting phenomenon among many who had become successful. They started with a dream – an assurance that they were going to make it. They willingly took the risks because they were convinced they could make their dreams come true.

I especially enjoyed the parts where they wrote about the dark days. Most of them had those experiences as they were near the end of the road. They reached the place where they weren't sure they would survive. Although they said it differently, the various statements went something like this:

"I reached the place where I didn't know if it was worth going on."

"I was ready to give up and go get a job with a guaranteed salary."

"I decided I was probably fooling myself and it was stupid to hold on."

Yet those people eventually became successful. They didn't quit, even though their candles burned low. Although the candles barely flickered, something kept them burning. They reported that holding on at the darkest point made the difference. "Once you've been to the bottom," one successful man said, "you're not afraid of risks again. You hang tight and you know that up is the only way to go."

As my friend, ultra-marathon runner Stan Cottrell, says, "I've often found that the difference between success or defeat is to hang on five more minutes. When all logic screams at you to quit, hold on five more minutes!"

Q: Feature articles are often defined by what they are not. For instance, they are not breaking news stories. Instead, a feature article can run the gamut of a profile to a how-to piece to a round-up on the best Chinese restaurants in the nation's largest airports. Many times personal references are avoided, but sometimes the personal "I" works well. How do you decide when to interject yourself?

A: Personal references work best when the subject is about issues only you, the writer, can address. You ask a source to describe the pain of the death of a loved one; however, if you know that experience personally, you may be able to say it as well as the source. It's a judgment call. The writer functions like the midwife who brings the ideas into the world. It can be a collaborative process where the writer works with the source or, in some cases, where the writer is the source. In those cases, it's legitimate to use yourself; however, feature writers often are best served by collecting information from others and using their words

Q: Are the people mentioned in your article real people? Does it matter in this kind of piece?

A: Yes. For some articles, a writer can use a composite character to advance the ideas, but it's always best to use real people and real quotations and real anecdotes. Real reactions may surprise you. A parent sees a son in a race car careen into a wall and explode. As a writer, you imagine the parent will react with horror. Not necessarily. She may see the action and show no reaction. It may not make sense, but it is real. Stay with reality and you will do more to help your article and help yourself.

Q: Do you have one piece of advice for someone who is writing a feature article?

A: Spend time with your sources. Too many writers think in terms of one question and one quotation. Treat each source as if she were the linchpin in your article. Your source will know you care and your article will be the better for it. You will have more information than you need, but it's all part of your education, isn't it?

Struggling to forgive
By Cecil Murphey
Used with permission

"Those who tell you they don't struggle with forgiving are lying to you or they're lying to themselves." I was a young Christian when Pastor Webb made that statement. At the time I thought he overstated the issue; now I believe he was correct.

I've learned through experience that forgiveness doesn't always come easily. This is especially true when pain rips through our hearts. Whether we feel betrayed or rejected, whether deceived or someone has smeared our reputation, whether they've lied about us or taken advantage of us, the suffering persists. Sometimes well-meaning friends imply the issue is trivial by urging, "Just get over it." If we've been deeply wounded, it's not trivial to us.

What those friends don't grasp is that it's not the seriousness of the offense, but our reaction that makes the agony intense. The deeper we feel wounded, the harder for us to release the pain and pardon the offender.

What happens when we're offended

Once we understand what happens when someone hurts us, we're ready to move toward forgiveness. If the injury cuts deeply, we wonder if we'll ever get over the emotional devastation. Sometimes distress so overwhelms our lives that we either don't function or we go through our tasks on autopilot.

We react in a variety of ways. One of them is to deny we've been hurt. We stuff the pain inside and lie to ourselves. What tends to happen is that the pain builds up below our consciousness. Later we may boil over in rage about what many would call a slight issue.

Another reaction is to retaliate. We've been crushed and we want to punish the offender for hurting us. We want to strike back and want that cruel person to feel worse than we do. Our revenge may be to speak against the one who offended us to anyone who will listen.

A third way is to wallow in our pain, and most of us do that for a while. We keep reminding ourselves that we don't deserve such treatment. We've been hurt too badly to push away our injury. Consequently, we relive and rehearse what happened and can't let go of it. Whenever the offender's name comes into our minds, we groan and suffer afresh.

We intensify our pain because we continuously recreate the situation in our mind and focus on what we might have said instead of

137

how we actually behaved. It's as if by trying to think of the right words (usually an insult) or making a pre-emptive strike, reality will change. However, no matter how hard we struggle, we can't remake the past.

A common response is to justify our outrage by crying out:

"Why did she do that to me?"

"I've always stood up for him and now he does this to me."

"I've been a faithful wife. He plays around, but I've kept my vows to God."

Such reactions may be normal, and as long as we focus on our agony, feel sorry for ourselves, and reel from our sorrow, we'll never take the first step toward reconciliation.

Why we forgive

First, we choose to forgive because it pleases God. Instead of asking, "Why should I forgive? It's his sin, not mine," we realize we want to be free of our pain because God commands us to forgive. We may not be able to release our pain immediately, and it may take much soul searching before we're ready. Ultimately, however, we forgive because it is the godly thing to do.

For example, Paul exhorts, "All bitterness, anger and wrath, insult and slander must be removed from you, along with all wickedness. And be kind and compassionate to one another, forgive one another, just as God also forgave you in Christ" (Ephesians 4:31–32 CSB).

In the Lord's Prayer, we ask God to forgive our sins in the same way we forgive others. Jesus then added, "For if you forgive people their wrongdoing, your heavenly Father will forgive you as well. But if you don't forgive people, your Father will not forgive your wrongdoing" (Matthew 6:14–15 CSB).

Second, we forgive because it's for our own good. As long as we refuse to let go of our hurt, we've tied that other person to ourselves. We have no inner peace. One person said, "We're giving that person free rent inside our heads." We need to consider the cost in not forgiving – how much energy and emotion we give to that hurt throughout the day or how much sleep we lose.

Third, we let go because we have experienced divine pardon for our sins. We have received God's grace – forgiveness – that we didn't deserve. No matter how wickedly we behaved in the past, God's grace wiped away every wrongdoing. The practical aspect is that our perception of God's grace shapes the way we treat others. That is, if we grasp the depth of our own failure and how little we merit cleansing of our offenses against God, we more readily release others.

Jesus taught this lesson when he visited Simon the leper. The host didn't offer him the common courtesy of having someone wash his feet. However, a prostitute came into the room, washed his feet with her tears, wiped them with her hair, then kissed his feet and put perfume on them. (See Luke 7:36-50.) The woman understood something that Simon did not: She knew how grossly she had sinned and how generously God had forgiven her. To make the lesson clear, Jesus says to Simon, "A creditor had two debtors. One owed him five hundred denarii, and the other fifty. Since they could not pay it back, he graciously forgave them both. So, which of them will love him more?" (vss. 41–42 CSB).

The answer was obvious. Jesus then pointed to the woman and said, "Therefore, I tell you, her many sins have been forgiven; that's why she loved much. But the one who is forgiven little, loves little" (v.47).

By little, Jesus means our perception of our sin. As long as we think we are morally superior to those who have wronged us, we'll have trouble erasing the pain. Once we perceive deep within that we are sinners, we realize there isn't much difference between us and the one who hurt us. The Bible is also quite clear to spell out that "There is no one righteous, not even one" (Romans 3:10b CSB).

How we forgive

1. *We confront our hurt.* Even if the offense is small, we don't ignore it or deny our pain. If we try, bitterness can begin to grow within us. We need to deal with the hurt as soon as we feel it. We don't suffer in silence and tell ourselves that we have forgiven. Until we confront our pain, it stays hidden in some subterranean part of our soul. In fact, it probably begins to fester. In the church, too often we deny how crushed we have been by another's actions. We force smiles on our faces and deny we've been offended.

Forgiveness begins when we admit, "I have been hurt, but I want to be free from this agony."

2. *We ask God to heal our wounds.* This doesn't happen automatically. Sometimes we have to pray for extended periods. We know God wants us to let go, but the deeper the pain, the longer it takes to be willing to release the offense.

3. *We need to allow ourselves time to heal.* We don't have to rush into forgiving. As long as the offense fills our hearts with grief, we're not ready. I liken this to the death of someone we love. We know it takes time for the grief to subside. We need to learn to be kind to ourselves and not push ourselves before we're ready.

4. *We need to ask God to give us a clean heart.* We pray for cleansing and ask God to remove any desire to hurt the other or to yearn for the other person to suffer. If we scrutinize ourselves, we're forced to admit how weak we are. How many times have we hurt or belittled others? Even though we tend to classify sins as small, large, or all-but-unforgivable, the Bible never makes that distinction. In God's eyes, sin is sin. The prayer of David after his adulterous affair makes the strong point that all sins are ultimately sins against God. "Against you, you only, have I sinned and done what is evil in your sight" (Psalm 51:4 NIV).

5. *We realize we no longer need the other person to be wrong.* This is difficult for many of us to admit, but once we perceive God's grace in our own lives, we also can acknowledge that we may have had some level of culpability. That doesn't justify another's sin or cruelty, but it does remind us of a powerful truth: Our sins may be different, but they are still rebellion against God. Once we can think objectively about our injury, we ask ourselves, "What if God rewarded me according to my deeds? What if God punished me for every wrong thing I did?"

6. *We need to pray for the person who hurt us.* Instead of crying out, "Repay them for their sins," we need to pray for their well being and for divine blessings on their lives. The more deeply hurt we are, the more difficult this will be to pray, but it's an important step. If we refuse to pray this way, it says we have set ourselves up as judges and have the right to decide what others deserve.

7. *We need to ask ourselves why this hurt so badly.* The answer may seem obvious. He committed adultery. She lied about me. This may be true, but when we scrutinize our emotions and attitudes more fully, we may have to face the reality that part of the hurt is because of our failure. This is not to excuse or overlook the offense, but it is to search our own hearts and ask God to help us see if we have any responsibility in what happened.

This isn't to diminish the wrongdoing of another. It is to challenge us to look at ourselves. Was I a silent contributor to this? Had I failed the other person – perhaps in a different way? Do I agonize over this because I don't want to face the evil in myself? If I can see myself as good then I can see the one who hurt me as evil.

For example, a friend once crushed me by accusing me of lying and turning people against him, and he called me terrible names. Although it took several weeks, I finally admitted to myself that I had been silent when others spoke against him. I had added a few judgmental comments about him in conversation and even repeated gossip. As long as I focused on his actions, I didn't have to examine my own heart. Until I admitted culpability, I couldn't understand the depth of my aching heart. I hurt because he was close to the truth about me.

My friend had, in effect, held up a mirror for me to stare at my careless words, minor hurts that I had kept hidden, and little resentments that had built up. When something evokes strong emotional reaction – good or bad – our response says more about us than it does about the other person or the event.

8. *We need to relinquish the offense.* Someone hurt us, but ultimately, the other sinned against God. This is God's issue and not ours.

Two biblical examples stand out. First, Joseph's brothers had hated him, conspired against him, thrown him into a pit, and sold him into slavery. After the death of their father Jacob, the brothers feared Joseph would retaliate. He said, "Don't be afraid. Am I in the place of God? You intended to harm me, but God intended it for good..." (Genesis 50:19–20a NIV).

Second, Jesus, in the midst of his own physical torture, cried out, "Father, forgive them." (See Luke 23:34.) He set the example for us to follow.

To follow Jesus' example may not be easy – and often it isn't. Despite how hard or long we have to struggle to forgive, we remind ourselves that as the people of God, we will and must forgive if we are to live in fellowship.

Exercises

1) In thinking about the astonishing career of Cecil Murphey, what strikes you as the one idea of his that would work for you?
2) The mind doctors say that working in isolation energizes introverts while extroverts gain energy by working with others. How do you see yourself? Based on this article, how do you see Cec Murphey?
3) What do you like best about the article? Do you think numbering the points helps the reader follow your organization? What about the use of "bullets?"

Writers' conferences

Writers' conferences are one of the best ways to **interact with writers and editors**. These venues allow writers of varying ability to interact with newbies and veteran writers. In a weekend, aspiring writers will learn about contracts, publication rights, publicity, rejection and other topics encountered in the craft. The Internet lists conferences and a quick search using the keywords "writers' conferences" will provide a number of hits. The cost can be as little as $75 for a day-long event to nearly $300 for a five-day meeting. The classes are valuable; the interaction is priceless.

Here's the story of one writer's experience at a conference. Karen Langley of Zion, Ill., sent me this anecdote of her success following a writer's conference.

I heard you speak at the 2001 American Christian Writers' Conference in Ft. Wayne. I was a shy college sophomore, it was the first writers' conference I'd ever attended, and I felt a bit out of my league as one of only a few under-30 attendees. I looked back through my conference notes, and I see that you talked about "Writing for the Secular Press." Honestly, I don't remember much about that, but I do remember thinking your suggestions for how to approach newspaper editors seemed pretty bold – too bold for my timid personality – but how cool if it could be that easy to get published!

That summer, my family took our annual vacation trip to Ocean City, NJ. I'd thought before about writing an article about our family reunion – a 27-year traditional "Pizza Blast" at a boardwalk pizza parlor. I remembered your suggestions and figured I had nothing to lose. So one afternoon before heading to the beach, I rode a bike to the newspaper office. I asked the receptionist if the editor was in; she went down the hall and brought him out front; I told him my idea; he said he was interested. He gave me a deadline, a word count and his phone number and said to call and let him know what time he could send out a photographer. So I interviewed my relatives and the pizza place owners, and wrote the story. A photographer came out and shot our family after the Pizza Blast (all 37 of us!), and I turned in my story along with a few pictures I'd taken (one of which appears with the story). I got a byline and my family has a nice memento of our reunion!

My article appeared in September 2001 in The Sure Guide. Since then I've published about a dozen articles in national teen magazines, another dozen or so on the web and a few devotionals. So, the idea works!

Making friends at conferences

When I spoke at my first writers' conference, I met Cec Murphey, the author highlighted in this chapter. He and I hit it off, and he remains a friend and confidant. These friendships are important to writers, who need ideas on moving their intent to write into action.

In the West is the Glorieta Christian Writers' Conference, usually held in October near Albuquerque, NM. In the East is Sandy Cove Christian Communicators, scheduled in October near Baltimore, Md. The Mid-Atlantic Christian Writers' Conference is held in late May near Washington, D.C. World Journalism Institute takes place around the nation and often offers scholarships. Classes are held at the headquarters in Asheville, NC, and points North and South. Workshops are where writers and journalists abound and you can find one near your home by checking the Internet and using the search term *writers' conference.*

Internships

College students nationwide have discovered that **internships** are as important as classroom training. More than half of all students who graduate took advantage of an internship while in college.[37] It works. It may amount to free labor, something most of us can't afford, but it is worth considering. Many of us offered our talents for free while we earned some bylines. The goal is to build a portfolio today. Don't wait. When your church or organization says it needs a feature article on the new president of the committee, a humorous article on the group's pet issue or a listing of coming events, volunteer, but insist on a byline. Parlay that byline into another byline. Keep a list of these successes with the most recent listed first. Before long, the volunteer work will yield to deadline work. When a publication is facing a deadline, the editor is more likely to ante up a paycheck to accompany the byline.

Whether volunteering or working as an intern, the ideal situation is to be paid; however, some writers have found that the free labor can lead to a paying job. The other benefit is that you get to test-drive your secret passion. Is it really for you? Writing isn't about a leisurely wait when the mood strikes. It is about collecting information, studying videotapes or poking into statistical surveys. It means getting to the scene, talking to people and reading documents. It's work, hard, fulfilling work that engages the mind and body like no other activity.

Internships can last a few weeks or a few months, part-time or full-time and can be formal situations with training sessions and performance reviews. However, you may have as much success by creating your own opportunity and asking an organization if you can work for it in a guided project. You supply the creativity and labor and the organization will provide the structure to nurse the project into a success.

---

[37] Altschuler, G.C. (2002, April 14). A tryout for the real world, interning is good for the resume. Better yet, it may get you hired. *The Chronicle of Higher Education.* p. 20.

For formal internships aimed at students, consider *The Internship Bible* by Princeton Review or *Internships 2005*, one of Peterson's Guides. Colleges and universities monitor internships for their students, but don't generally allow outsiders to see the openings. Among the benefits of writers' groups and writers' conferences is the network potential that can short-circuit these otherwise published internship possibilities. By asking friends and associates for help, you gain a degree of intimacy, and, possibly a better opportunity of breaking into the job. Once you land the internship, it's crucial that you do the job that the organization wants accomplished before you try more meaningful work. After the experience, it's good form to stay in touch with the organization. They know that you have ambition and all they need is an excuse to give you a chance to exercise your gifts.

A columnist on making the sale

To sell an article, a writer needs some good fortune and hard work, but mostly **hard work**. For columnist Don Feder, it amounts to reading, researching and re-reading.

Feder was a *Boston Herald* editorial writer and syndicated columnist from June 1983 until June 2002, when he took a sabbatical. Feder has been published in *The Wall Street Journal*, *National Review*, *Human Events*, *Reason* and *Reader's Digest*. His books include *A Jewish Conservative Looks at Pagan America* (1993) and *Who's Afraid of the Religious Right* (1996). Among Feder's suggestions for making the sale with a good article are:

Diction. Select the right word. This part of the process may be the technique that is most difficult to promising writers.

Work. "Good columns are paid off in sweat equity," Feder said. "It takes a time investment."

Humor. Feder urged the writers to use gentle humor, adding, "Nothing makes a louder sound than a joke that falls flat."

Read. Read history, current affairs, economics and material that is opposed to the conservative view. In addition, the columnist said some of the best writing and thinking can be found in speeches and poetry. He cited the Sermon on the Mount, Shakespeare's funeral oratory by Mark Anthony in the play *Julius Caesar*, Lincoln's "Gettysburg Address," Martin Luther King's "I Have a Dream" speech and Peggy Noonan's work for Ronald Reagan where the president said the ill-fated Challenger astronauts "touched the face of God."

Read some more. Read anthologies by columnists such as Chicago's Mike Royko who refused to write for a Rupert Murdoch newspaper for this reason: "No self-respecting fish would be wrapped in a Murdoch newspaper!" (Murdoch, the British media baron, is CEO of News Corp.)

Variety. Write whimsical prose. Write angry prose, but be ready to learn. "Don't be a Johnny One-Note," Feder said. "Don't always be angry or readers will think you are a crank and you tend to metamorphose into the Incredible Hulk."

Surprise. Surprise readers by providing something unexpected such as a magazine piece that Feder penned that discussed J.R.R. Tolkien of *Lord of the Rings* fame and his influence on C.S. Lewis, the greatest Christian apologist of the last century. "Tolkien was instrumental in Lewis returning to faith," Feder said. When columnists fail to surprise readers, their writing gets wooden, predictable. "Move readers by avoiding the steady stream of clichés," he said. "Keep it fresh." Too many columnists refer to Saddam Hussein as Hitler, abortion as the modern Holocaust and so on.

Personal. Among anyone's best prose are the personal narratives that describe the devastation of a drug addict, a homeless derelict or the quiet pain of a mother whose son overdosed. To get these portraits, Feder told the audience to visit a meeting of "addicts anonymous" to gain the vital research, scan newspapers, create files, study LexisNexis and search for authorities who can speak with credibility on topics.

Exercises

1) Visit the library and read six magazines with which you are unfamiliar.
2) Create a grid and record the number of quotations, the number of anecdotes, the number of sources used in each article and note the magazine's approach to statistics.
3) Write an analysis on the periodical based on your research. Explain the editorial slant.
4) Check the web for the writers' guidelines for each magazine.
5) Conceive of a feature article idea for this magazine. Write a 100-word query letter.
6) Then write the first page of a made-up article using the proper format.
7) Look up the copyright provisions on the Internet for the U.S. Copyright Office in Washington, D.C.

Biography of Jill Darling

Jill Darling

Jill Darling's love for writing began when she was a child. An avid letter writer, she corresponded with her father and 25 servicemen during the years he fought in the Vietnam conflict. Her efforts evolved into a fifth-grade class project that spread throughout the school.

As an adult, she honed her writing skills while homeschooling her two sons and working on assignments with them. Jill and her children wrote for *The Daily Review*'s "Teens' Page," a newspaper in Towanda, Pa. She has worked as a freelance columnist, feature writer and news correspondent for *The Daily Review*. In addition, she received a Year 2000 Amy Writing Award and is a national syndicated columnist for the Amy Foundation Syndicate. Additional awards came from the Associated Press Managing Editors of Pennsylvania in 2001 and the West Branch Christian Writers' Contest in 2002. She is a member of the National Society of Newspaper Columnists.

Darling contributes regularly to the *Press & Sun-Bulletin*, Binghamton, N.Y., and *Tioga County's Community Press*, Apalachin, N.Y. She is a contributing author to *50 Veteran Homeschoolers Share...Things We Wish We'd Known.*[38] Magazine articles include *Country Extra, Pennsylvania Magazine, Grit, The Teaching Home, The Mentor* and many other publications.

Darling assists her husband Pete in pastoring Faith Christian Fellowship, Apalachin, N.Y., where she served as children's minister for 18 years. They have two adult children, Greg and Keith, and daughter-in-law, Faith, and grandson, Andrew Gregory.

---

[38] Waring, B. and Waring, D. (1999). *50 veteran homeschoolers share . . . Things we wish we'd known.* Lynnwood. WA: Emerald Books.

Dads on duty help reduce school violence[39]
By Jill Darling
Used with permission

Whitney put on his black T-shirt and ball cap with gold logo and slipped on his gold satin jacket emblazoned with black letters as he prepared for his first day of school. This was his fourth year at Arlington High School in Indianapolis, Ind., and he was pumped. He drove early to school to beat his buddies so he could greet them as they bounded off the bus. He stood at the door and welcomed one special "bro," Whit, his 6-foot son, a new freshman at the school. The elder Whitney is one of 58 fathers at Arlington who volunteer for the Security Dads program.

Linda Wallace began the program in 1991. Wallace's 16-year-old daughter, Lena, wanted to attend the school's talent show, but their son told them she shouldn't go because of a rash of violence that had erupted on campus. He told them he didn't attend ball games or shows not because he wasn't interested, but because he feared for his own safety.

"This was supposed to be a fun time for them," Wallace said. "I decided I wanted to make a change, to give kids ownership of their schools."

That's when Wallace stumbled upon an idea to curb violence that has become a model for high schools around the country. Wallace had her husband, Anthony, don a school T-shirt and the entire family went to the talent show. The evening went so well that Wallace thought it would be a great idea to involve fathers in more events at the school.

Dressed in T-shirts or jackets with the Arlington mascot on the front and the words "Security Dad" on the back, the volunteer fathers walk the halls and interact with students on a daily basis. By mingling with students, their presence discourages inappropriate behavior and has improved the school's environment.

The dads also provide an example of strong, caring, involved fathers. Students often come to them for advice, or just to talk about problems in their lives.

Sue Bertrand of Towanda, Pa., graduated from Arlington High School in 1966 and was stunned to hear how the school had deteriorated when she first read about the Security Dads program in a magazine. "I could reasonably conclude that this could happen in any

---

[39] Darling, J. (2003, Oct. 4). Dads on duty help reduce school violence. *The (Binghamton, N.Y.) Press & Bulletin*, p. 4A.

school anywhere, even in Towanda," said Bertrand, whose son is a student in the district. "I would rather see the Security Dads program in place rather than policemen in Towanda schools, because a police presence adds to and perhaps confirms that the school is losing control."

"The kids are pretty well behaved when they know we're not out there trying to arrest them," said Security Dad Dennis Stansbury. "They are more responsive to us. If they see a police officer, they go on the defensive right away. With us, we're just other students' dads. It works great."

On Whitney's first day of school, commotion filled the hallways replete with high-fives and hugs from the kids as he greeted them with, "How was your summer?" and "Ready for this school year?" He roams the hallways for the entire school day, three days a week on his days off from work. He says the kids know his and the other dads' schedules, and if a schedule change arises the kids will ask, "Mr. Whitney, where have you been?"

"The students tell us when special events come up to make sure we know about it before the faculty has a chance to tell us," Whitney said. "They want you to be there 24-hours a day. [We] have 1200 to 1400 or 1500 kids. These are our kids. That's how we look at it."

Linda Wallace said Security Dads is not a formal program. "There's no money involved and there's no training," she said. "There's no way you can train a dad to be a dad. It's just organizing and giving them something to do."

Security Dads has received national attention. It's been featured on ABC's "Good Morning America", on CNN Headline News, and in articles in *Good Housekeeping* and *Parade* magazines. Wallace has helped direct hundreds of schools nationwide to organize and tailor the Security Dads program to their individual needs. I believe this program would benefit the schools in our region.

For more information, contact the Indiana Center for Family Schools and Community Partnerships www.fscp.org. Wallace is the associate director and project manager for the fathers' programs.

Interview with Jill Darling

Q: This article is an example of localizing, that is taking a news event that is in the national spotlight and given it local treatment. How did you get the background?

A: Towanda school officials contemplated having police presence to provide school security. This concerned Sue Bertrand who remembered reading about the Security Dads program in a magazine. An alumna of Arlington High School in Indianapolis, she thought the Security Dads program was worthy of attention. I contacted the magazine and got a phone number, which directed me to the Indianapolis public schools' partnership center. They gave me the Security Dads web site address. After researching that site and other related sites on the Internet, I had enough information for the base of my article. Then I contacted founder Linda Wallace and conducted an interview.

Q: As a freelance writer, what are the tradeoffs of work-for-hire?

A: There are no benefits unless you are highly compensated for your work. Under new corporate policy for the newspaper for which I contributed articles, I was faced with signing a work-for-hire contract. Signing it meant that I'd be giving the newspaper exclusive rights to my work (used anywhere and in any way with no further compensation) and I would no longer own the copyright to my material. Since my columns and articles are sold to magazines and appear online, I couldn't sign the contract and could therefore no longer write for the paper. Freelancers nationwide are faced with signing these contracts and ultimately forced out due to corporations wanting exclusive ownership, primarily due to publication on the Internet. A work-for-hire contract works well if, for example, a freelancer agrees to write a book on a prescribed topic for a particular company and the price is right. The writer is paid a hefty sum once and that's it. Exclusive rights to include the copyright belong to the company. If for some reason the company warrants, the writer is not even considered the author of the material.

Q: You write a column for an online service. What are some of the advantages and disadvantages?

A: The advantages of writing a column for an online service are that you get national exposure and your work is read by thousands more people. The disadvantages are that you don't have a rapport with readers like you do in your local newspaper. If someone writes in to agree or disagree, you'll never know it and can never respond. Writing a column in your local newspaper gives you a forum for debate and fodder for additional columns.

Exercises

1) How could the Security Dads story be re-packaged to sell a second or third time?
2) What else could help dramatize this kind of article?
3) What kind of color would you insert?

4) Identify the best quotation in the piece.

Summary
It is dangerous to write without an assignment and this chapter provided ideas on **selling the article first** before it is written. Some writers use email addresses or the telephone or both to contact an editor; however, many writers still use the old-fashioned approach of a query letter to make contact. A number of reference books such as the *Writer's Market* provide contact information. For a more personal approach, consider meeting as many editors in person as possible using a **road trip**. Once you land an assignment, the next step is to follow the protocol for submitting the work to garner as much goodwill as possible. In some cases, editors will mentor new writers on an informal basis. If possible, work with a more seasoned writer to learn as much as possible using writers' groups and writers' conferences. This chapter included an interview with Cecil Murphey, a writer who is known for his loving encouragement of fellow writers. The chapter ended with two articles that talk about various facets of the writing business, including **promotion**, and the **hard work** of studying other writers. In addition, writer Jill Darling talked about the pros and cons of work-for-hire.

Chapter 7

The ethical picture
FeatureWriting.Net/TakeNoPrisoners

Chapter at-a-glance

- ➢ Practicing the appropriate standard in news gathering
- ➢ Practicing the appropriate standard in news reporting
- ➢ Working with editors to achieve the proper balance

In E. Annie Proulx's Pulitzer Prize-winning novel, *The Shipping News*,[40] journalist Quoyle of the *Gammy Bird* newspaper finds his first publishing success when his feature article about a luxury yacht once owned by Hitler gains him favor, his first brush with acceptance. The sensation is short-lived when Quoyle learns that the owners of the craft stiffed his aunt after she carefully re-upholstered the vessel's ornate furniture. Does he use his newfound standing to crusade for his aunt, his closest living relative, or abide by a code that says the press should not be used for personal gain? Later Quoyle finds evidence of murder

Writers often show us a world that is dull and less alive than others know to be true. Climb reality from the inside and see the world from a balcony with truth encouraged by solid ethics. Don't settle for the broken-down fire escape of shoddy reporting.

---

[40] The novel explores the conventions of a second-rate newspaper in a narrative about an American family coping with life in a foreign port. Proulx, E. A. (1993). *The Shipping News*. New York: Charles Scribner's Sons.

linked to the yacht owners; does his duty to report the degrading details of the tragedy color his news judgment? Should he step aside and insist someone else write the grim report?

Codes of conduct questions sometimes are reduced to a phrase: **WWJD, what would Jesus do?** In recent years columnists have used WWJD to push the ethical boundary wider to ask what Jesus would drive – and vanquished the thought of a sports utility vehicle as wasteful. Nutritionists deplore processed food and ask what Jesus would eat, and authors wonder, "What would Jesus do as a writer?"[41]

That's not too hard. The only writing Jesus did was in the dirt. Remember that New Testament story of the woman accused of adultery?[42] As the mob deplored her (not the man), Jesus scribbled on the ground. Some speculate that Jesus wrote the sins associated with the accusing men, and one by one, the men left the scene of the passionate crime, robbed of an opportunity to stone someone. Whatever Jesus wrote was lost in the time it took a light breeze or a sandal impression to obliterate the marks.

Jesus didn't write, he did more. Author Madeleine L'Engle is reported to have said, "Jesus wasn't a theologian. He is a God who tells stories." Telling a strong narrative is a high and noble calling, and the mission of the best authors, the best reporters, and the best feature writers. Thinking of a deity as the creator of the ultimate story, the meta-narrative, may help us as we consider the standards we should embrace in the act of writing.

Al Janssen, writer of 22 books, often talks to writers about the power of the narrative. He knows that the best way to reach a culture is to share a gripping story that includes a timeless message. The secret? Art must precede argument. A well-told news story draws readers in. Trivial stories told well will get a hearing; profound stories told poorly won't. Perhaps the WWJD question can be rephrased: "What would Jesus have me do as a writer?"

---

[41] Smith, M. R. (2002). *The Jesus newspaper*. Lanham, MD: University Press of America.

[42] See the Gospel of John 8, verse 6, the *New American Standard Bible*, which says, "And they were saying this, testing Him, in order that they might have grounds for accusing Him. But Jesus stooped down, and with His finger wrote on the ground." The next verse says, "But when they persisted in asking Him, He straightened up, and said to them, "He who is without sin among you, let him be the first to throw a stone at her." John 8:8 says, "And again He stooped down and wrote on the ground." Nonetheless, at least one Bible commentary says, "It is useless to speculate as to what Jesus wrote. Nothing is made of the writing in the narrative" Harrison, E. F. and Pfeiffer, C. F., (1962). *The Wycliffe Bible Commentary*. Chicago: Moody Press, p. 1090.

Journalists in the United States are fond of recalling the days of colonial printers who defied governmental authority and printed articles that challenged those in power. The public's right to know is a guiding principle that is older than the nation, and the best writers these days temper this notion with a series of questions to position themselves on the side of angles. It's more than a list of do's and don'ts; it is a process of thinking about the need to obtain information and your reasons for it.

Among the oldest journalism groups in the nation are the Society of Professional Journalists and the American Society of Newspaper Editors, organizations that share a similar code of ethics. SPJ's code, heavily influenced by ASNE's code, includes three guiding principles: to seek truth, to minimize harm, and to remain independent. The complete code appears at the end of this chapter. In the 1940s, the Hutchins Commission[43] on the press urged anyone in the media to provide a truthful, comprehensive, and intelligent account of the day's events in a context that gives it meaning. In addition, the commission said it was the responsibility of the media to give a representative picture of the various groups in society while helping society clarify its goals and values. They called this model the theory of social responsibility. Since most of us can't print our own newspapers, magazines and books, it's up to the people who do to include all of a community's voices in the press.

Among readers' expectations of the press, whether inspirational or mainstream, is that it is committed to working for them.[44] The tacit contract is that the publication will provide information that is consistent with its editorial policy. In most cases, that means avoiding even the appearance of working for sources.

As a practical matter, the Poynter Institute in St. Petersburg, Fla., has developed some questions writers can use to think through the business of obtaining and publishing information. Keith Woods of Poynter used the question-approach of his colleague Bob Steele in explaining this process to the National Society of Newspaper Columnists at its Seminar on Ethics and Excellence in Column Writing. According to Woods, from the outset

---

[43] The Hutchins commission is named after educator Robert Maynard Hutchins who, in 1930, is quoted as saying: "I notice that in spite of the frightful lies you have printed about me, I still believe everything you print about other people." (2003, March 15). Quoted in *First Amendment Calendar*, Arlington, VA: The Freedom Forum.

[44] Woiwode, L. (2003, June 27). The ethics of writing. Asheville, N.C.: World Journalism Institute. Larry Woiwode refers to James R. Edwards and his idea that ethical systems often may be categorized as ethics of intention or ethics of outcome. Edwards found that the idea of *agape* combines both because the outcome conforms to God's nature and will be used to fulfill his eternal will.

of an article, writers should practice humility. They should ask themselves *what they know* and *what they need to know*. Humility suggests that as writers, we don't know everything. It requires the writer to consider the ethics involved in this situation along with the organizational policies and professional guidelines.

Better writers think about these basics and then ask, "Who else should be involved in the decision-making process?" A crucial issue today in the crisis communication model is the need to inform all the stakeholders in a decision, acknowledging that some stakeholders are more legitimate than others. One way to make sure that the writer possesses the right attitude is to ask, "What if the roles were reversed?" The process demands that writers switch roles with sources and think about the short-term and long-term consequences of the article.

Telling a hard truth may be the action that has the most consequence. A Hindu proverb says, "He who speaks the truth should have one foot in the stirrup." Anyone who has spent time in reporting news knows the danger of doing the job of reporting the truth and being rewarded with grief. Reporters must be ready to chronicle the good, bad and ugly with boldness as part of our cherished press freedoms. All writers, from the poet to the penny-a-word hack, enjoy the legacy of America's press freedoms. Once the writer considers the preceding questions, the final idea is to be prepared to explain the decision-making process to an editor, colleagues and others, including readers. The explanation may not win admirers; the goal is to ask the question and be prepared to provide a response, even a response that will have your hand clutching the reins while your foot slips into the stirrup.

The question-method allows a writer to think about macro issues that may not have clear-cut answers, but the press, which includes feature writers and freelance contributors, has developed a number of conventions to help writers gather and publish information with efficiency. Writers endure relentless deadlines, and the need to internalize conventions is a must. The following ideas are considered the basics of ethical conduct for writers.

Rules for quoting sources

Beginning writers tend to neglect attribution, but a good rule of thumb is to include attribution once every paragraph. Use speech tags such as "said." One editor in the Southwest would send his writers a note that urged, "Use said. Use said. Use said. Use said. Use said. Use said. Use said. Use said. Use said. Use said. Use said. Use said. Use said."

Got it?

The goal is to tell your reader the source of your information. Help her know that the information you are providing came from a source outside yourself. Using "said" or "according to" or similar phrases is the best way to establish that the information you are providing was from a source, not you. Answer the question, "Who says?" by connecting a quotation with a person's name and identity. The best speech tags do not unduly flatter or offend, which makes "said" the perfect verb. Avoid weak verbs such as "snipped," "sniffed," "sneered," "whined," "laughed," "hooted" and so on. Novelists like to use this kind of attribution and other attribution words such as "honked," "coughed," and "barked." These words are creative alternatives, but they can be inflammatory. The best idea is to play it straight and use "said." Believe it or not, readers will read over the "said," and the flow of your article will not be noticeably disturbed. Better to be overly cautious and use more attribution than less. These days writers are a little too cavalier in their writing. They use some attribution but make readers guess the source of the other information. Guessing games can be tiresome and rude, and lead to ethical mine fields, or as I like to say, *mind fields*, where vagueness is the enemy of clear thought.

In summary, cite a source for quotations but never lift a quotation from someone else's work. Do your own interviews. When you check a quotation from another writer's published interview with a source, you may be surprised to learn that the source will challenge the exact wording of the phrase. Finally, it may be obvious, but it's worth noting: never make up a quotation, and don't be tempted to fill in a quotation if a source says, "You write so well. Just have me say something witty." Not good and not ethical. Remember it is your credibility that will suffer.

Credibility demands that you always verify information, particularly in cases where some of the comments are in dispute. When one elected official accuses another elected official of improper conduct, the writer must get both sides. In most publications, no article of wrongdoing is written unless someone is charged with a crime; however, the nature of politics often leads to surly comments from opposing candidates. It's imperative that the writer finds out as much background as possible using official sources and unofficial sources. Remember that concept? Interview the people who are paid spokesmen (official sources), and those who are not on the payroll (unofficial sources). Check public records in the courthouse or on the web. See Chapter 8, *Using the Internet*, on searching the Internet for specific web sites. Above all, talk to the people who are being accused.

For writers who are new to interviewing, asking another person difficult or embarrassing questions seems impolite; however, many a person hasn't had a chance to explain because no one gave her an opportunity to go on the record. When the questions are too painful, try one of the following soft wind-ups. Say, "Your critics say…" This technique makes it sound as if the writer doesn't endorse the judgmental position but is just doing her job. Many variations exist for the same approach. "It's been reported…" Notice the passive construction of that sentence? Writers tend to avoid the passive voice as poor prose, but it has its uses when we don't want anyone to know the identity of the person who made a controversial statement.

Another approach that allows an interviewer to ask a question that may make a source uncomfortable is: "What do you say to those who claim…?" or, "Let me play devil's advocate and ask you…" These clauses allow the writer to gain some distance from the accusatory question to soften the source's potential anger at you for suggesting that she could do wrong.

Other writers use a direct approach and unapologetically plow ahead with a series of hard-hitting questions. Both methods have merit. In *The Shipping News*, Quoyle's first editor, while not taken with Quoyle, has to admit that his pathetic manner allows sources to open up and confess all the detail that is meant for a confessional. All writers have different approaches to obtain information. If you are reserved, use it to your advantage, and ask questions sheepishly by backing the car into a space. If you are bold, use your spirited high-speed chase to sail into the freeway on two wheels and a cup of coffee. Sources want to talk and writers must be ready to give them an opportunity. In those rare cases where a source cannot be located, explain to her colleagues, friends or family members that you are working very hard to include the source's viewpoint in the article. It's not good enough to call once and leave a message. You may risk becoming a nuisance, but you should call over and over if for no other reason than to let the office know how committed you are.

George Archibald, a newsman with several decades of reporting acumen, knows that his sources for the U.S. Senate and U.S. Congress must cross the capitol rotunda on the way to a committee meeting. When he needs a source, he finds a strategic spot and waits for the source to stroll by. The practice is not an ambush; it's a method of making sure his question to a valuable source gets to that person unfiltered by an aide and without delay. This style may not be yours, but it emphasizes the need to be vigilant.

Occasionally, your efforts fail. The source you need is on an airplane, in a meeting or just plain unavailable. Be honest. As I suggested earlier, tell your audience that you tried to contact Mr. X, but he could not be reached. You can tell the reader the number of times that you called. You can mention that you tried the telephone, facsimile machine, electronic mail, U.S. Postal service, personal contacts – the specific means that you used, but do your best not to suggest that the source was avoiding you. A good ethical rule of thumb is to give people the benefit of the doubt and never ascribe motives to their behavior. Only God and the person know the reason for an action. The motives may be tainted, suspect and dripping with malice, but you can't know another person's heartbeat.

To maintain accuracy, make it a habit of calling sources to double-check quotations. A tape recorder is no substitute for pad and pen or interviews typed directly into a computer, and many a sentence has been mangled from lips to ears to article. Check your quotation and you will be accurate, courteous and unusual. Typically, publications ask writers to avoid showing a source the finished article; however, no editor wants to publish inaccuracies. Learn your publication's policy and practice checking names, dates, quotations and other information that you did not observe directly.

Trust in the media

Trust in institutions continues to decline in the 21st century, but public confidence in the media is among the lowest. Since mid-1989, when communism fell in Europe, trust in the media went from 54% to 32%.[45] Among the problems for readers are high-profile cases such as Jayson Blair of *The New York Times* who resigned May 1, 2003 after he was accused of plagiarizing or fabricating 36 of 73 articles recently reported in the newspaper.[46] By May 28, 2003, Rick Bragg, a Pulitzer Prize-winning reporter for *The New York Times,* resigned over the use of his byline on an article largely the work of a freelance writer, J. Wes Yoder, a recent college graduate. The feature article concerned Florida oystermen and Yoder, an intern, did much of the work, according to the Associated Press.

By June 5, 2003, two leading editors of *The New York Times* retired following the back-to-back episodes. Executive Editor Howell Raines and Managing Editor Gerald M. Boyd resigned following questions over their judgment. In 2003, the 152-year-old institution faced national scrutiny with loyal followers pledging continued support. However, others such as conservative columnist George Will told the June 8, 2003 audience of ABC's *This Week with George Stephanopolous* that the idea that *The New York Times* is far superior to other metropolitan newspapers is fiction.

At *USA Today*, a report by a blue-ribbon group of editors found fabrications by former foreign correspondent Jack Kelley and led to

---

[45] Johnson, P. (2003, May 28). Trust in media keeps on slipping. *USA Today*, p. D1.
[46] Associated Press. (2003, May 29). Bragg's resignation is latest shadow at NY Times. *The Record Herald*, p. 12.

resignations of top editors in mid-2004.[47] From January through mid-2004, the press reported that Kelley, a reporter who was nominated for the Pulitzer Prize more than once, made up articles or purloined information from others. Kelley eventually released a statement that said, "I have made a number of serious mistakes that violate the values that are most important to me as a person and as a journalist." An independent panel of journalists found that Kelley lifted at least 100 passages from other publications in his articles. In late April, Hall Ritter, the managing editor for news at *USA Today*, resigned, and Brian Gallagher, the executive editor at *USA Today*, said he planned to step down. Earlier in April, 2004, Karen Jurgensen, editor since 1999, resigned over Kelley's reporting. Among the charges was the overuse of anonymous sources, a basic error in any kind of news reporting.

These lessons can't be emphasized too much. Checking information for accuracy is crucial and all writers – young, middle-aged and elderly – must do this duty. In all cases, verify information by attributing it to a source; however, the best approach is to find a second source to substantiate the information. It's hard, hard work but so worth it. The good news is that a *USA Today*/ CNN/ Gallup Poll showed that of 262 adults who said that they had been part of a story covered by the media, the perception that the media had been accurate was far more favorable: "78% found the coverage had been accurate."[48]

Gonzo reporting

Writers such as Hunter Thompson broke a number of conventions of source reporting. Along with anti-war sentiment and free love of the 1960s came the notion that straight reporting was straight jacketed reporting. To counter the approach of squeezing all the opinion from an article, writers retreated to the European model of reporting where journalists interject themselves into the poetry of the moment. They psychoanalyze the action and offer their interpretations. Some even express the thoughts of a source and that hidden motivation that I alluded to as deadly.

Don't try this at home. In the United States, this approach is best reserved for publications with editorial policies that can endure the heavy oar that stirs the waves of controversy. Fictional techniques such as repeated phrase, foreshadowing and dialogue are useful to the feature

---

[47] Bandler, J. (2004, April 23). Report cites 'virus of fear' at USA Today. , pp. B1-B2.

[48] Johnson, P. (2003, May 28). Trust in media keeps on slipping. *USA Today*, p. D1. The poll of 1,014 adults was conducted May 19-25, 2003 and included a margin of error of plus or minus 3 percent. The poll said that 62% of those polled said that the media don't get the facts straight.

writer, but once the writer steps into the shadows of fantasy, then she has failed in the craft of non-fiction.

Problem areas

The Society of Professional Journalists code says that nothing of value should be accepted from a source because gifts and favors can compromise the integrity of journalists and their employers. Retired cartoonist and editor John V. Lawing says that gifts are acceptable if they can be consumed on the spot. A professional sporting event is no less than a banquet without name cards. After a hearty dinner, writers can enjoy barley and hops and snacks throughout the match. Lawing's consumption rule tends to break down given that many calories. Each writer must learn her publication's policy or risk raising the ire of an editor who is convinced that free lunches choke free speech.

I once covered a Billy Graham crusade meeting where speaker John Wesley White gave me copies of his books. Overcome with guilt, I drove to his hotel and left a check for the evangelist with the night-shift manager. Later that night I confessed my lapse in judgment, and my editor laughed me to scorn. In her ethical calculus, evangelists often give books to anyone. Her rule: If the gift is for anyone, it's OK to accept it.

However, some sources give gifts of limited value to the participants – pens, notepads and trinkets, but reserve the wristwatch, tote bags and T-shirts for the press. Many writers accept these gifts anyway, but the more prestige a publication possesses, the more it will ban the smallest token.

Once at a dinner theater in south central Pennsylvania, I received an invitation for a complimentary meal for two and passes to cover the performance. The publication for which I worked considered the dinner and show to be a perquisite. That policy changed the night that found my wife and me at dinner to cover the season opening along with the publisher and his wife, and the editor and her husband – all on complimentary passes. No one knew the other was attending. How embarrassing for the publication. Covering arts, entertainment and sports requires that a publication formulate a consistent policy that includes paying its way. However, smaller publications with battered budgets are more likely to accept press passes as the price of staying in business.

Conflicts of interest

Some press organizations ask writers to avoid high-profile involvement in politics, community affairs, and social life to avoid the appearance of a conflict of interest. In the 21st century, the civic journalism model encourages writers to engage the community and be an active part of solving problems. In these cases, the writer is best served by seeking the sage advice of her editor. Editors may extend permission to deviate from the standard, but woe to the writer who engages in a political event or protest rally, writes about it, and then confesses. Forgiveness may be easier than permission, but with writers, it can cripple a reputation as a professional.

Your goal is to avoid appearance of conflicts as you pen your article. Help yourself by avoiding entangling alliances that hurt your primary cause – telling a story. A militant believer who covers an issue that she finds laudable may find solace in a publication that is committed to that cause, but the opportunity to sell the article a second, third, and fourth time will be hurt when the next editor learns of the trade-off.

Conflicts of interest manifest themselves in other ways. Consider the task of writing about a sniper who terrorized a city. Police authorities may think a journalist has information that can help the investigation. Should a writer share this information? It can be a tough call because public safety is at stake. However, most writers do their job and let the police do their job. As a writer gains a reputation, the temptation to trade information increases in a quid pro quo arrangement. It may work, or it may backfire. The only safe ground is to check with your editor. She may approve the exchange, or she may not.

Remember, your work is an honorable calling, and it can be accidentally sabotaged when the ethical code is jettisoned. When deals are struck between a writer and a source, a precedent is created. Should you need to contact that source again, she may think of your working relationship as a partnership that is subject to negotiations. Editor Frank Keegan once told me that friendships with sources must be handled with panache. A writer must be close enough to obtain reliable information; in some cases, the information may be provided to you over another writer. When the relationship gets too cozy, a writer will find it increasingly difficult to probe into a thorny issue.

Writers need sources; sources need writers. It's a marriage of convenience, and it's a mistake to think that sources are warm to you because you are charming and likeable. Columnists and opinion writers get inundated with telephone calls and email, and it's tempting to consider all this attention as recognition of a person's innate grasp of that cogent insight and gift for white-hot thinking. Once the person retires, the contact may stop. The reason is simple. The people who called wanted to influence public opinion; the contact with the writer, the conduit, was secondary. It is another part of the act of being humble for a writer not to believe her own public relations and not to think that her voice is more than pale dust floating on a summer breeze.

Think of the physician who is confronted with helping a family friend in an emergency. It may be easier to think clearly when the person is not a friend who is hurt, but a patient who needs care. The clinical approach helps the physician focus on the job at hand. It doesn't make her cold-hearted to be detached. It makes her more efficient, a better caregiver. Likewise, the writer who maintains professional distance from a source will find it easier to conduct routine business, and, in unusual times, do more of the same. Should the situation decay or become a friendship, the source and the writer may be better served by a change in assignment. Your audience will appreciate your desire to tell the story with as much impartiality as is humanly possible given that all of us are bound by our inherent mental maps that lead us in predictable ways of thinking.

The work of a writer can result in some unintended consequences. When a TV camera and fill light appear, the action may take a turn to the contrived. When a writer opens her notebook, a source may become self-conscious, and alter her behavior and speech in ways that she may be unaware. A more blatant example is a protest that gets heated only when the press is present. When the notebooks and broadcast equipment are stowed, the actors relax, drop their protest banners and glide over to Starbucks for refreshments. In these cases, writers must make a decision on the best way to characterize the action. Will the feature article take a light-hearted tone that suggests the protesters are pandering to an audience, and their commitment is subject to the presence of an audience? Or, will the on-again, off-again demonstration be ignored to avoid presenting a confusing picture of the rally? How much does a writer tell about the scripted nature of the protest versus the spontaneity? The Poynter process model may help you as you ponder these questions. While story telling is the goal, you must let the facts get in the way, and not resort to fiction just to jazz up the narrative.

Contests

Few writers will openly admit that they want a prize for their work, and more than one well-known journalist has denied the phrase "coveted prize." "I never coveted a writing award," they say, hurt in their rheumy eyes. For the rest of us, writing contests can be a mixed blessing. The legitimate ones enhance your marketability, and your sense of accomplishment. The weak ones prey on our need of acceptance in a business that is built on rejection.

A writer cannot go wrong by clearing a writing entry with an editor, particularly when the working relationship is ongoing. An occasional column in a publication doesn't merit asking permission for you to submit it to a contest. However, the marketing arms of companies are very sophisticated about planting product and service information in the mass media. Among the cleverest approaches by the less scrupulous jackals is to send out a notice of a contest early in the year that says the entry deadline is months away. The idea is that writers will have time to engineer an article that will be suitable for a contest about the dreaded X and ways to avoid it or the need to practice Y and ways to succeed at it. In some cases, the organizations that support these public awareness campaigns use these contests to advance their public relations mission at the expense of your credibility. The work you publish isn't a paid advertisement and readers will have no idea that you are subtly selling something. It's on the order of a product placement in a movie or TV show. Will you be complicit? You may win an award, but will it be the kind of recognition that will make you proud of your achievement?

Among the guidelines for selecting a reputable writing contest to enter is to evaluate the entry fee. Contest fees can exceed $100. Some places publish a writer's work with the hope that she will buy a copy of the publication. Writer Jill Darling calls this fraud "poetry.**con**." Some of the funnier submissions of poetry can be found at http://wockyjivvy.com /poetry/shame.

Contest fees in the $10-to $20-range are more acceptable. Next, consider the people who will evaluate the entries. Judges should be independent. They may be paid for their labor, but they shouldn't be beholden to the organization as board members or employees. Again, your best approach is to advise the publication for which you write of your intention to enter a contest, and allow the decision to be a cooperative one between you and an editor. A web site that monitors suspicious writing contests can be found at http://windpub.com/literary.scams.

Case study

The following case study actually happened. It highlights a number of ethical issues confronting writers. Perhaps the most egregious issue is the idea of sharing notes. It is customary for writers to not share notes, even negatives from photographs, with anyone outside the publication with which she is working. The idea is that notes are inchoate thoughts that may be misinterpreted as unduly offensive to people who are involved in the article. Should a writer be called upon to testify in a court case, she can argue that her publication makes it a policy not to reveal notes to outsiders. However, a court can prevail on the writer to share the notes, or punish the offender with a contempt of court order.

Beyond the notion of sharing information and questions of source reliability, the narrative explores the idea of showing compassion for others. In this case study, the writer put the publication at legal risk, but he did so in an attempt to perform a public good. For his violation of policy, he went on probation and later redeemed himself. It was I.

Rabbi-turned-evangelist provokes questions

Short of publishing a news story, is it ever appropriate to warn a source about the credibility of a speaker who an organization has hired?

Several years ago, I loaned a pastor some notes hoping to warn him and his church about an evangelist I suspected of phony credentials, but lacked the proof to print it. The offer backfired on me. Here's what happened.

In 1984 in Chambersburg, Pa., a rabbi-turned-evangelist came to town and *Public Opinion*, a 20,000-circulation Gannett daily, published a short press release on the speaker who was scheduled to preach in a nearby community.

"In an attempt to disprove the New Testament, he became a Christian," the article said, adding the speaker was a York, Pa., rabbi when his conversion occurred. "In the days following his decision to become a Christian, he was shot at, his home was burned and he and his son ... were beaten up."

Dr. Robert Chernoff, the rabbi in Chambersburg at that time, took exception to the account and questioned the newspaper's source, saying the article suggested the speaker encountered persecution from Jews following his conversion. Those questions prompted a yearlong investigation of the evangelist and included a flurry of letters from church officials and others. Many of the sources had a similar response: "He's clean but there's something unusual about his background. For instance, he had a family but now he doesn't," they said.

Most of the people wouldn't go on the record, but tantalized me with stories about county agencies that were investigating the man. One said that the man's wife died mysteriously shortly before he agreed to care for two children from a previous marriage. It was unclear if these were his children, or foster children. Some sources said the man was married more than once. The various narratives left the sequence in a vortex of confusion. When I asked the minister about the stories, he offered little explanation, and said others were using me to hurt his ministry.

The Jewish community where the man was a rabbi denied he ever worked in York. Later members of the York synagogue admitted the man had worked there as a rabbi for a few months, but he was fired because the congregation thought he was crazy.

The evangelist was said to have memorized a portion of the Old Testament as part of his rabbinical ordination, so I called Israel a half-dozen times looking for the rabbinical school he said he attended. I never found it, and the evangelist explained that schools open and close frequently in Israel.

As an ordained minister, the evangelist's credentials were more accessible. A church leader went on the record saying the former rabbi served a parish church in Central Pennsylvania for a time but resigned because he wanted more freedom to express himself as a charismatic believer.

When the traveling evangelist returned to Chambersburg in 1985 for a follow-up series of meetings, I discussed my findings with then executive editor Frank Keegan, now editor of a newspaper in Connecticut. We agreed the article would be incomplete if it didn't contain sources on the record alleging misrepresentation. We could have printed the church leader's remark that the evangelist was ordained and information from a Florida seminary, which praised the man's research on Hebrew-Christian parallels as scholarly, but the story would be woefully one-sided.

At the time, I thought that the information was sufficient enough to warrant a friendly warning to the pastor of the church where the evangelist would be speaking, but the pastor was unmoved. However, the pastor said he thought I was trying to trick him into making a remark, which might fuel some bad publicity. To the pastor, writers will stop at nothing, or in the words of former presidential candidate Ross Perot, the press is only after a "Gotcha" story.

Ignoring this rebuff, I told the minister about my file on the speaker and loaned it to him. Keegan learned of the transaction, and demanded the file be returned. He threatened to fire me, but at my $14,000-a-year salary, six weeks' probation seemed severe enough.

"I didn't fire Smith because it was not evil intent, but I put him on probation, so he'd get the point," Keegan told others. "He put the paper at risk. We gather information to print the news for all readers. It's immoral to do anything else with it. It's a violation of trust to gather information for private use. We later gave the story to the regular religion writer to follow up and that was as good as taking a gun and shooting it. That writer wasn't highly motivated."

Any writer on any beat for any time knows the value of quid pro quo when it comes to sharing information. Even Keegan, known in Chambersburg as Samurai editor for his animated defense of press freedoms, uses the maxim: "Sometimes you give a little information to get a little information."

I don't think I really expected the pastor to provide any new information because I shared my file, but I thought he might begin asking the same questions I was asking, and demand his own inquiry. Wasn't it my responsibility to share my concerns with this unsuspecting pastor? I thought so, but I was wrong. When a writer's gut tells him that something is amiss but he can't prove it, then it is old-fashioned gossip to repeat it. I may suspect someone is a hypocrite fleecing the flock, but it's wrong to point the accusing finger without a fistful of facts.

A telephone call may be appropriate, but only to explain that a story won't appear either as an announcement or an in-depth story because the reporter can't verify some information. That's all. If pressed, the reporter shouldn't divulge the unsubstantiated information, but might suggest where a person could look to find what the reporter found. The best response, however, is to keep digging until that one person steps forward or the relevant document appears to provide the missing piece or pieces.

At last report, the traveling evangelist was faring well, and his reputation remains unsoiled. Press critic Frank Kelly says society is a tremendous cave of sound, in which voices bounce back and forth with the puny journalist listening to the roar in the chamber trying to form his own judgment.

In our mass-mediated world with no lack of voices, writers are too aware that no one has to listen. For you and me as writers, our goal is to offer solid information that may help readers make good decisions. If a reporter can't nail down the information, he shouldn't serve up unsupported specifics hurting innocents and damaging the reputation of a press working for all readers. What would you have done in this case and why? How does the question-approach suggested earlier in this chapter help in this case study? The following code is used widely by journalists, but it is apropos for feature writers as well.

The SPJ Code of Ethics[49]

Preamble

Members of the Society of Professional Journalists believe that public enlightenment is the forerunner of justice and the foundation of democracy. The duty of the journalist is to further those ends by seeking truth and providing a fair and comprehensive account of events and issues. Conscientious journalists from all media and specialties strive to serve the public with thoroughness and honesty. Professional integrity is the cornerstone of a journalist's credibility. Members of the Society share a

---

[49] Code of ethics for the Society of Professional Journalists. American Society of Newspaper Editors web site. Retrieved February 18, 2003, from http://www.spj.org/ethics_code.asp. Used with permission of Society of Professional Journalists, Sigma Delta Chi Foundation.

dedication to ethical behavior and adopt this code to declare the Society's principles and standards of practice.

Seek truth and report it

- Journalists should be honest, fair and courageous in gathering, reporting and interpreting information.

Journalists should:

- Test the accuracy of information from all sources and exercise care to avoid inadvertent error. Deliberate distortion is never permissible.
- Diligently seek out subjects of news stories to give them the opportunity to respond to allegations of wrongdoing.
- Identify sources whenever feasible. The public is entitled to as much information as possible on sources' reliability.
- Always question sources' motives before promising anonymity. Clarify conditions attached to any promise made in exchange for information. Keep promises.
- Make certain that headlines, news teases and promotional material, photos, video, audio, graphics, sound bites and quotations do not misrepresent. They should not oversimplify or highlight incidents out of context.
- Never distort the content of news photos or video. Image enhancement for technical clarity is always permissible. Label montages and photo illustrations.
- Avoid misleading re-enactments or staged news events. If re-enactment is necessary to tell a story, label it.
- Avoid undercover or other surreptitious methods of gathering information except when traditional open methods will not yield information vital to the public. Use of such methods should be explained as part of the story.
- Never plagiarize.
- Tell the story of the diversity and magnitude of the human experience boldly, even when it is unpopular to do so.
- Examine their own cultural values and avoid imposing those values on others.
- Avoid stereotyping by race, gender, age, religion, ethnicity, geography, sexual orientation, disability, physical appearance or social status.
- Support the open exchange of views, even views they find repugnant.

- Give voice to the voiceless; official and unofficial sources of information can be equally valid.
- Distinguish between advocacy and news reporting. Analysis and commentary should be labeled and not misrepresent fact or context.
- Distinguish news from advertising and shun hybrids that blur the lines between the two.
- Recognize a special obligation to ensure that the public's business is conducted in the open and that government records are open to inspection.

Minimize harm

- Ethical journalists treat sources, subjects and colleagues as human beings deserving of respect.

Journalists should:

- Show compassion for those who may be affected adversely by news coverage. Use special sensitivity when dealing with children and inexperienced sources or subjects.
- Be sensitive when seeking or using interviews or photographs of those affected by tragedy or grief.
- Recognize that gathering and reporting information may cause harm or discomfort. Pursuit of the news is not a license for arrogance.
- Recognize that private people have a greater right to control information about themselves than do public officials and others who seek power, influence or attention. Only an overriding public need can justify intrusion into anyone's privacy.
- Show good taste. Avoid pandering to lurid curiosity.
- Be cautious about identifying juvenile suspects or victims of sex crimes.
- Be judicious about naming criminal suspects before the formal filing of charges.
- Balance a criminal suspect's fair trial rights with the public's right to be informed.

Act independently

- Journalists should be free of obligation to any interest other than the public's right to know.

Journalists should:
- Avoid conflicts of interest, real or perceived.
- Remain free of associations and activities that may compromise integrity or damage credibility.
- Refuse gifts, favors, fees, free travel and special treatment, and shun secondary employment, political involvement, public office and service in community organizations if they compromise journalistic integrity.
- Disclose unavoidable conflicts.
- Be vigilant and courageous about holding those with power accountable.
- Deny favored treatment to advertisers and special interests and resist their pressure to influence news coverage.
- Be wary of sources offering information for favors or money; avoid bidding for news.

Be accountable
- Journalists are accountable to their readers, listeners, viewers and each other.

Journalists should:
- Clarify and explain news coverage and invite dialogue with the public over journalistic conduct.
- Encourage the public to voice grievances against the news media.
- Admit mistakes and correct them promptly.
- Expose unethical practices of journalists and the news media.
- Abide by the same high standards to which they hold others.

The SPJ Code of Ethics is voluntarily embraced by thousands of writers, editors and other news professionals. The present version of the code was adopted by the 1996 SPJ National Convention, after months of study and debate among the Society's members.

Sigma Delta Chi's first Code of Ethics was borrowed from the American Society of Newspaper Editors in 1926. In 1973, Sigma Delta Chi wrote its own code, which was revised in 1984, 1987 and 1996.[50]

---

[50] Copyright © 1996-2002 Society of Professional Journalists. All Rights Reserved. Society of Professional Journalists Eugene S. Pulliam National Journalism Center, 3909 N. Meridian St., Indianapolis, IN 46208

Holly G. Miller

Biography of Holly G. Miller

Holly G. Miller is the travel editor for the Saturday Evening Post, publications consultant to Lilly Endowment, adjunct professor of communication at Anderson University and a frequent speaker at writers' conferences.

Miller has written or co-written 13 books including *Write on Target, The freelance writer's handbook,* and *How to earn more than pennies for your thoughts.* In addition, her textbook on angles and anecdotes for students interested in magazine writing was scheduled for release in 2005 by Iowa State University Press.

In addition to her books, Miller has written more than 2,000 articles for publications such as *TV Guide, Modern Maturity, Writer's Digest, Reader's Digest, Arts Indiana, The Christian Herald, Virtue* and many others.

She holds a graduate degree in journalism from Ball State University and is chairman of the Ball State University Communication Advisory Board as well as a member of the Midwest Writers Workshop. She is a member of the Hall of Fame at Ball State University and received awards for her writing. Among them was a first place award in feature writing for the Associated Press of Indiana, an award for her travel writing by the Indiana Department of Commerce and the Society of American Travel Writers and many other organizations.

As a speaker, Miller talks to writers around the nation at conferences such as the Pacific Press Writers Seminary, Cape Cod Writers Workshop, the Mount Hermon Writers Conference and others.

Interview with Holly G. Miller

Q: Define travel writing. Doesn't it amount to writing a review just like a film critic may do in film?

A: Travel writing is much more than visiting a destination and then reviewing it. Travel features can take the form of how-to articles – how to beat jet lag, how to travel with toddlers, how to fly high on a tight budget. They can take the form of roundups – the five best children's museums in America; the most romantic French restaurants in Old Quebec; and so on. They can be seasonal pieces – Christmas on Nantucket, the great Passion play of Eureka Springs (Easter). They can mark anniversaries – the Eisenhower homestead in Kansas marks the former president's 100th birthday. They can be what I call "travel with a twist" – Sam Spade's San Francisco or Ernest Hemingway's Key West.

Q: As the travel editor, what are some of the ethical considerations of making a press trip to review?

A: Travel reporting is also known as "fam trips" for "familiarization trip" and publications either have a "no-fam-trip" policy or they don't. What that means is whether or not a magazine or newspaper will publish an article that resulted from free travel supplied by an airline, destination, and so on. Unless a writer is able to produce several articles from a single trip or sell the trip many times to many markets, she really can't afford to underwrite all expenses without some kind of "press rate" from various venues.

Q: What do you do when the destination doesn't live up to the hype? Do you still write a review?

A: Every writer has an obligation to be honest with his or her reader. In travel writing, we have to understand that readers may elect to visit a place based on our recommendations. Thus, of course, we must tell the good, the bad and the so-so. Some publications prefer not to pan a place. Rather than write a negative story, the editor may opt to publish nothing.

Q: What are three tips you have for a new writer in snagging and preparing the travel article?

A: A few tips:

1) Pick out-of-the-way places and then focus on a single small aspect of the destination such as a restaurant where all the locals go but tourists don't know about;

2) Always include sidebars and hotboxes to embellish the package; avoid the encyclopedia version of a place;

3) Concentrate on senses – tastes, sounds – rather than facts that are available in any guidebook; don't gush! Remember, you are a travel journalist out for a good story, not a tourist out for a good time.

Peter Island offers comfort and a taste of adventure
By Holly G. Miller
Used with permission

A high-powered business executive once arrived on the Caribbean's very secluded Peter Island and quickly issued two orders to the resort's check-in staff, "I want to lose ten pounds, and I want to get a tan." Wayne Kafcsak, general manager and chief greeter, overheard the request and knew he couldn't deliver. With an award-winning chef in the kitchen and a 34-member culinary crew determined to pamper the resort's 100 guests, "I could only guarantee the tan," said Kafcsak.

Half an hour by boat from the nearest "city" – if that's what you call Road Town or nearby Tortola – Peter Island is a pristine speck of heaven that is too small to accommodate cruise ships and too remote to attract tourists bent on a party-packed weekend. A visit typically stretches over ten days and often includes nothing more stressful than a slow sail among little-known islands with colorful names. Depending on the wind's direction, your boat is likely to glide past Fallen Jerusalem, whose rocks are reminiscent of the tumbled-down walls of Jericho; Norman Island, legendary model for Robert Louis Stevenson's Treasure Island; Jost Van Dyke, where "Main Street" is a sandy path; Necker Island, a pricey hideaway favored by royalty and rock stars; and Dead Chest, where Blackbeard once stranded 15 mutinous sailors with only a bottle of rum, a sword and the motivation for a song ("Yo, ho, ho and a bottle of rum").

"We struggle under the name "Virgin Islands" because people automatically think of St. Thomas," explains Kafcsak. But Peter Island – unlike St. Thomas – is part of the less-populated British Virgin Islands, not the teeming U.S. Virgin Islands. It is privately owned by Americans, which means that all development plans undergo double scrutiny. The government carefully monitors growth and immigration, while the island's owners meticulously supervise expansion and enhancements. A recent multimillion-dollar "millennium makeover" boosted the amenities of the resort without sacrificing its privacy. With only 52 guest rooms and three villas clustered on the property's 1,800 acres, crowded beaches and restaurants are never a problem. Nowhere will you find a parking lot, a structure rising higher than the mast of a 40-foot yacht, or more than one vacationer per ten acres. Island shopping is limited to a single, well-stocked boutique.

"Guests are fiercely loyal to this place," says Kafcsak, who personally welcomes visitors within 24 hours of their arrival and has been known to volunteer his services as a guide for island-hopping excursions. Vacationers come back year after year, lured by the seclusion, the friendly staff, and the opportunity to sample such delicacies as snapper filled with spinach and herbs, tuna wrapped in papaya, seafood brochette, chilled coconut soup, and mango mousse.

"One couple has visited 35 times, always specifying the same suite, which they refer to as 'our room,'" says Kafcsak.

If the relaxed lifestyle on Peter Island is typically Caribbean, the conveniences are all-American. A spa and air-conditioned exercise center are within steps of one of the five beaches, a fitness trail winds along the shore, and each guest suite is equipped with a CD player and a take-home disc of island music. Only after a day or two in this tropical paradise do perceptive guests detect a subtle Michigan presence. Clues include icy containers of mineral water bottled in Grand Rapids and stocked in the mini-bars, as well as complimentary packages of soap, shampoo, and conditioner supplied by Amway Corporation, also based in Michigan, and arranged on shelves in the bathrooms. Grand Rapids? Amway?

The connection between balmy Peter Island and chilly northern Michigan is real and was established two decades ago when the resort changed hands. Once the property of Norwegian millionaire Peter Smedwig, the entire island was purchased in the late 1970s by Michigan entrepreneurs Jay Van Andel and Rich DeVos, cofounders of Amway Corporation. The current owners and their families are frequent visitors, flying by private jet to the airstrip on Tortola or sailing into the resort's harbor on their spacious yacht. When in residence, they occupy the very private Eagle's Nest, a villa located on the island's highest point. Although they are rarely seen by Peter Island guests, Amway's owners have a positive influence on the resort's operations – customer service is first-rate.

"We don't say no to a guest," says Chef Wilford ("Willo") Stoutt, who sometimes staffs the omelet station at the morning buffet just to hear guests' comments. His menus change daily, so diners always have new choices. Vegetarian entrees are mainstays, and he frequently adds to the day's offerings as fresh seafood and produce become available. Variety is important because room rates are based on a full American meal plan (all breakfast, lunches, and dinners are included). Guests can dine at Tradewinds, the resort's main restaurant overlooking Sir Francis Drake Channel, or at the more casual Deadman's Beach Bar and Grill, located close to the shore under towering palms and a cedar-shake roof.

"Our clientele is easy to please," he says, "because we give them what they want."

Chef Willo is one of a handful of resort employees who actually live on Peter Island. After the launch departs for Tortola at 11 each night, resort guests have the island to themselves. Not until the breads-and-pastry staff arrives aboard the 5:30 a.m. boat does the island's population swell slightly. This serenity appeals to vacationers who are serious about their need to "get away from it all" and to veterans of Caribbean cruises who have "done" the islands endless times. Activity options exist, of course, and vacationers can pick and choose their pastimes. A boat makes the 65-minute trip to St. Thomas weekly (twice a week during high season), and the Tortola-to-Peter Island water taxi crisscrosses the channel several times a day. Thursday excursions take snorkelers to the Bath – huge granite boulders – on Virgin Gorda, and special packages combine five nights on Peter Island with two nights aboard a luxury sailboat.

But for all the possibilities, perhaps the best activity available is also the simplest: walking. The views are spectacular, and because private cars are not allowed on Peter Island, the narrow paths belong to strolling and jogging pedestrians. The best time to explore the property is early in the morning after a stop at the Library, the freestanding building with louvered doors that open to the beach on one side, the pool on the other. Here you can sip juice, sample a muffin, and (if you haven't weaned yourself from the news back home) catch one of the morning shows on the island's only public television. Better yet, you can claim a lounge chair, contemplate your day's agenda, and then celebrate the fact that you really don't have one.

For additional information, call 800-346-4451, or visit the resort's Website at www.peterisland.com.

Exercises

1) Re-read the article. Does this piece feature the "travel-with-a-twist" angle?

2) What is the news peg in this piece? As you may recall from chapter one, *The chocolate-covered almond*, a news peg is the reason that the article is being written. That reason may be said in a subtle tone, but it helps the audience discern the reason the article is being presented now rather than next week, next month or next year.

3) Based on this article, think of another article that you could write that is similar to this piece. Next, think of an article that is unlike this one, but could be a travel piece based on your region.

4) To maintain your high standards, what are some of the points that you must make about the ideas in number 3 so you won't violate an editor's trust?

Summary

Some writers argue that if a quotation doesn't have just the right snap, it should be reworded to capture some panache, but that principle just won't work in feature writing. We are bound by standards on quoting sources, protecting sources, checking information found by other writers and areas of conflict. Among the most difficult ideas to internalize is the one about providing accurate information even when the facts may not flatter a source. Feature writing isn't about puff pieces that can be used by public relations offices to promote a sanitized vision of person, organization or event. Warts, hair lips and receding hairlines are all apart of the portrait, and airbrushing only adds to the sense that feature articles are merely ramped-up news releases. For this reason, better writers are judicious about contests, free lunches and gifts from sources. This chapter included an interview with writer Holly G. Miller who offers some additional advice on a very specific kind of feature writing, the travel article.

Chapter 8

Using the Internet
FeatureWriting.Net/Com

Chapter at-a-glance

> ➤ Understanding terms associated with the Internet
> ➤ Appreciating the need to check for accuracy
> ➤ Perusing the best sites for writers

With a computer, modem and service for the Internet, any writer can get a sense of the big picture as part of her feature story. The problem with the Internet isn't too little information; it is a matter of overkill and worse, deception that can prove embarrassing for the downy types.

Michael Gorman captured the zeitgeist of the Internet in the following observation:

> *The 'Net is like a huge vandalized library. Someone has destroyed the catalog and removed the front matter, indexes, etc. from hundreds of thousands of books and torn and scattered what remains ... 'Surfing' is the process of sifting through this disorganized mess in the hope of coming across some useful fragments of text and images that can be related to other fragments. The 'Net is even worse than a vandalized library*

The Internet can be swamp gas – a powerful weapon that can harm when the wind shifts ever so slightly – or it can be the tide that brings that elusive idea to shore.

> *because thousands of additional unorganized fragments are added daily by the myriad of cranks, sages, and persons with time on their hands who launch unfiltered messages into cyberspace.*[51]

The goal of this chapter is to let a person who has little understanding of the Web get her bearings. For writers who have some understanding of the Internet, the first part of the chapter may be skimmed. For you, the main event is the dozens and dozens of sure-fire Web sites that will make you a writer of power. You will find information that only the most prolific researchers had available just a few decades ago. The chapter ends with my picks for the top 10 Web sites for writers and journalists. Netward!

Terms

People often speak of the Internet and the World Wide Web as if the two were one in the same, but one refers to the hardware that supports this system and the other refers to the computer rules that allow users to go from site to site. The **Internet**, usually capitalized, is the plumbing: the pipes, the faucets and the valves. It is a network of networks. The network consists of computers, the physical structure, where stored information can be accessed. Typically, organizations have computers called *servers* to form a network. The networks are linked to one another to form the Internet, a kind of global water system, but instead of fluid traveling through the pipes, it is information.

If the Internet is the plumbing, then the **World Wide Web** is the science that the system uses to operate. It includes the computer language and computer rules, called protocols, that allow users to connect from one network to another, to move the water – the information – from a distant place to your personal faucet. The Web uses hypertext links to go from one network to another. Each network contains its own content, words, graphics and pictures, often referred to as **JPGs** (pronounced *jay pegs*) or TIFF files. Some sites include movies, audio files and other information that users can download, replay or search using commands such as "word search."

---

[51] "The Corruption of Cataloging." (1995, September 15). *Library Journal*, 120, 34.

Browsers and operating systems

To begin using the Internet to find information on the World Wide Web, computers must have a software package called a **browser.** Browsers allow users to search and view a Web site.

The computer world is generally bifurcated into personal computers (PCs), such as the IBM-brand computer and clones, and the Macintosh computer. Each has a different operating system, which means some of the instructions vary from computer to computer. However, when a user is searching the 'Net, often called surfing, the Web sites do not appear radically different on either a Macintosh or a PC. Nonetheless, the most common browsers are **Internet Explorer,** used more often by PC owners, Netscape, Mozilla, and Opera, often used by Macintosh users. However, both browsers will work on either operating system. Online providers often have a browsing system. For instance, America Online has its own browser.

Searching the Internet

Looking for information on the Internet may be compared to trying to find information in the public library. Many people like poking around, randomly going from stack to stack, and selecting a volume as the mood strikes. Others want a more systematic approach. Perhaps the best way to begin is to log onto the Internet, and open the browser on your computer. The information at the top of the screen that begins **http://** is the beginning of a Web address. When an address is underlined on a Web page, that is an indication that it is "hot," and can be clicked to drive the user to that Web site. The http:// address is known as a **Uniform Resource Locator**, or **URL**. Often, a user can type in a topic and guess what the Web page theme will be. If a user wanted information on a college, she would type the college name along with what is called the site designation, **.edu** (which is short for education), and the college's Web site may appear, like so: campbell.edu. When speaking of this designation, users say "dot edu," as in, "Visit me on the Web at campbell dot edu," and listeners are supposed to interpret the "dot edu" as ".edu."

Users must use caution in guessing the names of URLs because innocent sounding names can result in some chagrined faces if the page that opens turns out to have suspicious content. It happens. I often shudder when I see a black background opening on my computer screen for fear that the content is not family-friendly. In some cases, these Web sites load more than one page, so extracting yourself by closing each page, sometimes called a pop-up window, becomes a time-consuming chore. Filters, some free, are available to block unwelcome content. Unwanted electronic mail also can be blocked.

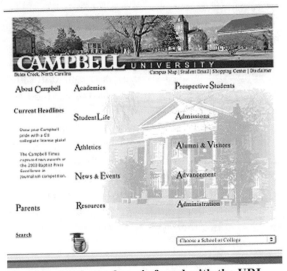

The website shown here is found with the URL Campbell.edu and is an example of an educational website.

A more systematic approach is to use a **subject directory** such as the one on Yahoo.com. This page allows users to type in a topic in an open area called the search field and look for that subject. The user could select "autos," click "enter" or "go," and let the computer search the World Wide Web for Web pages on automobiles. The computer is looking for pages that have imbedded words, called **metatags**, in them to help people with their searches. When you type "auto," the browser searches for that metatag.

Search engines combine subject directories for a high-speed approach. This type of search tool is called a metasearch engine. Dogpile.com, for example, allows users to search several subject directories just by typing in one topic in the search field. The Web pages that the computer finds will include a domain name, and, often, a country code. The domain name extension that is most common on the Internet is **.com**, which suggests the organization that is supplying the information, the host, is selling something. Many organizations with nothing for sale also use the .com ending, however. Other popular domain extensions include the following:

Domain names	**Country codes**
.edu – education	**.au** – Australia
.gov – government	**.ca** – Canada
.org – organization	**.es** – Spain
.mil – military	**.uk** – United Kingdom
.net – network	**.us** – United States
.info – information	**.mu** – Mauritius
.tv - television	

The Web page for Taylor University in Indiana is www.tayloru.edu. The "edu" tells the user that the host institution is involved in education.

However, an organization that services journalism education such as the Association for Education in Journalism and Mass Communication has the name **aejmc** and the Web address of www.aejmc.org. "Org" tells the user that the Web page is hosted by an organization, but it also suggests that the site isn't commercial. Knowing the suffix can help you decide the mission of the organization, but .com doesn't necessarily mean that the site won't be unduly forthcoming on the trade-offs of products or services that they are promoting.

Evaluate

Understanding the components of the URL can help you evaluate the Web pages you find. For example, government information from the United States is generally considered by librarians to be some of the most reliable information on the World Wide Web. When you encounter the site name **.gov** and it is associated with the United States, you can be confident the facts are correct. Having praised Caesar, it's now time to offer a warning. Government sites typically support the administration's agenda; therefore, a .gov site should be evaluated in terms of the prevailing administration's point of view.

TIP: When using e-mail, you can sometimes guess at the contact person for public information if he or she works in government. Ken Wheeler, a public relations expert in Portsmouth, Va., has this suggestion. Reporters and writers use public relations contacts for much of the background that they use. These people go by many names – public relations counselors, media relations directors or communications spokesmen; in government, however, these people often are known as public information officers or PIOs. To contact a PIO using email, use PIO and the following address formula. Use pio@ci.[name of city].[abbreviation state name].[us]. "Ci" stands for city. For a contact in Portsmouth, for instance, use pio@ci.portsmouth.va.us. For a county, use "co" and the name of the county, and the abbreviation for the state as in pio@co.spalding.ga.us. In this case, the "ga" stands for Georgia. Use the U.S. postal abbreviations for names of states.

This formula doesn't always work, but it's a useful idea that you can try when you are in a jam.

Don't be discouraged. A writer may offer an informed conclusion when crafting commentary or news-opinion. In most cases, however, the writer must use the reportorial approach to writing, meaning all the salient information must be attributed to a source. When reporting information from a government Web page, the best writers will cite the page. This practice tells the reader, listener or viewer where the information originated, and the attribution gets the writer off the hook. If a writer suspects that the facts are woefully sloppy or inaccurate, more research must be done to avoid perpetuating false information. Finally, it's important that the writer follow-up a Web page by contacting the source either by electronic mail, U.S. Postal service or telephone to confirm the information. Too many writers are relying on Web reports without resorting to old-fashioned fact checking. Double-check. Triple-check. The reputation you save may be your own. Believe me. A reviewer of one my books gave me a sound editorial thrashing for misspelling a name of an editor from the 19th century. (Big sigh. Alas, I deserved it.)

General Internet search tools

Typically, **search engines** (special sites that take a user to specific Web sites) include **subject directories**. Browsers allow users to save favorite Web sites under a pull-down menu for "favorites" or "bookmarks." If you are like me, you tend to find a search engine that you enjoy, and never bother to check the others. However, if you browse through the following list and *save* a number of these sites as favorites to which to return, you will have an edge over most writers. Why? Because writers are always in a hurry. They can't take time to do too much background work, which is too bad, because editors delight in the unexpected morsel of odd information. They relish it. Some get so giddy that they leave their seats, dance a little soft-shoe and hum to themselves. They are delighted when you make them smile in appreciation for the work you did. You work hard, so the editor (and reader AND viewer) can savor an easy smile. See? Experiment with these Web sites as you write your article, and you will be more creative, write better prose, and sell more copy! Trust me.

Caution. Too many writers find a site, save it and then find that their list of favorites is too long to be helpful. In this case, it may be worth your while to create a Web page of your own with categories for Web sites. Most online services allow users to operate a Web site. In addition to building an online identity, your personal Web site page can be loaded with tools to help you build a page of online sites that will help you succeed as a writer. You can group sites according to topics such as news services, fast facts, resources and so on. Short of your own Web site, consider subdividing lists within your favorites list. Some browsers allow you to subdivide your favorite Web sites into categories to achieve the same kind of system that allows you easy access to sites that you will want to peruse again and again. On the Internet Explorer browser, favorites can be arranged using the "Organize Favorites" pull-down menu.

Subject directories include ready-to-go topics, which are **clickable**, meaning that the user can click on the word or phrase and be taken to a series of sites. In addition, the subject directory provides a quick list of Web sites on a subject that the search engine has already compiled. The topics include *sports*, for instance.

More and more often, however, frequent users of the Internet prefer to pick their own topic for a search using a search engine. The sites below are search engines that use a search field where the user can type in a specific topic, such as "early American furniture," and then click "enter" or "go" to get a list of Web sites that are associated with that topic. Be advised. Overlap exists and the findings may not differ markedly from one page to another.

AltaVista – http://www.altavista.com
Excite – http://www.excite.com
Google – http://www.google.com
HotBot – http://www.hotbot.com
Infoseek – http://www.infoseek.com
Lycos – http://www.lycos.com
Northern Light – http://www.northernlight.com
Yahoo – http://www.yahoo.com

Many writers often begin their work with a Google search, or use a meta-search engine such as dogpile.com, the search engine that was mentioned earlier in this chapter. Search engines are said to **crawl** specified databases to retrieve documents relevant to your search terms. Directories consist of links to documents arranged by subject. For instance, beaucoup.com includes a directory of topics on computers, software, employment, society, geography, references and arts and entertainment. Under government, it lists links to the White House, the United Nations, the World Bank and more. Other sites of directories include (and all are preceded by www.):

LookSmart.com
Galaxy.com
Infomine.com
Webcrawler.com

Keep in mind that the designation, .com, means that the site is commercial. You should expect to see advertisements on the page or surprises called "pop-up advertisements" as you use the service.

Metasearch engines, also known as multi-threaded search engines, combined some of the search engines above for a comprehensive search. Debriefing.com uses a convenient button system to allow users to search the Web for news, music and pictures.

In addition to dogpile.com and debriefing.com, other metasearch engines are (and, again, all are preceded by www.):

TheBigHub.com
Mamma.com
MetaGopher.com
ProFusion.com
SavvySearch.com
Go2Net.com

A reference for new words is wordspy.com, a page that lists new phrases entering the language.

Business and finance

For business sites, consider b2bexcite.com and find links to human resources and personnel, e-commerce such as credit card processors, insurance, telecommunications, travel and real estate. Bpubs.com is a thorough index with categories for information on entrepreneurs, intellectual property, marketing and much more.

For financial sites, whispernumber.com includes a free service that allows the user to log into lists of financial earnings and other financial information. Other financial sites include:

DailyStocks.com
Moneywebsearch.com
FinancialFind.com
TradingDay.com
JustQuotes.com

Government

The site www.nwbuildnet.com/nwbn/govbot.html allows users to search for government documents and public records. A similar site is searchgov.com, and it allows users to search for documents on the federal, state and local level and access reports from independent agencies.

For political information and links to other sites on public policy, try politicalinformation.com.

At fedstats.gov, users can see an alphabetical list of topics, arranged like the list at the end of this book. From the home page, users can select topics from A to Z. For the letter "C," the site listed Cancer and had the following:

Atlas of Cancer Mortality in the United States
  Breast
  Cervical
  Lung
  Mortality maps
  Prostate
Charitable trusts
Census, The
Children
And many, many more.

Law

Among the chief business of government are public policy and the formulation of legislation for the state. For the individual interested in the legal terrain in general, there's findlaw.com. It lists legal subjects, legal careers, experts and consultants and more. Under legal subjects, it contains an alphabetical list. Among the topics are:

Administrative Law
Admiralty
Agriculture Law
Antitrust & Trade Regulation
Banking Law
Bankruptcy Law
Civil Rights
Commercial Law
Communications Law
Constitutional Law
Construction Law
Contracts
Corporation & Enterprise Law
Criminal Law
Cyberspace Law
Dispute Resolution &
  Arbitration
Education Law
Energy Law
And many, many other topics.

Law.com features news, a lawyer locator and links to resources such as the dealmaker that includes information on the latest and the biggest deals, and information on financial deal statistics such as arbitrage.

At lawcrawler.findlaw.com, users can find information on law schools, case law, U.S. law, U.S. federal case law, U.S. state case law and forms such as sample contracts.

For writers who want to brush up on copyright issues, consider copylaw.com as a source for information on the use of material in the public domain and the idea of fair use among other considerations important to anyone who is a freelance writer.

Experts in general

Among the growing number of Web sites that feature experts include askanexpert.com, a site that appeals to children; experts.com, is designed to highlight experts who are qualified to speak in court; and yearbooknews.com, is quite a find for journalists and authors. It advertises itself as, "the Yearbook of Experts' website, America's Favorite Newsroom Resource in print, on the Web and via LexisNexis® since 1984."

Trust and verify

As stated earlier, credibility is crucial in delivering information, whether hard news or soft, feature news. I once wrote a feature article on household hints. Among them was an idea that I read about for recycling coffee grounds by adding them to plant soil. I used that idea in my feature article and only later tried the practice with my own indoor plants. As the article went to press, here's what I learned: Coffee grounds may be great for some outdoor plants, but they can create mold in some indoor plants. At the very least, my article should have warned readers of this possibility. Readers trusted me, and I let them down. Rather than repeat an idea from a source, I could have checked it out by interviewing a landscaper, a florist, someone at a plant nursery or by conducting more research to verify that the coffee-ground disposal technique I recommended worked without complications.

Trust and verify, President Reagan once warned the United States as he described his policy of missile disarmament with foreign powers. Be sure to evaluate the information, he urged. Good writers must evaluate information, using the criteria of authority or credibility of source, accuracy of information, objectivity or point-of-view, currency of information, coverage or relevance of information.

Librarian Karen Robinson agrees with Reagan's mantra and instructs researchers to apply that principle to print and electronic sources including the Web site's visual perspective. Is the page easy to read? Are the links clearly visible? Do the images add to the content? Do they download within a reasonable amount of time? These are questions that help a good writer assess the overall value of the site.

Full-text articles and e-books

The quality of Web sites runs the spectrum from first-rate to lousy. For writers, the best sites direct a writer to background she needs with convenience. For many writers, the best sites are those that allow a user to access full-text articles from journals, magazines and newspapers. Here are a couple of sites that can provide full-text copy.

The Gutenberg Project may be found at www.promo.net/pg. This site contains full-text books known as electronic books, or e-books. Authors include Shakespeare, Arthur Conan Doyle, Edgar Rice Burroughs (who wrote the Tarzan books), and Lewis Carroll (who wrote *Alice's Adventures in Wonderland*), to name a few. The site features books published before 1923, a benchmark year for some copyright laws. Some Web services charge to download books, others do not. The Gutenberg Project is free.

Digital library links can also be found at: dir.yahoo.com/reference /libraries/digital_libraries.

This Web site can be a little busy, but it allows users to find full-text books. It led me to The English Server Web site at http://eserver.org, where I clicked books and found a listing including G.K. Chesterton's novel, *The Innocence of Father Brown* at http://eserver.org/fiction /innocence.

Books and references

At Bartleby.com, another Web site that offers full-text books, writers can learn about good writing style using William Strunk Jr.'s *Elements of Style* at www.bartleby.com/141. This book is considered required reading for all serious writers. You will learn that possessive in "Charles's voice" is preferred to the missing "s" in "Charles' voice," and learn grammar with little pain. This site includes many reference works. For an encyclopedia on world history, for example, consider: www.bartleby.com/67.

And don't forget the fun sites that contain unusual information such as the edgy salon.com, a site not known for using the King's English. Another favorite site among the computer leaders of the day is slashdot.com, odd information of interest to serious computer users. For instance, in early 2004, a student in the eighth grade made the page because he successfully sent the message "Hey!" to every computer in the school. He was suspended! Finally, fark.com may be too racy and too odd for the mainstream but it does carry the Best of the Web from the Wall Street Journal Online, which makes the ordinary reader wonder, "Why not just read the Wall Street Journal Online and skip the intermediate step? But you're no ordinary reader.

Journalism Web sites

University libraries also provide a number of helps for writers. For instance, Regent University in Virginia Beach includes a grammar program among other writing tools. To use it, go to the home page at www.regent.edu and click on university library. Next, click on the "virtual research desk" at the bottom right-hand corner. It lists great helps for writers including grammar help, quotation search, encyclopedia and other online resources. In addition, try regent.edu/lib/theo/html for a generous list of religious periodicals. For writers who want to peruse periodicals and Web sites read by the working press, access a page of links by going from the university library page www.regent.edu/lib and clicking on subjects. After clicking on subjects, go to "communication." It lists the following links that can be valuable for writers.

American Journalism Review NewsLink provides access to newspapers around the nation and an employment list at newslink.org.

Fairness and Accuracy in Reporting reviews the political slant of coverage. It is a national media watch group and tends to criticize mainstream mass media at Fair.org.

The *Editor & Publisher* magazine Web site is considered one of the best sources for journalists on issues affecting the press. It is located at mediainfo.com. Among its many features is a listing of full-time employment opportunities across the nation.

The Society of Professional Journalists is one of the oldest and most respected journalism organizations in the nation. Its site provides news links and news on issues of interests to writers at www.spj.org.

Political information

For political information, try think tanks such as The Heritage Foundation at heritage.org for conservative views, or The Brookings Institute at brookings.org, which features more liberal views. The Cato Institute conducts public policy analysis and may be found at www.cato.org. For information on the financial aspects of politics, try the following site, opensecrets.org. The Hoover Institute examines freedom and other issues associated with democracy. It is located at hoover.org.

Reporting

For resources on **computer-assisted reporting**, try Virginia Commonwealth University (VCU) School of Mass Communications, at www.people.vcu.edu/~jcsouth. It links to Facsnet at www.facsnet.org where writers can learn about issues and read news coverage related to those topics. The site bills itself as education for journalists. For an A to Z of topics and related Web sites, similar to the list of feature ideas at the end of this book, try the "power reporting" site that can be accessed from VCU at www.powerreporting.com/category/beat_by_beat.

Under R for religion, for instance, the site listed links to "a journalist's online glossary of religion" and "information on anti-Arab sentiment" collected by The Southern Poverty Law Center. In addition, the site provides statistics on Arab Americans including a primer on Islam and the basic tenets of the religion.

It also includes several full-text versions of the Bible and links to the Congressional Quarterly Terrorism Resources including Islamic fundamentalism and related topics.

From the VCU site, a writer can access the content-rich "journalist's toolbox" that features links to maps, shareware, health and medical sites, government information, and many more helps for aspiring writers. See www.csne.org/toolbox.html.

Writer Web sites

Writers can help other writers, and writing groups can be a place where ambitious ink spots pool their knowledge, critique each other's work and provide all-important encouragement through a writers' group on the Internet. Many writers maintain a Web page as part of their overall identity, called **branding**, and use their pages to post ideas for others to peruse. These Web pages often have links to resources and include announcements about writer's groups, writer conferences and other helpful ideas. For

James Watkins shows what "brand" of writer he is through a website that furthers his public exposure.

instance, author James Watkins has an author's site at www.jameswatkins.com. To build traffic, Jim offers an exclusive list of references for anyone who receives his weekly columns via email. The exclusive reference page includes links to fellow ink writers. The sites often include ideas on getting published.

For instance, James Watkins's site links to John Riddle's www.ilovetowrite.com. This site provides some practical ideas on breaking into print and suggests that writers browse a bookstore for ideas. Riddle also offers his own list of Web sites for freelance writers. The one that has provided him the most writing opportunities is www.craigslist.org. This site provides free classified advertisements. The area that is of interest to writers is labeled "writers and editors," or may be under arts, media and design. In addition, opportunities for "education writers" may be listed under "education." The site is freshened up daily and the classified advertisements are arranged by metropolitan area.

A site devoted to freelance writers who are looking for paying assignments and other links for writing work is www.writingcareer.com/freecontent.shtml.

Journalismjobs.com is another site for journalists and freelance writers. This site is sponsored by *Columbia Journalism Review* magazine and features links to events, writing, reporting and editing jobs for print, broadcast and online. It includes articles and links to periodicals including student newspapers. A similar site for freelance writers is freelancewrite.about.com, which has a fair amount of commercial content but delivers nonetheless. It contains articles such as "Seven mistakes new magazine writers make" and links to jobs, grant writing, even greeting card writing.

For publishing information, consider Sally E. Stuart's Web site at www.stuartmarket.com for lists of periodicals and book publishers. Each year Stuart publishes the *Christian Writers' Market Guide* through Shaw Books, and it is considered the best source for publishing in the inspiration press.

For background and information on film including the names of characters and casts along with plot summaries, visit the Internet Movie Database at www.imbd.com.

Sources of a general nature

Need an almanac, dictionary, encyclopedia or an atlas? Try infoplease.com. This site provides reference helps, but it contains a few pop-up advertisements that can interfere with your search. For the dictionary reference, I typed in "vita" and the computer presented a number of phrases with that word, including

cur•ric•u•lum vi•tae *Pronunciation:* (ku-rik'yu-lum vI'tE, vE'tI; *Lat.* kOOr-rik'oo-loom" wE'tI), —*pl. cur•ric•u•la vi•tae Pronunciation:* (ku-rik'yu-lu vI'tE, vE'tI; *Lat.* kOOr-rik'oo-lä" wE'tI). [key]

1. Also called vita, vitae. a brief biographical résumé of one's career and training, as prepared by a person applying for a job.

2. Latin. the course of one's life or career.

Another valuable source for writers is a timeline that focuses on highlights from years past. For the year 1900, for instance, the U.S. population was 76 million people, Henri Matisse led the Fauvist movement in painting, and Austrian psychiatrist Sigmund Freud published *The Interpretation of Dreams*. The site includes detailed information under each of topic, including a note that the term *Fauvism* is from French meaning *wild beast*, and that this movement yielded to Cubism.

Bigchalk.com can be a worthy tool for writers. It is designed for children and youth, but it can help writers obtain full-text articles. Users must register and a trial service is available. However, many public libraries use this site, making the cost of a full-text search of a database amount to the expense of a library card and a visit to your community's best place for research – the library. A trend these days is for young students to do research at large bookstores. If the bookstore managers only knew that those young people are doing their homework when they browse. Perhaps a business opportunity exists in that environment. For the rest of us, the library allows books and lots of electronic databases that will give you full-text articles.

Bartelby.com is the place for the hard-to-find quotation. Remember that great line, "I'm sorry to have written such a long letter, but I didn't have time to write a shorter one?" Who said it? George Bernard Shaw. This site may help make those kinds of connections, but it takes some time to search; nonetheless, it features an electronic version of *Bartlett's Quotations* and dozens of other reference books.

For reference information, try www.refdesk.com for fast, family-friendly information without advertisements. It has search areas for a dictionary, thesaurus, headlines, links to commentary by dozens of opinion writers, sports writers and more, the word of the day, links to TV networks and the Daily Writer's Almanac, a site that provides inspiration for new and veteran writers. It has a link to a free IRS tax preparation service, a white page telephone directory and a reverse white page directory, where users can obtain telephone information from a street address.

As an experiment, I used refdesk.com to see what I could find for an explanation for A.D. and B.C. and found a good summary on A.D., Anno Domini, the year of our Lord, and what it claims is the "preferred use" of B.C.E. (Before the Common Era) and C.E. (Common Era) instead. B.C.E. is a usage that some believe more accurately reflects the Western calendar with a sense of scholarship. Others, however, see it as an attempt to cloud the connection between the current calendar and Christ's birth. The site, www.radix.net/~dglenn/defs/ce.html, provided a fine summary with some commentary on preferred usages.

When interviewing an author of Christian books, try Christianbook.com/html/authors/index.html/98320402. This site provides an alphabetical listing of many authors and background on each.

For information on the top 150 best-selling books, try www.usatoday.com/life/books/top-50.htm. The list examines a book for this week's sales and last week's sales. Some titles include links to the books, most do not.

For a review of the trends in books for Christian audiences, try the entire online issue of *World* magazine at: www.worldmag.com/world/issue/07-07-02/.

For book reviews in general, *The News York Times* on the Web is a reliable source. You may be required to provide a username and password, but it is a free service although it does ask for your income level and occupation. One writer I know always chooses the highest income that is offered thinking she will get on the stellar mailing lists! The mail-order catalogues alone make for lots of fun at the holidays if you're on the A list for mass mailings. The site is nytimes.com/pages/books/index.html.

For writers, one Web site that is sure to provide quality is the online site of the writer's magazine, *Publisher's Weekly*, at www.publishersweekly.reviewsnews.com. This Web site covers the business side of publishing, an area that you may want to monitor to have that insider feeling. Other good writer sources include www.writersdigest.com and www.writersmarket.com, two sites that cater to the professional writer. Professional does not have to mean a writer who has published hundreds of articles. The articles are aimed at writers who are growing in their craft.

From time to time, a writer needs to know the day of the week from a distant year. **Perpetual Calendar** can help. This resource, as much of interest to academics as anyone, is at www.my.execpc.com/~mikeber/calendar.html and allows users to select the year and determine the date. Want to know the day of the week for Feb. 21 in the year 1955? Change the year to 1955 on this Web site, and you will find out that Feb. 21, 1955, fell on a Monday. It is on a Monday again in 2005 as this book is published.

Need to look up a name in a community newspaper? Try newspaperarchive.com. It appears to have access to Midwestern newspapers primarily, but it can be a valuable source for a name search, particularly family history. For the more prominent person, try www.s9.com/biography. This site allows the user to locate a well-known person and obtain some modest background. A search of "Michael Smith" located the astronaut who died in the Challenger space tragedy.

A search engine that combines the commercial site of Amazon with a partner is archive.org, one of the Web's best-kept secrets. From the archive.org home page, I clicked on alexa.com and entered the title of a recent book and found dozens of pages that included references to this little-known title.

Confused by all those worldwide agencies that find their way into news articles? Try the following Web site: www.odci.gov/cia/publications

/factbook. From this page sponsored by the Central Intelligence Agency, you can access the appendix that lists in alphabetical order of international organizations such as the following.

ABEDA – Arab Bank for Economic Development in Africa
ACC – Arab Cooperation Council
ACCT – Agency for the French-Speaking Community
ACP – Group African, Caribbean, and Pacific Group of States
AfDB – African Development Bank
AFESD – Arab Fund for Economic and Social Development

The page also provides a summary of countries around the world in a World Factbook. When I reviewed an academic book on the press in Nicaragua, I brushed up on that country's history using a list from the World Factbook. The summary listed the country's geography, people, government, economy, communications, transportation, military and transnational issues. The flag of the country also is included with facts about elected officials. Also useful for checking information is the History of the World Timeline feature found at www.historychannel.com, which lists events from 401 B.C. to the present.

From time to time, you will be required to know the value of money from country to country. The Universal Currency Converter provides accurate rates at a Web site: www.xe.com/ucc. I entered 10 for United States dollars and learned that in late 2004 that amount would buy 7.84 Euros and 5.44 United Kingdom pounds. Naturally, these figures fluctuate constantly, all the more reason to save or **bookmark** the page to have ready access to conversion figures. It provides conversions for South Korean Won, Sudanese Dinars, Mexican Pesos, Japanese Yen and, it claims, all the world's currencies.

As a writer, you are a curious person who initiates conversations with strangers, looks beneath tables and takes notice of the books on a person's desk. (Ever look in someone's medicine cabinet?) In short, you're part of a peculiar people. At times that curiosity can be satisfied when writing about technology and science using www.howstuffworks.com. This Web page has animation on how an engine works and articles on how ATM machines operate, background info on aerosol cans, the delights of an electric dimmer switch, and more. The page may stimulate you as you think of ideas for articles.

Occasionally, you will need to find information on medical issues. www.drkoop.com provides a search function for topics within the Web site, or it can search the Web or another medical Web site. This medical site contains news articles on aging, diseases and preventive medicine.

Like all Web sites, it is not a substitute for interviewing an expert, but it may acquaint you with enough information to help you understand an issue as you collect information from a source. When using information from an Internet site, treat it as you would information from a publication. Cite the source, and check it for accuracy. Never lift a quotation or a statistic from a Web site and drop it into your article without citing it. Why? Two reasons. One, courtesy. Someone did the work to put that information on the site, and she deserves recognition. Two, if the information is inaccurate, you are responsible for disseminating an error. That is the last action that you want to take as a writer. Be accurate. That's a noble calling, and you are worth the effort.

Medical information in particular is problematic and should be verified over and over. Among the top medical frauds of the decade is one that concerns AIDS. At www.quackwatch.org, users can read about the claims and use this information as they conduct interviews. According to this Web site, "Victims of incurable diseases are especially vulnerable to the promises of charlatans. AIDS is a prime example. Underground or 'guerrilla clinics' offering homemade treatments have sprung up in the United States, the Caribbean, and Europe." The site cautions readers to view cures with skepticism.

Not long ago a magazine assigned me to write about a professional baseball player, easy enough. The hard part of doing an article on a public figure is characterizing the wealth associated with the person, an element that may or may not be important to your audience. In my case, I contacted the National Baseball League and asked what the average starting salary was for a first baseman. That worked. How about ordinary people such as bankers or somewhat unusual vocations such as acting? Try www.salary.com. This site, which sells resume-writing services among other services, provides a guide on average salaries for a job in a specific geographical area. In addition, it offers advice, self-tests and other helps on careers and earnings. The site could be helpful for you as you prepare for an interview or write an article on cost-of-living, unemployment, job creation, job losses and so on.

Scams, urban legends and the paranormal

A Web site that helps you find background on scams is www.scambusters.com. The site monitors Internet hoaxes and urban legends and had the following report in 2003.

Urban Legend #3

On Saturday, 24 January 1998, Naval Air Station, Joint Reserve Base, New Orleans' Quarterdeck, received a telephone call from an individual identifying himself as an AT&T Service Technician who was running a test on our telephone lines. He stated that to complete the test the QMOW should touch nine (9), zero (0), pound sign (#) and hang up. Luckily, the QMOW was suspicious and refused. Upon contacting the telephone company, we were informed that by using 90#, you end up giving the individual that called you access to your telephone line, and allows them to place a long distance telephone call, with the charge appearing on your telephone bill. We were further informed that this scam has been originating from many of the local jails/prisons. Please 'pass the word.'

Scambusters.com reported, "Strangely enough this story does have some truth to it. BUT it only works on telephones where you have to dial 9 to get an outside line AND the system allows you to make a long distance call once you've gotten that outside line." I accessed this link: www.scambusters.com/Scambusters22.html#Nike to get that information in 2003. I mention the year because links change frequently and what's up today may be gone tomorrow. It's called **link rot.** Be aware of the mercurial nature of the Internet because it's another facet of your pilgrimage for truth. Be passionate about accuracy.

For similar information on those slightly eerie bits of urban drama, you may want to experiment with www.snopes.com. It covers entertainment among other issues. Snopes.com recently reported the following background about *Amazing Grace*, a popular Gospel hymn.

Having survived a horrific storm, a slave trader promptly gave up his livelihood, became a Christian, and penned the hymn Amazing Grace in thanksgiving.

The order of events may be off, but the gist of that Snopes.com report is true; however, the following is false, although the Web site reported it as true. In early 2003, the Web site reported, "Bob Dylan stole the song *Blowin' in the Wind* from a New Jersey high school student. "

According to Scott Marshall, that rumor is untrue. Marshall wrote *Restless pilgrim, the spiritual journey of Bob Dylan* with Marcia Ford, published by Relevant Media in Lake Mary, Fla., in 2002. Marshall said, "For the record, Dylan, as a 20-year-old in the early days of 1962, penned *Blowin' in the Wind* himself." According to Marshall, Dylan said, "It was just another song I wrote and got thrown into all the songs I was doing at the time. I wrote it in a cafe across the street from the Gaslight [Cafe in Greenwich Village]. Although I thought it was special, I didn't know to what degree, I wrote it for the moment, ya' know. I remember running into

Peter of Peter, Paul, and Mary on the street, after they had recorded it. 'Man,' he said, 'you're going to make $5,000.' And I said 'What? Five thousand dollars?' Five thousand dollars, it seemed like a million at the time. He said, 'It's amazing man. You've really hit it big.' Of course, I'd been playing the song for a while anyway and people had always responded to it in a positive way to say the least. Money was never a motivation to write anything. I never wrote anything with 'this-is-gonna-be-a-hit or this-isn't-type of attitude.' I'm not that smart anyway."[52]

Again, this kind of information must be checked and re-checked, but snopes.com can be one of the sites that you use on your quest for accuracy.

In the ruthless pursuit of accuracy, sites such as www.csicop.org can help with scientific explanations of the paranormal. The site is hosted by the Committee on the Scientific Investigation of the Claims of the Paranormal. When the popular movie, *Signs,* opened, renewed interest in crop circles led the Web site to post the most recent evidence to discredit the appearance of these circles. That link is: www.csicop.org/si/2002-09/crop-circles.html.

U.S. Census information

As stated earlier, the government provides some of the best information. The U.S. Department of Commerce provides census figures at www.census.gov. This Web site is rich for mining feature stories. It includes an A-Z list on topics. It includes information on genealogy, news releases and statistics for income figures. Using the alphabetical list of topics, I examined "T," and chose "tutorial." There I learned about the best ways to use the site. From the home page, I choose "2001 Area Profiles" and went to the "American Community Survey" page. From there, I selected the "narrative and tabular profiles" to peruse data from the U.S. Census of 2001, the most recent year for the available data. Of the geographical areas available, I selected Sevier County, Tenn., and learned that residents there tend not to move, 59% are married families and the leading age group is 25-44 years of age. This kind of information is valuable for an article on the graying of America, the mobility of Americans, and the changing identity of family. The information is from the federal government, making it a highly reliable source; however, in the interest of accuracy, a good writer could have another source such as a

---

[52] From Cameron Crowe, who interviewed Dylan about the individual songs that appeared on *Biograph*, a 5-record compilation (now 3 CDs) filled with Dylan originals., Crowe's work appeared in the 1985 liner notes to *Blowin' in the Wind*, New York: CBS.

university sociologist comment on the strength of the findings. That's good reporting.

Another commendable page for statistics is robertniles.com. This page, designed to help writers, breaks down the complicated business of statistics and gives easy-to-understand explanations along with articles on agriculture, crime, economics, education, energy and more.

Investigations

Reporters and writers do the job of so many other like-minded people. We do sleuthing using many of the techniques of law enforcement, even private investigators. For the would-be P.I.'s is the Web site virtualgumshoe.com. This site has a fun feel but it links to some powerful searches with the added bonus that the hot buttons on the left remain while you use the main window for a search. For instance, from the categories on the left side of the home page is FAQ, or frequently asked questions. Under this page, is a link to U.S. vital records where a user can search birth, death, marriages and other records. The topics include adoption resources, archives, area codes & zip codes, associations and attorneys. And, that's just the A's. The page has links to missing persons, sex offenders, gangs, cults, fraternities and sororities and more.

Under "General Resources or how to information," the site will take the user to inet.investigation.com and allow her to conduct a number of searches including a people search or an email search. Tutorials will help the new user think through a strategy. This site includes a number of commercial products, but it has enough free searches that the imaginative writer will be well served.

A site that is sometimes frightening for its revelations of personal information is www.anywho.com, and it allows users to obtain maps, telephone numbers and other information using a reverse directory. When the street name is known or some other information, a writer can sometimes find the crucial telephone number that she needs. To contact a neighbor of a source for a slightly different viewpoint on the topic in a news story, for instance, the reverse telephone directory is handy. Also consider www.switchboard.com.

Public opinion polls

Among the best source for reliable polling information is www.pollingreport.com. It provides up-to-date information on the state of the union in the United States, elections and trends.

Another source for public opinion polls is from a troika of information heavyweights –TODAY/CNN/Gallup Poll. It is: www.usatoday.com/news /poll001.htm. Or go to www.library.csun.edu/mfinley/polls.html. Another is www.nationaljournal.com.pubs/nj/index.htm. Polls are listed on the side of the home page.

A polling mine on spiritual concerns is sponsored by the Barna Research Online and may be found at www.barna.org/cgi-bin/MainArchives.asp. This page lists 40 topics on beliefs, the Bible, church attendance, money, religious differences, family and others. This site reflects George Barna's interest in religion and the public opinion surveys often examine some aspect of Christianity.

Electronic databases

Electronic databases often are subscription-based, and too expensive for the ordinary person. Nonetheless, many public libraries and university libraries allow guests to access this information.

Factiva is a Dow Jones electronic database, and users must pay to access it. Some college and university libraries have this service, global.factiva.com, and may allow guests to use it to search full-text articles in magazines and newspapers. An even better full-text electronic database is **LexisNexis**, but it is a very expensive. For most of us, it is only available at good college libraries at web.lexis-nexis.com. It features "Comprehensive resources for business, news, politics and government, medical information, legal information, case law, U.S. and state codes, biographical information, and accounting and tax information."

Associations

Associations such as groups dedicated to horseback riding, to disability issues and just about any pet cause of any kind abound in the United States. For example, enter the name "Mark Twain," and you will find a site for the Mark Twain Boyhood Home Association in Hannibal, Mo.; Mark Twain House in Hartford, Conn.; the Mark Twain Democratic Club in Whittier, Calif.; an appreciation society in New York City and two Mark Twain Foundations.

In addition to ordinary brick-and-mortar offices, these lobbying organizations have Web pages and live to interact with reporters and writers. Gale Group publishes a reference available at most public libraries, *Encyclopedia of Associations, an association of unlimited references.*[53] However, many libraries also have the online version known

---

[53] Hedbland, A. (2003). *Encyclopedia of Associations, an association of unlimited references.* New York: Gale Publishing.

as **Associations Unlimited**. This electronic database allows users to conduct a custom search on a keyword that you pick. It can lead you to groups that advocate positions on topics for which you are writing. This publication remains a favorite of journalists because it points writers to sources who are well informed and articulate about a topic. Often these sources will send you press packets of background, photographic slides, fact sheets, maps, graphics and other useful information in their attempt to get their side of the issue publicized. Gale's publications are some of the writing industry's best-kept secrets, and now you know!

The online version has a number of ways to access information. For instance, by typing the word "bells" into the association name blank, the directory provided the names of four organizations that deal with bells. One organization is known as AIDS Memorial Bells and included an address in Largo, Fla. However, Bells of the Lakes listed a U.S. Postal address and email address along with the number of members, the president's name, the amount of dues, its budget and this description: Music and education through the medium of hand bells.

Gale Group also produces these reference works:
- Biography and Genealogy Master Index
- Contemporary Authors
- Gale Database of Publications and Broadcast Media.

My top 10

At this point, you are thinking, "Ah, too many Web sites exist out there!" To narrow it down a bit, here are my personal top 10 favorites in alphabetical order.

1) **Alexa.com** for archival information.
2) **Associations Unlimited** for names of lobbying groups or advocacy groups in this subscription-only electronic database. It's available at college libraries at galenet.galegroup.com.
3) **Barna.org** for public opinion polling information on spiritual issues.
4) **Bartelby.com** for quotation help.
5) **Ilovetowrite.com** for inspiration.
6) **LexisNexis** for full-text articles in this subscription-only electronic database. It's available at college libraries at web.lexis-nexis.com/universe.
7) **Refdesk.com** for reference help.
8) **RobertNiles.com** for statistics.
9) **Scambusters.com** for fun content on urban legends.
10) **Virtualgumshoe.com** for searches of public records.

Netward

Freelance writing coach Norm Rohrer used to urge his followers on with the word, "Onward." The word is packed with power and optimism. It suggests energy unleashed. That is the idea of "Netward." You now have the Web sites to access the best information, but you'll have to do the work. And you'll have to do the other important tasks of interviewing sources and observing for graphic details that can transform limp prose into bold writing. From today forward, use the Internet every time you write an article. Set a goal of finding one drab of information that makes you smile. If it makes you say, "Wow," "No kidding," or "Dawg," then probability is in your favor that others will say the same. Netward!

Julia Duin

Biography of Julia Duin

A veteran writer and reporter with nearly 20 years of experience, Julia Duin (pronounced "Dean") is assistant national editor at *The Washington Times* and the author of *Wholly Single, Purity Makes the Heart Grow Stronger* and *Waiting for True Love.* She has worked fulltime for five newspapers and part-time for a sixth one. Duin has taught journalism at Patrick Henry College in Purcellville, Va., and she has earned degrees from Lewis and Clark College, Portland, Ore., and Trinity Episcopal School for Ministry, Ambridge, Pa. She has published thousands of articles in her writing career.

Editor's note. The following article by writer Julia Duin appeared in The Washington Times early in 2003 when the United States and others fought Saddam Hussein in a war to liberate Iraq from a dictator suspected of using poisonous gas on Iraqis and others.

Hillary given "pink slip" for stance on Iraq War[54]
By Julia Duin
Copyright © 2003 News World Communications, Inc.
Reprinted with permission of The Washington Times. This reprint does not
constitute or imply any endorsement or sponsorship of any product,
service, company or organization.

Sen. Hillary Rodham Clinton was handed a "pink slip" – a frilly piece of lingerie – yesterday from an enraged group of female war protesters who told her to quit her job because she was not doing enough to oppose military action against Iraq.

"Hillary is getting the pink slip," said Medea Benjamin, an organizer from New York, "because she is not representing her constituents. She should get another job."

The New York Democrat spoke calmly during a 10-minute repartee she had with about 50 women from Code Pink, a feminist anti-war group planning demonstrations this weekend in Washington.

Dressed in all manner of pink berets, boas, shawls, scarves, coats and even a bathrobe, the group members roamed the halls of Congress all afternoon, giving out pink slips to various legislators and hoisting banners such as "Real Democrats Listen to Peoples' Calls for Peace."

The pink lingerie, which demonstrators obtained at thrift shops, were decorated with anti-war slogans and inked-on pleas such as "Hillary, do the right thing."

The women first appeared at Mrs. Clinton's office at 2 p.m., singing, "Hillary, show some spine/We're putting our bodies on the line."

"We'll vote in 2008," vowed one demonstrator, alluding to Mrs. Clinton's rumored presidential ambitions.

The senator's staff finally agreed to make Mrs. Clinton available at 4:45 p.m.

Mrs. Clinton, who arrived 45 minutes late and insisted that all reporters leave the room before she addressed the protesters, explained her reasons for not trusting Iraqi leader Saddam Hussein.

"I admire your willingness to speak out on behalf of women and children in Iraq," she said. "The only way to change this is for Saddam Hussein to disarm, and I don't think he will. We are in a very difficult position right now. I'd love to agree with you, but I can't."

---

[54] Duin, J. (2003, March 7). Hillary given 'pink slip' for stance on Iraq war. *The Washington Times*, p. A4.

But when one of the protest leaders, Jodie Evans of Venice, Calif., tore off her full-length pink slip and presented it to Mrs. Clinton, the senator walked out.

"I am the senator from New York," she said, "and I will not put people's security at risk."

"But you are," the demonstrators shouted at her as she exited.

Another pink slip was handed to staff at the office of Sen. Dianne Feinstein, California Democrat, where demonstrators hoisted a sign reading, "Dianne Have Mercy on the Children."

"We don't think it's fair to the Iraqi people that she wants us to go to war," Miss Evans said. Feinstein spokesman Howard Gantman mollified the demonstrators by explaining that out of the 50,000 phone calls her office had received since August, 48,000 have been against war.

The demonstrators, who were mostly over 30 and from various states around the country, presented "badges of honor" to Democratic politicians who oppose war with Iraq. Recipients included Sen. Edward M. Kennedy of Massachusetts, Reps. Marcy Kaptur of Ohio, Barbara Lee of California, Eddie Bernice Johnson of Texas, John Conyers Jr. of Michigan and Jim McDermott of Washington.

The publicity stunt was a walk-up to more anti-war activities, starting with a "teach-in" today at Shiloh Baptist Church at 9th and P streets NW and a women's march to the White House on Saturday. The National Organization for Women has loaned out a portion of its 15th Street NW offices to Code Pink organizers.

> **Tip:** Among Julia Duin's favorite Web sites is commentary sponsored by Florida's Poynter Institute called Romenesko's Media News, www.poynter.org/column.asp?id=45. This site, popular among writers and journalists, features media criticism and lively opinion pieces on topics of salience to writers and others.

Interview with Julia Duin

Q: How did you get the story idea?

A: I receive email from a number of groups and Code Pink, a feminist, anti-war group alerted me to this protest days ahead.

Q: Other than email, how do you use the Internet for your work?

A: I do searches using Google and Profnet, and whitepages.com provides telephone numbers, some of which are unlisted, for sources. I enjoy visiting Web sites such as Mediawatch.com or Poynter.org and checking out the buzz. For instance, Poynter.org provides helpful information for working journalists and writers. It has information on interviewing, columns and ongoing discussions about ethics.

Q: The group wore pink slips, that is undergarments, as part of the protest. How did that look?

A: The protesters wore pink slips and big bras over their street clothes and it made them look like homeless people, but it added to the protest message that they wanted to send.

Q: Once you were on the scene, Sen. Clinton's staff tried to eject you. What did you do?

A: The lesson here is to outwait them. Sen. Clinton made the group wait in a U.S. Senate hearing room but called it an extension of her office space. That way she could argue that the group of nearly 40 people were just waiting for her in her Senate office and she has the right to bar the press from a meeting in her office. Code Pink organizers told me the senator was refusing to grant them an audience if the press was present. So they kicked out my photographer, who like me had been waiting for hours. The organizers were between a rock and a hard place because Hillary's people were using me as an excuse for her not to show. I told them I didn't want to leave, but the choice was up to them, as it was their event. While we were still dickering over this, Hillary finally walked into the room. The stand off was a free press issue and in this case, the press won. I just out-waited her.

Q: How long a day was it?

A: I started the day around 10 a.m. By the time Sen. Clinton stopped talking with the protesters, it was nearly 6 p.m. I went back to the newspaper, lobbied for the article for page one and had it written in 45 minutes. But by that time the decision on page one was made and my story ran on page A4. I worked very hard to get that article but timing is everything and by the time Sen. Clinton showed up for the meeting, it was after 5 p.m. and at that point, the page one layout for the next day is hard to break. In this business, writers must be aggressive and fast, not to mention accurate and creative. At one point, I donned a pink beret just to blend in with the group to get the story!

Exercises

1) Re-read the article. What search terms can you suggest to use in an Internet search when writing about an anti-war group?
2) What observation did you find in this article?

3) What is your opinion about a journalist or writer trying to blend into a group?

4) Identify the conflict in this article.

Biography of Terry Mattingly

Terry Mattingly

Terry Mattingly, known at "tmatt" to his friends, is an associate professor of Mass Media and Religion at Palm Beach Atlantic University in Florida and senior fellow for journalism with the Council for Christian Colleges and Universities (CCCU) in Washington, D.C. He also writes the weekly "On Religion" column for the Scripps Howard News Service, which is sent to 350 North American newspapers.

Mattingly holds degrees from Baylor University and the University of Illinois in Urbana-Champaign. His homepage at http://www.tmatt.net features archives of his syndicated columns. Among the best links on his Web site is his freelance work that spotlights the tension of religion reporting at http://tmatt.gospelcom.net/tmatt/freelance.

In addition to his classroom duties at Palm Beach Atlantic, Mattingly lectures at Gordon-Conwell Theological Seminary in South Hamilton, Mass., the Torreys Honors Program at Biola University, Baylor University in Waco, Texas, and in other settings across the nation. With the CCCU, Mattingly is founder and co-director of the Summer Institute of Journalism, a four-week undergraduate program in late May and early June at its headquarters in Washington, D.C. His writing also appears in Current Thoughts & Trends, Beliefnet.com, Touchstone, The Lookout, the Amy Foundation Syndicate and other publications.

Terry is married to Debra Bridges Mattingly, a librarian on the Palm Beach Atlantic faculty, and they have two children. Among Terry's hobbies is collecting vintage guitars. His family is active in the Antiochian Orthodox Church, especially in music, missions and evangelism.

Ten years of reporting on a fault line
By Terry Mattingly
Used with permission

Back in the 1980s, I began to experience deja vu while covering event after event on the religion beat in Charlotte, Denver, and then at the national level.

I kept seeing a fascinating cast of characters at events centering on faith, politics and morality. A pro-life rally, for example, would feature a Baptist, a Catholic priest, an Orthodox rabbi and a cluster of conservative Methodists, Presbyterians, Episcopalians and Lutherans. Then, the pro-choice counter-rally would feature a "moderate" Baptist, a Catholic activist or two, a Reform rabbi and mainline Methodists, Presbyterians, Episcopalians and Lutherans.

Similar line-ups would appear at many rallies linked to gay rights, sex-education programs and controversies in media, the arts and even science. Along with other journalists, I kept reporting that today's social issues were creating bizarre coalitions that defied historic and doctrinal boundaries. After several years of writing about "strange bedfellows," it became obvious that what was once unique was now commonplace.

Then, in 1986, a sociologist of religion had an epiphany while serving as a witness in a church-state case in Mobile, Ala. The question was whether "secular humanism" had evolved into a state-mandated religion, leading to discrimination against traditional "Judeo-Christian" believers. Once more, two seemingly bizarre coalitions faced off in the public square.

"I realized something there in that courtroom. We were witnessing a fundamental realignment in American religious pluralism," said James Davison Hunter of the University of Virginia. "Divisions that were deeply rooted in our civilization were disappearing, divisions that had for generations caused religious animosity, prejudice and even warfare. It was mind-blowing. The ground was moving."

The old dividing lines centered on issues such as the person of Jesus Christ, church tradition and the Protestant Reformation. But these new interfaith coalitions were fighting about something even more basic – the nature of truth and moral authority.

Two years later, Hunter began writing "Culture Wars: The Struggle to Define America," in which he declared that America now contains two basic world views, which he called "orthodox" and "progressive." The orthodox believe it's possible to follow transcendent, revealed truths. Progressives disagree and put their trust in personal experience, even if that requires them to "resymbolize historic faiths according to the prevailing assumptions of contemporary life."

That's what I was seeing at all of those rallies and marches. And that's why, whenever I covered separate meetings of Catholics, Jews, Baptists, Episcopalians or whatever, I almost always found two distinct camps of people fighting about the same subjects.

About the same time Hunter began "Culture Wars," I began writing this column for the Scripps Howard News Service. The column turns 10 years old this week and, almost every week, I have seen evidence that Hunter has found a fault line that runs through virtually every set of pews in contemporary religious life.

Ask any big question and this issue looms in the background. Is the Bible an infallible source of truth? Is papal authority unique? Do women and men have God-given roles in the home and the church? Can centuries of Jewish traditions survive in the modern world? Can marriage be redefined? Is abortion wrong? Can traditionalists proclaim that sex outside of marriage is sin? Are heaven and hell real? Do all religious roads lead to the same end? Is there one God, or many? What is his or her name or names?

Many in the orthodox camp disagree on some of the answers, but they are united in their belief that public life must include room for those who insist eternal answers exist. Meanwhile, progressives are finding it harder to tolerate the views of people they consider offensive and intolerant. This is not a clash between religious people and secular people, stressed Hunter. This is a battle between two fundamentally different approaches to faith.

"We may soon reach the point when religious conservatives will long for the time when real, live, secular humanists ran the show," he said. "At least those people believed in something specific. At least they believed in reason and universal principles."

Today, secularism just doesn't sell in the marketplace. This approach to life has been tried and found wanting. People hunger for spirituality, miracles and a sense of mystery. But the core question remains: Should believers defend eternal truths or follow their hearts?

"The momentum is toward experience and emotions and feelings," said Hunter. "People are saying, 'I feel, therefore I am.' This is how more and more people are deciding what is real and right and true."[55]

Interview with Terry Mattingly

Q: Your work may be found at a number of Internet sites. What are some of the advantages and disadvantages of this kind of exposure?

---

[55] Mattingly, T. (1998, April 15). Ten years of reporting on a fault line. Gospelcom.net. Retrieved July 15, 2003, from http://tmatt.gospelcom.net/column /1998/04/15/.

A: First of all, the legal issues are a fog bank. People are posting the actual texts of columns all over with no permission from me or from Scripps Howard. It is one thing to publish a link to a column. Publishing the actual text is something else. People are supposed to seek my permission.

The advantages? Readers.

Q: What kind of reader reaction did you receive on the column above? What kind of reaction do you receive from 'Net exposure in general?

A: It is impossible to judge without knowing what is happening to other writers. I will simply say this – consistently, the columns I write about worship and especially music draw the highest number of responses. I also receive quite a bit of feedback on my columns about faith issues in popular culture.

Like it or not, pop culture rules.

Q: How do you use the Internet for your columns?

A: I could not write the column I write – a national and global angle column – without the Internet. I work at one location, with my speaking engagements taking me on the road. I cannot live on a long distance telephone line. In addition to research, I use email to exchange documents, forward questions and line up the times for interviews. I cannot imagine doing any of what I do without it.

Q: Do you see feature writing overlapping with column writing?

A: I have always been a deadline reporter, working in deadline lengths, who only occasionally wrote true feature-length stories. Today, I write an analysis column with a strict wire-service length requirement. I guess that I use elements of feature writing in these columns – primarily using interview materials to recreate scenes and details. But most of my writing is by telephone, document and email. This is not the natural terrain of true feature writing, in my opinion.

Q: What's your best piece of advice for new writers?

A: I know little or nothing about writing. I am a reporter. That says what I want to say!

Exercises

5) Re-read Julia Duin's work and Terry Mattingly's column. How are they similar; how are they different?
6) Are they feature articles? Explain.
7) What can Terry Mattingly do in his writing that straight-news writers can't do?
8) Do you have a preference in your writing?

9) If you had to write a straight-news piece, could you?

Summary

This book is built on the use of the Internet to get the best information possible for your article. Understanding the terms is important in the name of getting the information right! Writers use search tools to access electronic databases and specific Web sites for the best possible information. As writers search for information, they practice the discipline of checking it for accuracy. Web sites exist for nearly every topic from business to law to experts in areas such as politics, medicine and more. Writers can learn much from perusing Web sites for writers and journalists and online publications designed for all kinds of readers. Scams and urban legends can be debunked using the Web, but writers must be ever vigilant to double-check information that they cull on the Internet. (Are you sensing a repetitive disqualifier here? Be careful when you use the Net.) Among the best information available is from the U.S. government. While it may reflect the foreign policy position of the administration, it is considered reliable. For instance, U.S. Census figures are available on the Web and can be a rich source of feature story material. Polling information is another source for ideas. For instance, Barna Research Online provides thoughtful survey research. This chapter included an interview with an editor who uses the Internet for her research.

Chapter 9

Eight habits of highly effective photographers
FeatureWriting.Net/Photo

Chapter at-a-glance

> ➤ Enhancing your freelance income with photography
> ➤ Mastering the habits of good composition
> ➤ Thinking visually as you write

Writers tend to be poets at heart. They feel deeply and use words to circle a thought, then creep up on it, and sometimes actually capture it. The best writers speak for all of us, and say what we feel and think, but in powerful, memorable ways. Taking a photograph is to seize the mood, an idea, a feeling, an issue – all of which is involved in producing a winning feature, but as a visual representation. For the freelance writer and journalist, producing a quality image may mean doubling your paycheck. When done well, the photograph tells a story. It's a visual narrative that uses facial expressions, light, actions and more to provoke a mood, a feeling that moves an audience to identify, to question, to pause, to feel at peace.

These days publications and online services are as concerned with the visual art elements as they are the article, and you may be able to double your money by submitting a photograph that assists you in telling the story. Editors need graphic art, line

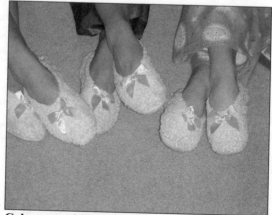

Color, repetition and the odd angle are among the considerations in composing your photograph. Think background-foreground.

art, info graphics, tables of statistics, maps – and, most of all, pictures: either black-and-white photographs, colored slides or prints, or digital images that can accompany the words of your article.

This chapter will explore a step-by-step approach for taking good quality photographs. By applying the seven timeless principles suggested in this chapter, you will be equipped to see the photograph that is required for the article, and bring it to market. These ideas will work whether you are using a **disposable** or **35mm camera**, which uses film and a developing process, or a **digital camera**, which uses a floppy disc or a memory stick in tandem with a computer. Each camera has its trade-off, but the digital camera allows you to ship your art from your computer to an editor's computer without the delay of processing the film. Whatever format you use, the goal is to tell a gripping story with words and pictures to move your audience, to help them see the wonder of life in all its tragedy, surprises and joy.

This chapter will explore technical issues in passing only. The primary goal is to consider composition principles to improve the art you submit with your article.

Habit 1: Move in.

The theme of this chapter is **composition**, the way the parts of the picture are arranged. Getting close to your subject can enhance composition, your first step in becoming a highly effective photographer. For our purposes, most of your photographs will be of people, and your editor will want to see the person's face – not her back, but her face. Think head and shoulders for a photograph of a single subject. Consider the

photograph of three-year-old Alanna from the playhouse. To remember the idea of the perennial need for headshots, think about Alanna popping out of the playhouse window. That idea alone will allow you to remember that most publications want a clear shot of the person's head. While it may be ordinary, it is a desirable picture that a publication can use. For now, concentrate on taking the

Solid-colored backgrounds work well, but most of all, get close to your subject.

photograph about four to five feet from your subject. That task alone will keep you busy. Call it the **triple F rule**, the **four-to-five-feet rule.**

The Black Star picture agency began taking photographs of the world's hot spots in the 1930s. A 1997 review of their work in Hendrik Neubauer's *Black Star, 60 years of photojournalism*, shows hundreds of graphic still photographs across more than six decades – and all are of people engaged in dramatic moments. Audiences want to see the **person's face**. A close-up of a hand or jewelry can work, but most publications want to see your subject's face. You will become a highly effective photographer with the practice of photographing a solid close-up shot of the person's face. As you gain confidence, ask your subject to avoid posing, and let him or her talk or show some kind of facial reaction. Let the subject react to your question and wait, pause just a beat or two, and allow the subject to laugh, look puzzled, express sadness and so on.

Most of all, however, get the person's face, either as a three-quarter profile, or by allowing the person to face the camera head on. Take a photograph of the person looking at the camera; next take a photograph of the person facing forward, but not looking at the camera. Depending on the goal of the article, the eyes-forward or eyes-away look will take the day. In most cases, the portrait approach of the subject caught in a casual moment is the pose your audience will appreciate most.

When using digital or disposable cameras, be aware of getting too close. Four feet is about as close as a photographer can get with those cameras. In summary, practice the **Triple F rule** for the shot that is most likely to be used with your article.

Habit 2: Monitor the background and the foreground.

Highly effective photographers look at all the parts of the photographs and see life through a rectangle, a **frame**. Better photographers see the clutter in a photograph, particularly the background, and next, the foreground. You now know to get close to your subject; next, monitor the background behind the subject's head. Be wary of the painting on the wall, the stray light from another light source or the busy traffic of the nearby street. The best background is a blank wall or a solid color background.

I photographed Alanna in a playroom, full of bright blues, vivid reds and sunny yellows, but nearly every angle, while colorful, contained a distraction in the background. I moved around to center the camera on her face, but the background contained a bulletin board, a shelf, or some other objects that interfered with the subject, what we call the **focal point** of the photograph.

Beware of busy backgrounds and foregrounds.

Look at this shot of Alanna, taken the same day as the photograph of her in the playhouse. While the shot is a close up and features her childish delight, the background intrudes. Notice the computer monitor and window in the background and the sip cup in the foreground. Do you see how distracting these objects can be if the subject is the focal point? Yes, it's true that the objects provide some sense of Alanna's environment, but a better picture is available for the photographer who is willing to wait for the right shot.

Beware of busy backgrounds and foregrounds.

Another issue associated with backgrounds and foregrounds is the idea of framing. In the first photograph, the window of the playhouse frames the subject. Windows and doorways can be used to frame your subject, meaning the shape of the opening works like a picture frame to draw the viewer's eye to the focal point. Look for these **natural frames** as you take your photograph. A limb on a tree works to frame the top of your photograph when you are working outside.

Getting close to your subject may not be difficult, but finding an uncluttered background may take some work. Get in the habit of moving around to eliminate distractions. Try getting higher than the subject's head by standing on a sturdy piece of furniture and looking down on the subject. By contrast, try kneeling and looking up toward your subject. Select the angle that works best. As a last resort, have your subject move. With some creativity, however, the photographer can get close and avoid a busy background by adjusting the angle, the direction of the camera shot.

Tip: When shooting outdoors, try to keep your subject in the shade and use the flash to provide what is known as **spot flash** to flatter your subject. Avoid taking shots when the sun is at its zenith to avoid harsh shadows. For the best light, consider shooting a color photograph at sunrise or sunset when the amber rays of the sun cast the warmest light. Be advised, however, this light fades within a few minutes.

Keep in mind that the camera vision is different from your vision. The human eye can zero in on an object and ignore the objects that are unimportant. A camera sees all the objects the same, forcing the photographer to visually point your audience in the right direction. The most obvious way to direct your audience's attention to the subject matter is by reducing the number of elements in the photograph, thereby making the subject matter clear to us.

Once you begin getting close to the subject and looking at the background, you can begin to experiment with more dramatic approaches. At first, concentrate on the **triple B rule**, **Background, Background, Background**. Using the Triple F and the Triple B will give you the FB, foolproof beauty.

Habit 3: Look at shapes and lines.

The doorway works as a picture frame in a photograph, but it also can be thought of as a **shape**, a rectangle. It is one of the many shapes found in man-made environments, or in nature. A student's desk may be square; a book, a rectangle; a clock, a circle; a lampshade, a triangle. Natural and man-made objects can be reduced to shapes; boards, bricks and shadows can be thought of as lines. As you compose your photograph, consider the shapes and lines to arrange them in a pattern. Remember, as a photographer, you must move around to compose the picture inside the frame. Look for lines that lead the viewer's eye to your subject. **Leading lines** are one of the best composition principles of good photographers.

In this photograph of Shaun, shapes are evident. The fence to his back forms a large rectangle. The box on which he sits is similar to a square.

Now look a little more closely. Imagine that the fence and box are connected. Together the shapes make a kind of backward "L." Shaun's posture also makes a kind of "L" with his back as the longer part of the L and his legs as the shorter part of the L.

In this photograph, the lines move in an up-and-down motion in the fence and in a back-and-forth

Rectangles and lines can lead the eye to a focal point.

motion of the box. In the background are saplings that form a vertical pattern with the stray fence post to the left working as a kind of frame. The branch above his head helps frame the shot. Together, the fence post and tree limb create another crude L shape that goes in the opposite direction as the fence and box. The lines on Shaun's pants and coat break up the static, straight lines and give the picture some rhythm. In short, the photograph contains a series of shapes and lines. As you take a photograph, become aware of these shapes and use them to arrange your subject in a pleasing pose. Shape your writing success by lining up good quality photographs to submit with your copy.

Habit 4: Look for the Z pattern, or the S pattern.

A Z-shaped pattern can lead the eye to the focal point.

Among the most pleasing patterns to the human eye are the shape of an "S" and the shape of a "Z." In each case, the line curves from either left to right or right to left. In the rectangle represented by the frame in a camera, the S or Z is a way to allow the eye to move from top to bottom in the frame. The mind sees the line and intuitively traces it throughout the photograph.

In this photograph, the fence shape suggests a kind of rudimentary Z, with the top leg of the Z connecting to the gray-colored fence in the background. The bottom part of the fence cuts across the frame in the foreground to suggest the bottom leg of the Z. At the most severe angle of the Z is Shaun who helps suggest motion by leaning into the area that the most severe angle of the Z is pointing. The fence helps point the viewer's eye to Shaun, the focal point of the picture. The lines from the sidewalks tend to converge where Shaun is standing, and those lines help the viewer see that Shaun is the subject.

This next photograph relies on the steps and the railing in the stairwell to

This photo, taken as part of a seminar on photography, uses the Z-shaped pattern as well.
Photo by Mathew Berman. Used with permission.

212

suggest the Z pattern. Winding country roads work as S patterns. Mountain ranges work as Z patterns. A series of clouds can create an S or Z pattern, even the gangway on a ferryboat can make the pattern. The playground equipment may imitate an S or Z. A rope, a walkway or a driveway can do the same. Fabric, jewelry and other objects also may be arranged in an S or Z pattern. Force yourself to look for these patterns and you will create a photograph that others will enjoy and that will draw them to your words.

Habit 5: Look for contrasts – winner-loser, big-small, light-dark.

Contrasts often help tell a story. Imagine a photograph of an athlete who is jubilant in victory with her hands stretched over her head, but beside her is her defeated opponent; shoulders slumped, holding back the tears. That's a contrast.

Look for contrasts as you compose your shot. Note the solid colors in this subject's wardrobe against the landscape background. The natural colors of the vegetation and the rust of the farm machinery provide a contrast for the brighter colors in Taylor's outfit.

Or perhaps you'd like to think of this shot as a contrast between new and old. Taylor's clothes

The solid colors in the subject's attire contrast with the weeds and disabled farm implement.

reflect modern comforts: store bought sweatshirt and scarf, modern necklace. Compare this to the era of the farm tool, which seems to have been sitting there for half a century, perhaps before the modern department store made Taylor's outfit readily available.

Overall, the photograph is well-balanced and possesses a nice Z pattern as suggested in the last habit. These attributes are enhanced by the contrasts. Consider contrasts as you select your subject matter.

Habit 6: Use the rule of thirds.

The viewing area in the viewing frame of a camera can be reduced to a kind of tic-tac-toe board with lines dividing the area of the frame into three equal parts, both horizontally and vertically.

Can you see it?

According to the **rule of thirds**, the subject of the photograph works best by placing him or her where the lines intersect. The rule says that a major element placed at one of their junctions will create the more dynamic picture. Usually, you will have to impose the imaginary lines on the viewing area and move yourself around to put your subject either to the top left, bottom left, top right or bottom right. However, sometimes the lines occur in nature and you can use them to guide your composition. For instance, horizons could be on one of the horizontal lines just above or below the center of the frame.

The subject is in the corner of the frame, not the center.

In the photograph of Shaun sitting on the bench, the idea of the tic-tac-toe board is suggested, but, in this case, the thirds resemble quadrants. His head and trunk are in the bottom, right quadrant. The principle would work better had the photographer moved back a few more feet. However, the focal point is concentrated in one corner and that's the idea you want to consider. Practice putting the subject of the shot in one of the corners to create a pleasing composition. Avoid placing the subject in the center of the frame. In photography, the sweet spot tends to be **off-center**, not the bull's eye.

Do you see the leading lines in the photograph? Notice the lines of the fence that move vertically across the background. The slats of the bench move horizontally. They intersect where Shaun is sitting. Those leads intuitively tell the viewer that Shaun is the focal point.

An alternate photograph of the same subject shows more of the foreground and

Lines intersect to point the eye to the focal point.

background and suggests a slightly different mood. The ivy seems to be climbing toward the intersection of the bench, the grass, the fence, and, most importantly, the focal point, Shaun. As you take a photograph, pause, take a deep breath and look for the photograph that can be. Place the subject where the imaginary lines of the thirds intersect and your art will begin to have a professional feel about it and your editor will remember you fondly.

Habit 7: Look for repeated patterns.

Anyone who decorates knows the benefit of repeating a pattern in the rug, sofa and other areas in a living area. The use of a similar colored wood or a stand of various sizes of candles creates a cozy feel to a room.

The best composition uses **repeated patterns** for a well-balanced feel. The patterns can be dramatic such as a checkered pattern on a floor, on a pillow and in your subject's shirt; however, the better patterns are subtler and have the power of a whisper over a shout.

At first glance, the picture of Taylor may not reveal repetition until you see the picture as a series of lines and shapes. In particular, see the arm rail leading from one corner of the photograph, moving at a sharp 45-degree angle to the porch railing. Taylor's right arm rests on the porch railing, which leads to her left arm, which angles toward her face. The arm rail and the position of Taylor's arm repeat the line, but one mirrors the other.

The subject's left arm makes an angle like the railing.

Perhaps easier to see is the repetition of the spindles in the porch supports, the rectangles in the shutters, the horizontal lines on the clay pots, and the repetition of the lines in the vinyl siding. In a color photo, repetition could be found in the colors too.

Habit 8: Saturate the scene with a variety of shots.

In **saturation photography**, a highly effective photographer takes a series of photographs from long range, middle range and close up. Habit 1 of highly effective photographers taught you to move in; now you may want to consider two other angles. The idea is that your editor may want to show a **panoramic view**, a long shot. To play it safe, it's good form to take a long shot.

The long shot provides lots of visual detail, but notice how small the subject appears. That's the trade-off in these kinds of photographs. In general, it's a good practice to keep your subject's head about the size of a quarter. In this photograph, you should see the rule of thirds operating. The subject is in the bottom, right-hand third of the shot. The subject could have been photographed deeper in the right-hand corner, but the cabinet on the right and the piano on the left provide a natural frame to force the viewer's eye to the focal point. Note also that the subject is facing into the photograph, which is considered part of good composition that suggests balance.

A long shot provides detail of a room.

In the next photograph, Taylor's entire body can be seen, but the appearance of the room is minimized. Now the editor must decide if she wants to include the room to give a sense of environment, or compromise and settle for some room and the entire subject.

In the long-range photograph and the medium-range photograph, the photographer dropped to one knee to shoot the subject's face straight on. Most people shoot photographs from eye level. For a novel effect, consider getting very low or very high. Lie down and shoot a photograph from the worm's eye view; then take the same photograph from the bird's eye view. The results will surprise you, and, more importantly, your editor.

A medium shot is a closer shot of the subject.

This third photo of Taylor may be too much of a close-up for the article that it accompanies; however, if you submit the long shot, medium shot and close-up shot, your editor will have a choice. This choice will provide a variety of layout and design solutions to play the article. The saturation approach can only improve the chances of your work getting published.

A close-up shot gives the picture a different feel.

You now know the seven habits of highly effective photographers. These ideas can be summed up with the three **C**'s:

1) Choose a strong focal point.
2) Close in on your subject.
3) Capture the moment.

Test yourself

For fun, examine the photograph to test yourself. How many of the seven principles of composition can you find in the photograph? The answer appears following the picture.

How many composition principles can you find?

Answer: This photograph is a caricature of good composition.

1) **Foreground and background.** The foreground and background include some repetition, wood and lines either moving horizontally, vertically or diagonally.

2) **Lines.** The shadow from the post and railing are lines that push the eye to the focal point, enhanced by the white in Taylor's shoes and jacket.

3) **Z pattern.** The furniture forms the Z pattern.

4) **Contrasts.** Taylor wears a contrasting black and white outfit.

5) **Rule of thirds.** She is located at the top right-hand corner of the photograph where two of the lines in the rule of thirds intersect.

6) **Repetition and patterns.** The wood slats and boards are a repetitious element as is the pattern in the gingham fabric on the bench and table.

7) **Saturation.** The photograph was taken from a high angle, a kind of long shot.

Biography of Eva Marie Everson

Eva Marie Everson

The work of award-winning author, Eva Marie Everson, includes the novel trilogy *Shadow of Dreams, Summon the Shadows*, and *Shadows of Light*. Her nonfiction includes *Intimate Moments with God, Intimate Encounters with God*, and *Silver and Gold*. In 2005 look for *The Pot Luck Club* and *What Your Kids Won't Tell You*. Eva Marie is a contributing author to a number of publications. She has worked as an editor and teaches at various writers' workshops and seminars. Eva Marie Everson is a member of Advanced Writers & Speakers Association and the recipient of the Member of the Year Award for 2002. She writes for a number of magazines and has a regular feature at Crosswalk.com's faith channel.

Eva Marie Everson grew up in a rural southern town in Georgia just outside of Savannah. She is married, has four children and three grandchildren, and lives in Orlando, Florida. She taught Old Testament theology for six years at Life Training Center in Longwood, Florida. She has written articles for Crosswalk.com including the *Falling Into The Bible* series, and has had regular columns in *Christian Bride Magazine* and *Christian Retailing Magazine*. Eva Marie has been featured on *Decision Today* radio broadcast. She was a guest speaker at the *Louise Mandrell Theater*.

Interview with Eva Marie Everson

Q: In 2002, you and six other journalists toured the Holy Land on assignment. Your photographs of the Holy Land were used with the article you wrote for an online news and commentary page. Talk about the photographs that you took in the 10-day tour. How many were worth publishing?

A: I took about 350 photographs. I'd have to say nearly all of them were worth publishing, though some were of interest only to those of us who went and others were duplicates.

Q: What is the most difficult part of writing and taking photographs when on assignment? Is it that you miss a quotation as you aim the camera? Or, is it that you can concentrate on one at the expense of the other? Or what?

A: I used a 35mm camera used by professional shooters. Several of the other women took small digitals, but I took a 35mm camera and a variety of lenses, which meant lugging them. But I said over and over, "You just wait until you see my photographs. You'll be so jealous." And they were. My photos were just absolutely fabulous. The other difficulty was that I missed a few prime shots because we were in a van and I'd asked so many times to "Stop!" that I hated to ask again and again. Now I regret it. When we were driving north along the Dead Sea, we came around a curve and there was a spectacular sight! A mountain reflected so perfectly in the water, one couldn't tell where the real mountain stopped and the reflection began. I regret that I didn't say, "Stop." Even our tour guide said later that was a regrettable miss.

Thirdly, when we were at specific locations, I always had to wait for the rest of the tour group to "get outta' the way!" Or, I'd have to run ahead of them. I didn't want the raw beauty of the land to be interrupted by humans. However, I realize that a subject can enhance the photograph and provide scale. For my purposes, I wanted to show the rugged scenery with its timelessness.

Finally, I found that many shots just couldn't be obtained. I could TAKE the picture, but I couldn't grasp what was happening inside of me, the emotion. It's a shame we can't bottle the emotion and bring it back with us.

Q: What fictional techniques can be seen in this article on Israel?

A: With fiction you paint a picture with your words that tell a story. I used that same technique in this article here. I wanted to tell both the story of Mary and the story of "the reader."

Q: More writers like fiction writing than feature writing. What is the better way to begin as a writer? Do fiction writers sacrifice their craft when writing feature articles or vice versa or neither?

A: I like fiction writing, of course, but I found that I love feature writing! This was the experience of a lifetime! As a fiction writer, I used the tools of the trade to convey the emotion of what we experienced while in the Holy Land. One does not merely tour the Holy Land. It is experienced!

I would never suggest beginning as a fiction writer. The competition is too great and it's such a difficult genre. I tell writers in my workshops to begin by writing for their local newspaper or church paper. Write a neighborhood watch newsletter and pass it out to the neighbors or a similar type of thing. Start small. I wrote a ton of devotional articles for online publication without making a dime before I ever got paid, and you know? It was a great experience. No regrets.

Q: Do fiction writers sacrifice their craft when writing feature articles?

A: Absolutely not. The only time you sacrifice your craft is when you quit writing all together. But it's rare to find a writer, or so I'm told, who can write both fiction and nonfiction. So my biggest suggestion is to find the genre you are good at – not the one you think you want to write in – and give it your best.

Cutlines

The pages ahead feature photographs taken by Eva Marie Everson when she worked as a journalist in Israel. You may recall from Chapter 4, *Developing the article and more*, that the information under a photograph is called a **cutline**. It is commonly known as a caption, but some publications use other names. For instance, high-quality magazines such as *National Geographic* call this information a **legend**. Legends are written by someone other than the writer of the article and the legend writer conducts her own research to amplify the photograph. The goal of a good cutline or legend is to tell the reader something beyond what is visible in the photograph.

In the second photograph featuring a panoramic view of the Jezreel Valley, Eva Marie Everson could have written the following: "The Jezreel Valley has some of the most fertile farmland in Israel and is a place where, atop a mountain such as Mt. Tabor or Mt. Gilboa, the scenes are breathtaking! It is rich with agriculture and natural springs and it's at one of those springs that a famous story from the Bible took place."

Remember Gideon? Judges 7 says Gideon and his men were camped at the spring of Harod, which is in the Jezreel Valley. It was there that God told Gideon to take the men down to the water, then have them drink. Gideon was to look for those who drank the water like a dog vs. those who drank hand to mouth. Three hundred men did the latter, and these were the men God used in the battle against the Midianites. The others got the consolation prize of going home.

Israel photo #1

This unidentified woman working in a pottery shop was photographed in Safed, a town known for art and mysticism in Israel. The subject is smiling, which is a modest distraction; however, she isn't looking directly at the camera and that makes the photograph publishable. The colors and textures create a contrast and the photograph is framed by the railing. As you photograph subjects, work hard to get their names and ask them a question. Ask about the activity or reactions that the person received as they work. Ask an open-ended question that may help you create an exciting cutline. If possible, try to get the subject to tell you a story, an

Photograph by Eva Marie Everson
Used with permission.

anecdote, about the first day on the job, the hardest day on the job, the funniest day on the job – anything that will enhance the cutline information. Remember: You are a storyteller.

Israel photo #2

This next photograph shows the Jezreel Valley from atop Mt. Tabor. Notice the S pattern in this long shot. If needed, Eva Marie Everson could have added the information mentioned above to create a second story, a mini-article within the article.

Photograph by Eva Marie Everson
Used with permission.

Falling into the Bible: Mary's well
By Eva Marie Everson
Used with permission

Editor's Note: In June 2002, author Eva Marie Everson toured the Holy Land as a journalist and photojournalist. This article is one of a series that she wrote for Crosswalk.com, an online service.

We were on our way to Nazareth, to a place called Mary's Well located at the northern end of Rehov Masqobia. As our van wound along the curving roads and up along the rolling drives, I gazed out the window at the modern architecture and tried to remind myself this place had once been the boyhood home of Jesus. It wasn't computing... and then we came to a stop and our tour guide said, "This is Mary's Well." And just like that, I was transported to another time and a very different lifestyle.

Water is a vital part of my daily life, but fetching it isn't. I get up in the morning, turn on the faucet in the bathroom sink and brush my teeth. I then pad into the kitchen, pour water into the coffeemaker and voila! Coffee. During the day I shower in water, drink water, cook with water, saturate my lawn with water, and never give it a second thought. Once a month my husband and I pay the water bill, but even that's not bad enough to make me ponder over the source of it.

But in Mary's day, a young girl or woman had to go to the town's water supply – a well – to draw water for the use of her family and for herself. While we were in Hazor, we climbed into one such well, treading carefully down narrow steps that led nearly 135 feet into the earth. Climbing down wasn't such a chore. Climbing up was another story.

"Now imagine doing this while carrying jugs of water," explained our tour guide Miriam Feinberg Vamosh, author of *Daily Life at the Time of Jesus*. I couldn't. I was too busy working at catching my breath.

Biblical history

The Hebrew word for well is "beer" and is the forename of places like Beersheba (Beer'Sheva) where Abraham's Well is located. Many of the ancient wells found in the Holy Land were dug from limestone and oftentimes had steps that led into them. Some were supplied by springs. Women and young girls went to the wells to draw water typically in the early hours of the day, in order to have water to prepare bread that would be taken out into the fields.

"The girls would have to be physically strong, in order to lift the skins or jars that were quite large," reports Miriam. "They would also have to be aware of their surroundings, especially if the well or spring were outside of the town, in order to protect their property and themselves from marauders and mischief-makers."

For centuries there was only one well in Nazareth. During the period in which Mary lived there as a young girl and later as a wife and mother, she would have walked to this well daily, never dreaming, surely, that one day it would carry her name as a memorial.

According to tradition, Mary had gone to the well when the angel Gabriel visited her. "In the sixth month, God sent the angel Gabriel to Nazareth, a town in Galilee, to a virgin pledged to be married to a man named Joseph, a descendant of David. The virgin's name was Mary. The angel went to her and said, 'Greetings, you who are highly favored! The Lord is with you.' Mary was greatly troubled at his words and wondered what kind of greeting this might be. But the angel said to her, 'Do not be afraid, Mary, you have found favor with God. You will be with child and give birth to a son, and you are to give him the name Jesus. He will be great and will be called the Son of the Most High. The Lord God will give him the throne of his father David, and he will reign over the house of Jacob forever; his kingdom will never end.'" (Luke 1:26-33 NIV)

Of course the Bible doesn't tell us where Mary was when she received the news, but the traditional story of Mary's Well is generally accepted. Scholars can argue about location, but they must agree this well was the only source of water during those days.

There are several biblical stories of women who went to wells to draw water and had life-altering experiences. Rebekah's trip led to her marriage to Isaac (Genesis 24). The Samaritan woman (John 4) came at an unusual time of day (noon, when fewer people would be present) and ended up confronting the Messiah.

According to the story, Jesus, who was resting at the well, asked the woman for water. Because He was Jewish and she was Samaritan (bitter enemies), the woman questioned His request. We can imagine the crinkle around His eyes as He said to her, "If you knew the gift of God and who it is that asks you for a drink, you would have asked him and he would have given you living water." (John 4:10 NIV) Before their conversation had come to an end, He explained to her:

"Everyone who drinks this water will be thirsty again, but whoever drinks the water I give him will never thirst. Indeed, the water I give him will become in him a spring of water welling up to eternal life." (John 4:13,14, NIV)

Coming to the well for these two women meant life would never be the same.

Falling in

Today in a catacomb of an elaborate church known as St. Gabriel's Greek Orthodox Church of the Annunciation, a first century spring of water continues to flow. One can walk from the square where Mary's Well stands, through the Grotto of St. Gabriel's and into the cool sanctuary of the church. The architecture is rich and dark. It's easy to feel transported within these hallowed walls and to imagine a young virgin coming to this very area to fetch water for her family. But is it accurate?

Few viewers of Franco Zeffirelli's *Jesus of Nazareth* can forget the picture actress Olivia Hussey made in her portrayal of Mary the mother of Jesus. Early in the epic film, the young Mary, sleeping soundly in her modest bedroom, is startled awake by the angel Gabriel. She grips the sheets in her tiny fists as her hair cascades over her slender shoulders and her lips and eyes form a look of anxiousness.

Over the years many have held such a vision of the annunciation, that little sneak preview Gabriel gave to the virgin betrothed to a carpenter named Joseph, letting her know life would never be the same. Tradition, on the other hand, gives us the story of Mary at the well.

If tradition is truth – and I have to admit to having my senses tantalized by such a story – then Mary came for water that would not satisfy and left knowing she'd be the mother of the One who'd one day say He was Living Water.

The question for me is not whether or not Mary was at the well or asleep in her bed. The question for me is whether or not I look for God's purpose and plan for my life in the every day activities that I do.

An additional question is whether or not I spiritually protect myself from my "enemy," that age-old mischief-maker himself, Satan.

Jesus has beckoned us to come, to drink, to be satisfied. Not because it's a daily chore, but because it's a daily desire. Each day, as we seek to know God more intimately – to reach His heart, even – we draw from the well of His Word; we drink from His sustaining presence in prayer.

You never know whom you might meet when you come to the water.

And this is part of what I learned when I fell into the Bible.

Exercises

1) Re-read the article and ask yourself what photographs does this article suggest?
2) If you could use three photographs, what would you imagine would be the best picks? Would it be a long shot, a close-up shot of a woman going to a well or a close-up of the well mechanism or what?
3) This article is written as a personal reflection and a feature. What do you like about it, and what would you like to change?
4) Notice Eva Marie Everson's use of the present tense in her quotations. What is the danger of present tense?
5) Can you think of a topic you could write about that would include this kind of technique?

Summary

Writer Vie Herlocker does well as a writer but found that she could enhance her freelance income by taking photographs to accompany her articles. "I had never taken a photography class, or even read anything about taking photos before learning the seven habits," she said. "The best way I know to express how helpful that information was to me is to let you know that I won second place in a photography contest this year!"

Whether the camera is a 35mm, disposable or digital, good photographs are possible using seven basic principles. Photographers should strive to follow as many of the following principles as possible: get close, monitor the background and foreground, look for shapes and lines, look for Z patterns and S patterns, look for contrasts, use the rule of thirds, seek repeated patterns, and practice saturation coverage of close ups, medium shots and long shots. This chapter included an interview with writer Eva Marie Everson who writes fiction, but knows how to create a powerful feature article. She took photographs while in the Middle East on assignment and found that a few simple ideas made her work publishable.

This chapter has presented seven habits of highly effective photographers, ideas that you can use to make your work more attractive to an audience. To practice these timeless principles of visual composition, take a walk and stop periodically and compose a photograph. Try the rule of thirds. Think about contrasts. Consider repetition, lines and shapes. In all these cases, you may not find an ideal photograph, but you'll come close. Look for the photograph that is there. Really look and you will see it, although it may not include all the composition principles.

It is like a game of golf. A hole-in-one is rare; however, the shot that is closest to the pin is considered excellent golf. As you take a photograph, concentrate on the ideal, but be ready to take a solid photograph that meets at least one of the composition principles. Over time you will find that your eye will improve, and then your photographs will improve, enhancing your sense of fulfillment and your paycheck.

Chapter 10

SHOP talk for writers
FeatureWriting.Net/Strategy

Chapter at-a-glance

> Using a mnemonic as you write
> Applying Selection, History, Observation and Perspective in your feature article
> Inserting color in all your writing

When writers meet, the conversation often turns to shop talk, the business of writing. When a new writer gets a chance to talk to a shopworn veteran writer, she may ask, "What is your greatest piece of practical advice?" eager to plum the fiery wisdom from all those trips to Mt. Helicon and visits with the writing muse. The answer: avoid over-reliance on one source when preparing an article. It's the most common mistake of new writers, new freelancers and new journalists.

The following is a strategy for developing an assignment for general-interest and specialty publications using a multi-source approach. The following strategy uses the acronym SHOP to emphasize the steps good writers review in preparing an article. SHOP stands for:

- **Selection**
- **History**
- **Observation**
- **Perspective**

Finding your angle sometimes feels like spotting a frog in a birdhouse, but look hard enough and the angle may reveal itself.

The approach

In the next chapter is an A-to-Z list of topics that can be fashioned into a timeless feature article. For the most part, these ideas include the **SHOP** approach. As a writer, you can use the SHOP formula to get a sense on how to write the piece. In some cases, you may not need the entire sequence, but always consider the various stages of story production to make yours full-bodied: a metaphor here, dialogue there, rich details, the telling quote – all meant to transform your words into pictures and ideas and scenes that leave your audience thrilled, exhausted, perplexed and satisfied.

Selection

For each assignment, think about **Selection**. Selection is the topic that you will cover, but it considers the idea, the thrust. Think of Selection as unwrapping the layers of an onion. You peel off the top layer, revealing a second layer. You peel back that layer and you find yet another, then another. Story selection is like that. You select a topic and then realize that the topic is a little deeper. You may choose not to go deeper. You may want to stay with the top layer, but you sense you have a direction. You have an angle, one that you selected.

Let's examine an example to illustrate the point. Suppose you discover a schoolhouse more than 100 years old that is in the final stages of remodeling by a man who once attended classes in it. You think SHOP. Let's say that the restoration of the old schoolhouse meant pulling back layer upon layer of linoleum flooring to reveal the rich grain of original hard wood floors. Think of your research as going deeper and deeper into the project.

Selection is the first part. For this assignment, you select as the thrust of your article the care and attention that the man has invested in the project. You set up an interview and visit the man at the schoolhouse, now in his possession. You dress for the part, knowing that the building may be like a construction site, with sawhorses, dust and paint. You bring a notebook, camera, flash with fresh batteries, a pocket tape recorder and a list of questions that you formulate in the planning time before the interview.

If you're not careful, you may stall here and think of this primary source as the only source you need. That approach is called the one-source article, and must be avoided. Most publications want much more than one voice quoted in an article. However, other publications want art – photography, graphics, maps, charts and so on – and only a modest amount of information, and may settle for one source. Others want lots of art and lots of copy. For this reason, it is much better to check with the editor before the assignment, but all editors will be impressed with authoritative sources that help supplement your primary source. In short, get in the habit of always exceeding your editor's expectations. Never settle for a one-source feature article.

Let's look at a one-source piece that is based on a real article, but changed to fit the considerations of this chapter. The article is not italicized while my comments are in italics. Many of the comments concern style as well as the SHOP strategy. When you are unsure about the appropriate style to use in writing an article, reach for the *Associated Press Stylebook and Briefing on Media Law*. It reads a bit like a dictionary, but it answers all those questions about when to abbreviate, rules on city names combined with states, and the preferred approach to capitalization. Your publication will have its own style, but many publications default to AP style when they have no firm policy. For instance, one newsletter publisher drops the article "the" in all its copy. It may sound odd, but the publisher said that her "the"-free articles possess a breezy tone to them, a quality that she finds attractive. Now to the article.

One man's love for a one-room school

Good idea to provide a headline for the editor. It helps all of us to know what the article is about before we start reading. These days we also provide a second, smaller headline and a paragraph of summary of the article. We are doing these at-a-glance helps to make reading the article as easy as possible for the audience. In online writing, the idea is called "chunking."

It's been a real labor of love for Tom Howard. *Indent the next paragraph for effect. Many feature articles resort to a tight lead, also spelled lede, that uses 15 words or less. The anecdotal lead is in demand, but you are the wordsmith, so it's your job to select the lead that is best for your story.*

> **Tip:** Use lowercase when you are unsure if the word should be capitalized. Most publications don't capitalize words in headlines, commonly referred to as titles. Also, most publications don't use capital letters or caps for much of anything beyond proper names. It's called down style.

Now 70, Howard studied as a third-grade student in a one-room schoolhouse, known as the Curtis School in Spalding County, when it closed in 1942 in this rural part of western New York. *(If the article appears in a publication in the mythical area of Spalding County, New York, most readers will understand the building's location; however, if the* article will be published in a regional or national periodical, it's better to give a location that nearly any reader can understand. Also, note the correct use of "a" in "a one-room schoolhouse. According to AP style, the rule for "a, an" says that the article "a" should be used before a consonant sound as in "a one-year term.") After years of renovating, Howard will celebrate the grand opening of the schoolhouse next month. *(Give the precise month. Readers will know to look at the top of the page for the publication's date.)*

"Third grade is a time when the imagination is full tilt," said Howard. "Restoring Curtis School was like restoring that part of my imagination that just needed dusting off to get back to full strength."

Three generations of Howards attended Curtis School and a few will be present Sunday when the public is invited to an open house from 10 a.m. to 4 p.m. *(We call this information the news peg. It is the reason that the article is being published now. When a news peg is not as apparent, you have to be more creative to invent a reason for the article to be of relevance. Perhaps it is an anniversary of the first schoolhouse ever built, the one-year anniversary of the project's beginning, or it is an offbeat link to the national debate on rising construction costs of new schools.)*

Howard of Palachin, New York, *(Use abbreviation after city name, Palachin, N.Y. Is that the correct spelling of Palachin? If so, write "stet" or "cq," old-school phrases that let the editor know that you double-checked the odd spelling.)* is the fourth generation to live in this part of New York, just yards from the schoolhouse door. Built in 1870, the schoolhouse rests on the family farmstead.

"I lost out on a reason to miss school," Howard said. "I just opened our front door and strolled a few steps to the schoolhouse door."

Because he lived so close, Howard had the morning job of carrying water in a pail from the family's springhouse to supply the school's water cooler for the day.

Howard's brother, Joseph, acquired the building when the state auctioned off one-room schoolhouses in the 1950s. *(Be cautious here. We have now introduced two men with the same last name. We must be careful not to confuse the reader in future attribution. Sometimes a writer must use both first and last names to keep the identifications straight. Since Joe Howard is deceased, the reader will understand that the quotations must be from the surviving Howard.)* The structure was used for storage and Joseph planned to turn it into a machine shop, which *(good use of "which." Use "that" when no comma appears.)* he successfully avoided, Howard says with a laugh. *(How much did Joseph Howard pay? In many cases, these structures are sold for $1 to rid the school district or* *municipality for the liability of a dilapidated building that is unsound for use.)*

Howard bought it after his brother's death and wanted to restore the building to its original 1870s state. *(Note the correct use of the "s" for a decade.)* He spent the last seven years researching the school's history as he repaired and painted the building.

A 1932 photo of the classroom shows rows of 21 students sitting at their desks, including Howard's brother, Joseph; and sister, Jill; along with the teacher. This photograph served as a blueprint to help Howard redecorate. Two of the desks are intact from 1870, but most were reconstructed from wood, using the original ornate metal frames found in a storage building on the family farm. The original school bell, several books, bookends, pictures, records and report cards tell the story of the by-gone era.

"At first people were reluctant to come around or get involved in the project because they wanted to find out if I was serious about it," Howard said. "But in recent years, it's really brought the community together. People have stopped by just about every day that I'm here to see what I'm doing and tell me about their memories of the school." *(Quotations read best when the speaker's identification is placed after the first sentence as it is in this paragraph.)*

In this article, the writer interviewed Howard. For her, the **Selection** revolved around the remodeling of the schoolhouse. The writer provided some modest history, but she didn't give the reader an in-depth explanation on Howard's reasons for remodeling the schoolhouse. Howard mentioned his imagination as a factor, but the audience may want more explanation. The writer could have improved the article by asking other questions that help the reader identify with Howard's motivation.

Remember the five W's – who, what, when, why, where? The *why* question is usually the most interesting, and in this case, it could have provided a robust psychological profile for this act of restoration.

In this article, the writer's thrust was the refurbishing project. She selected this angle as the main direction; however, she could have pulled back for a wide-angle shot of the action, and featured the universal elements of Tom Howard's work. Selection includes thinking about the way the audience will relate to the article. Some may find Howard's labor significant, and be inspired to imitate it. Others will vicariously experience the work, and share in a sense of satisfaction for preserving a historic artifact. The narrative is replete with nostalgia. That feeling will appeal to some readers, but the writer who selects well can appeal to tiers of audiences, some of whom are curious about bygone days and a person's passion to reclaim the past. What drives that kind of ambition? Do each of us see ourselves in that kind of activity? Thinking through these kinds of questions will help you select a primary, secondary, and perhaps a tertiary angle for your opus.

History

To make this story more informative, the writer could include **History**. For our purposes, history refers to background. What is the history of the structure, or what background can be provided to make the reader better appreciate the novelty of a one-room schoolhouse? To get this information, the writer is compelled to seek other sources. A good rule is to force yourself to talk to at least three sources if you can. It makes for a better article. Imagine a quotation on the history from the teacher who instructed Howard!

To learn information on one-room schoolhouses, I opened Associations Unlimited electronic database at http://galenet.galegroup.com. Remember these databases are too expensive for ordinary people to use; therefore, you have to use a university library or use the paper edition, *Encyclopedia of Associations, an Association of Unlimited References,* at the public library. Using the Associations Unlimited database, I entered the term, "one-room," into a search, and found nothing. Then I tried "school house," two words, and obtained the following result:

1850 School House Foundation
c/o Carl F. Greenler
198 Locust St., Ste. 201
Lynn, MA 01904-0000 USA
Phone:(781) 593-3942
Primary Contact: Carl F. Greenler, Contact
Founded: 1997. **Members:** 8. LOCAL. **Description:** Works to restore and reuse the oldest schoolhouse in the city, built in 1850.
Conventions/Meetings: annual board meeting.
SIC: 8641 - Civic & Social Associations
Subject Descriptor(s): Historic Preservation
Subject Category: Northeastern States; Cultural Organization.

While this organization appeared promising, contact with it would require a toll call, so I entered another term. The subject descriptor above noted "historic preservation," a term that I tried next and found 42 national and regional organizations that could provide background on the history of one-room schoolhouses.

I chose one that I thought was the best fit and sent the contact person an email.

National Trust for Historic Preservation, Northeast
6401 Germantown Ave.
Philadelphia, PA 19144 USA
Phone: (215) 848-8033
Fax: (215) 848-5997
E-Mail: adrian_fine@nthp.org
Affiliated With: National Trust for Historic Preservation

Next, I conducted an Internet search using dogpile, the metasearch engine. I entered "one-room schoolhouse" as a search term, and found a site called the "One-Room Schoolhouse Resource Center, a compilation of historical one-room school resources throughout North America that are available on the Internet" and located at: http://sites.onlinemac.com /kcampbell/One_Room Schoolhouses.htm.

The best part of this web page were links to one-room schoolhouse projects around the nation, but most of the sites did not include contact information, which means that the web site information could not be checked. In addition, the resource person who may know about the area was impossible to contact. However, the home page for the One-Room Schoolhouse Resource Center included an email address, and I sent that person a note asking for suggestions on experts who I could interview on one-room schoolhouses.

This entire online searching process took about an hour, but it paid dividends. If nothing else, the article on Howard could mention the One-Room Schoolhouse Resource Center web site and describe some of the pages and links. For instance, a bulletin board on the home page described families who are living in the schoolhouses, and how they use them beyond a domicile. One couple operated an antique store; others had just purchased a one-room schoolhouse and wanted information on ideas for adding plumbing and electricity without unduly disturbing the historic integrity of the structure. A curious writer could explore the pages to gain an appreciation for the swell of national interest in these buildings. For instance, many of the sites described the curriculum used at the turn of the 20th century as reading, arithmetic and writing; others commented on the typical school day. These details can supplement Howard's recollections.

A web page for Calvert County, Md., at http://calvert-county.com/school.htm, included detail that could be rewritten for an article. The article included a contact person and her telephone number, which allows a writer to double-check the information for accuracy. The page said students from the one-room schoolhouse era read from red-and-tan *McGuffy Readers*, wrote on slates and ate mid-day meals from tin lunch pails. At recess, they played games of "Annie Over" and "Bug in the Gully." During cold weather, an iron chunk stove in the center of the room provided heat. This detail enriches an article, but it must be checked.

Observation

Observation includes all the stimuli from your five senses. Tell the reader what you saw and heard. Describe the texture of the exterior of the one-room schoolhouse. Be precise. Tell the type of wood used for the floor planks. Give colors. If the door creaks, try to relate it to a sound that others may recognize – aluminum bending, typing paper being crushed, or a can of evaporated milk being opened with a screwdriver. Help us experience the moment. How does the chalk sound as it is applied to the slate board once used by students? Count the stars on the American flag. Are there 50? Have insects invaded the walls? Does it remind you of other sights that you can recall to help your audience see what you see, hear what you hear or smell what you smell? The stove odor may be long gone, but buildings can absorb scents, and your cultivated senses can help your reader live the moment along with you.

Be judicious in your use of adjectives and work to be very precise about the nouns. "The wood is faded" is passable as a sentence, but the exact type of wood is so much better. Now describe the pattern on the planks. Help us see the discoloration, the wear, their battered quality that reminds you of those wizened faces of old men who lived full lives, short on regret, long on the suffering that makes people strong.

When you insert observation into your feature article, allow yourself to draw on free writing. Bring to mind those feelings that you associated with the moment. As novelist William Forrester (Sean Connery) tells his young charge Jamal Wallace (Rob Brown) in the film, *Finding Forrester*[56]: "You write your first draft with your heart, and you rewrite with your head."

This advice must be tempered by adding that it works best for free writing where you let yourself draw from your inner voice, unrestrained this time. Once you have dropped the veneer, you can reclaim the observations in their fullness. Practice free writing as soon as you can unload your notes. Write unrestrained. Take a break. Drink some cool water. Now re-read the words and begin editing. Savor the lines that are the strongest, but most faithful to the observation. Resist the temptation to

---

[56] Rich, M. (2000). *Finding forrester*. Directed by Gus Van Sant. Produced by Dany Wolf and Jonathan King. Culver City, CA: Columbia Pictures.

make almost right, right. If the pattern on the floor resembles a Rorschach personality test, don't make it into a Simpson's cartoon character.

In an interview with Evangelical Press Association, actor Tom Key of the award-winning *Cotton Patch Gospel* musical said:

> The great temptation is to be sentimental, rather than to tell the truth. It's the opposite mistake that the writer who is not a believer in anything can make, which is to be nihilistic and look at the universe and life and not see any evidence of grace or hope. That's the reverse of sentimentality. Sentimentality on one level is a great heresy; it looks like the truth and makes you feel like the truth, but it's not. I think that's great practical instruction from the angel who inspired John's vision: write down what you see. It's very tempting to write down what you want to see. Or what will sell better. It's tempting to write down fantasy that does not reflect reality – often that sells better.[57]

Record your impressions as factually as is humanly possible, and the impact will be memorable if you strive to release your creativity with honesty. Descriptions from senses can be evocative by their absence. Describe the quiet of the schoolroom or the vacant walls; by contrast, write about the noise that shoes make when steps echo off the cavernous foundation, or tell about the doodles printed ever so faintly on the desktops. Avoid using opinion words such as "a *cheery* color." Instead, examine the log timbers that made up the rear wall. What kind of lumber was used? Are they planks of rough cherry wood, or walnut or spruce or some other material? Smooth or choppy? Pitted? Weathered? You tell us.

Mine for anecdotes. Did anyone carve his or her names in the clapboard siding, spray paint gang letters, or post yard sale notices? Can Howard recall some playful moments in the building that you can craft into an anecdote that breathes life into the forlorn solitude of a long-abandoned building? Ask Howard if anyone hauled parts of the structure West for use by wagon trains. Be offbeat. Be inventive. Use your imagination to ask a series of questions that may irrigate Howard's memory. Don't be satisfied with a cursory look at the various parts of the building. Study the structure on a ladder and get on the ground and look at the foundation. Is it fragile and full of insects?

---

[57] Trouten, D. (2003, February 23). Key: Art is about evoking the truth. Evangelical Press Association. Retrieved February 23, 2003, from http://www.gospelcom.net/epa/html/q_a.html.

Ask Howard to comment on what you are seeing. Put him in situations that are likely to make him recall some distant memory that will make the kind of short story that leaves your audience smiling with identification. Howard may have never smoked his first cigarette, but as he leans down to inspect the foundation, he may recall the naughty boys who once hid near the timber foundation to practice their cigarette moves à la Humphrey Bogart.

As you leisurely investigate the structure, use the time to prod Howard. Ask him if anyone else wanted the building besides his brother. Did anyone mind that the Howard family bought it? All the time, look, listen, collect information from all your senses including that unnamed additional sense that tells you when people are sad, fulfilled, edgy or uncomfortable. Be sure to ask your source about those impressions. As Howard relaxes, he will begin confiding some of his innermost impressions that will help your audience appreciate his need to restore his old schoolhouse. Be ready to record those thoughts.

Perspective

The final part of the acronym is P for **Perspective**. In this case, the writer wants to show us the micro picture that highlights the macro picture. Howard's one-room schoolhouse restoration, the smaller picture, is part of the bigger picture, one-room schoolhouses across the nation, education of yesteryear, preservation projects and the curious human need to recall the past with homage.

For **Perspective**, the writer may want to contact the state to get the quantity of one-room schoolhouses surviving in the state or the nation versus the number originally built. Did the state provide a design that all the school districts adopted? Perhaps the state government has a department of historic preservation where you can ask about these structures and their history. Ask the state expert when one-room schoolhouses were the most popular. Ask how many are still in use. You may get a contact for someone in Amish country who can explain how the buildings remain in use in those communities, but faded as populations soared in numbers with the post-war baby boom.

When a state expert isn't available, try a historian at the nearby university. Ask her if anyone knows if any luminaries were educated in one-room schoolhouses. Mine for statistics including the number of one-room schoolhouses that may still survive but in secondary uses.

A good source for information on experts, particularly academia, is ProfNet at http://www.profnet.com. As a freelance writer or reporter, you will be required to enter some basic information on the topic along with your deadline. In return, your request will be sent to the United States or around the world. This web site is an ideal place to start your search, even before you do your primary interview. The expert can send you information via electronic mail. Once you have the first response, you can always ask follow-up questions in a second response. The expert benefits by having her name and specialty recognized in your article. You benefit by using a high-quality source who has studied the issue systematically.

Be sure to check LexisNexis. What other articles have been written about one-room schoolhouses? Read the competition in the press to get names of sources. Call these sources or email them, and ask for others who are knowledgeable about the topic and contact them. Keep peeling back the onion until you have enough great material to write.

As you know, LexisNexis is an electronic database that you'll have to access from a public or university library. As of 2003, an Associated Press article retrieved from LexisNexis said one-room schoolhouses may still be found in operation including one in the town of Shirley and six others on Maine's islands. Of the 125 articles that mentioned one-room schoolhouses, most contained little background on the history of the buildings and didn't quote an authoritative source such as a historian. A review of the list shows that a trend is underway to restore these structures. By reading a series of these articles, the ambitious writer can confidently report that communities from Canada to Chicago to Milwaukee, North and South, are reviving one-room schoolhouses. This finding alone may make the feature writer rethink the direction of the article.

Once we understand that one-room schoolhouses are a popular rehabilitation project, Howard's work becomes the narrative that personalizes a national trend. By mentioning the other restoration efforts, the writer can propel her modest feature article into a "reader" of interest to a national audience. Naturally, she will have to make some contacts with the other regions to capture the flavor of those areas and to verify the information that she has gleaned from her database research.

Once you have gathered all your information, you are ready to write. The finished article will have a meaty quality, editorial heft, the kind of piece that is likely to have shelf-life. Isn't that what you want from your work? By investing in it with some substance, you are creating the kind of prose that your audience will want to preserve and recall when the topic of the next wave of learning standards cascades over weary parents and teachers and families become sentimental about the good old days. As a writer, you have the ability to construct an article of note; the only question is if you are willing to invest the time and energy in crafting a feature article that will endure.

One writer I know praised the SHOP approach, but wondered about the practicality of incorporating all four steps in every article. Good point. A savvy writer is judicious in her pursuit of the elusive feature story. At times, the primary source will be the focus of the work. At other times, the article demands a more global approach. The choice is dictated by your own creativity, your editor's bias and prejudice, and the space and time limitations of the assignment. Naturally, it is easier to cut material than it is to invent it on deadline, so I favor leaning to overkill at the onset.

When I started my career in my slender 20s, writer Craig Massey manhandled a fistful of my recent work, studied it with a grunt, and said, "You're going to make it." How could he know? He didn't. What he knew is what you need to burn deep into that ethereal part of you that would be a pinch of dust if it were visible. That's the part of you that is the deepest you, and it's where you make commitments to yourself. If you commit to explore like Meriwether Lewis of overland expedition fame, you will discover the rarest of connections that will make you the writer of the hour. You can do it. The SHOP formula is just a technique. The real writer succeeds because she is on a mission and she won't relax until she's unleashed that creative energy and given it a voice. That voice is yours and we are all waiting for your unique utterance.

Biography of Wes Pippert

Wesley G. Pippert

The Director of the University of Missouri journalism program in Washington, D.C., Wesley G. Pippert, worked as a foreign correspondent, writer, speaker and educator. He is one of a handful of print reporters in the United States who have had extended assignments covering state capitals, Congress, the White House and an international posting.

Wes spent nearly 30 years with United Press International. He was a Congressional Fellow and also had year-long fellowships at the University of Michigan and Harvard University's Kennedy School of Government. He has an honorary doctorate from Gordon College. In addition, he was a Fellow at the Institute of Politics, and Fellow at the Center for Press, Politics and Public Policy, Kennedy School of Government Harvard University; and Journalism Fellow, National Endowment for the Humanities, University of Michigan.

Wes has written more than 100 articles in publications such as the *New York Times* op-ed page and *Chicago Tribune*. Among his six books is *Land of Promise, Land of Strife.*

Interview with Wesley Pippert

Q: This article contains a number of sources. Did you interview them all at once for the article, or is this a case of working on an assignment a little at a time and combining the interviews?

A: The article was the result of a series of visits throughout Israel, along the Mediterranean, along the Lebanon border, along the Dead Sea and inside a rural area. I took a lot of notes from each location and combined them in a piece that drew from each of the visits.

In reporting and writing, you find that every experience prepares you for what follows. Everything we do is based on what we've done to that point. We store impressions away in our memories and we draw on these experiences when we write.

Q: The reader can see the images of sandy beaches and fresh fruit and appreciate the preciseness of the costs, distances and numbers. When you are selecting color, how do you decide how much to include?

A: Yes, I learned early in my career to gather color. When I covered the White House, for instance, I made a point of noting the weather just in case I needed it later. The senses can add to an article by providing vivid detail. All reporters and writers tend to be observant by instinct. When we're working, we sharpen our senses and tune into the color to help the reader appreciate the moment.

Q: What are your suggestions for writing a good feature article?

A: I have four suggestions for the feature writer. Prepare ahead of time.

1) Do as much preparation ahead of time using previously published clips of articles and the Internet, but always check this information for accuracy.
2) Next, practice being observant. Look for relevant detail that will make your story vivid.
3) Include a variety of perspectives. When conducting a profile piece, for instance, talk to a person's detractors as well as her friends.
4) Finally, work to find some new peg, a new angle, for the article. Make it vivid. Make it fresh. And give the reader a multi-perspective that he or she doesn't know.

Editor's note: Among the many feature articles filed by Wes Pippert in his years as senior correspondent is the following account of a kibbutz. The story records life in the mid-1980s. Little has changed since then in this Middle Eastern country where conflict is part of the day-to-day existence.

Lifestyle in flux on Israel's kibbutzim
By Wesley G. Pippert
Used with permission

Change is sweeping the kibbutz, Israel's grand social experiment. Nowadays children stay at home overnight instead of living separately and their parents go off to work in factories.

The 120,000 men, women and children on Israel's 250 kibbutzim still keep customs and values the first kibbutzniks had at the turn of the century when they worked the land and lived communally.

But change is obvious. Some is a return to the traditional. Instead of the children living, eating and sleeping by themselves, many of them now eat the evening meal and spend the night with their parents.

"It boils down to the night. Where will the children be?" said Raphael Lancer, a member of Nof Ginosar. Previously children were considered "the property of the kibbutzim," Lancer said. "They ignore the needs of the mother."

Now many kibbutzim provide the parents with apartments large enough to let the children eat the evening meal and sleep overnight.

"The parents like children sleeping at home," Lancer said.

"It was the mothers' struggle. It never came from the children," said Yuval Peleg, a member of Kittutz Shefayim.

Peleg has a 14-year-old son who he says decides where he will stay.

"I have never made a decision for him since he was 2," Peleg said. "He decided to stay home until he was 13. All his peers stayed at the children's home. But he had gotten his own computer and didn't want to."

The homecoming has occurred gradually. The orthodox Kibbutz Lavi in the Galilee voted in 1957 to let children live with their parents and spend only the working hours of the day in the children's houses.

"This 'revolutionary' step is one we have never regretted," a Lavi member said.

Most of Israel's kibbutzim still have herds of dairy cows, hundreds of chickens and lush fruit groves. A typical kibbutz has several hundred members and several hundred acres.

The kibbutz cares for every need for its members. There are no salaries, but the kibbutz has annual individual budgets for such things as vacations, clothing, books, gifts, cosmetics and coffee.

Peleg's kibbutz, a "club-type" resort village on the Mediterranean nine miles north of Tel Aviv, is typical of the change in the economy of the kibbutzim.

Twenty-five kibbutzim have guest houses – the largest hotel chain in Israel – with pleasant accommodations and prices that attract not only hard-pressed Israelis but thousands of tourists.

Journalists crossing into Lebanon through the Rosh Hanikra checkpoint frequently stay overnight or eat breakfast at Kibbutz Gesher Haziv, nestled among the hills of Lebanon, the hills of Galilee and the sandy beach of the Mediterranean.

The price: $21 per person for bed and breakfast. Guests occasionally pick their own grapefruit for breakfast or an avocado to take home.

Gesher Haziv's main source of income, however, is a factory that makes high chairs, rockers and play tables.

At orthodox Kibbutz Lavi, the 600 to 700 members eat communally. More than half the guests in its guest house are religiously oriented – and 70 percent of these are Christians who can make a roundtrip to Jesus' hometown of Nazareth or the headquarters of his ministry at Capernaum on the Sea of Galilee in a single day.

Lavi was founded on a barren hilltop in 1949 by 50 settlers from England. It planted trees, built a synagogue, furnished it – and now makes synagogue benches and supplies for export to the United States.

Biography of John Carpenter

John B. Carpenter

John B. Carpenter is editor of *The Herald-News*, Dayton, Tenn., part of the Jones Media Group. A journalist for nearly two decades, John is originally from New England but has lived in Tennessee since 1979.

In 1986 he earned a bachelor's degree in history from Bryan College, Dayton, Tenn. He was editor of the student newspaper there, the same paper that he now advises. In 2002, he received a Master of Science degree in communications with a concentration in journalism management from the University of Tennessee at Knoxville.

Under John's leadership, *The Herald-News* has become an award-winning newspaper. Three times he has won the Tennessee Press Association's first-place award for editorial writing and has also won first-place awards for both his news and feature photography. In addition to being editor, John continues to write for *The Herald-News* and has penned hundreds of feature articles since 1987.

Among his memberships, present and past, are the Tennessee Press Association, National Newspaper Association, East Tennessee Chapter of the Society of Professional Journalists, Chattanooga Press Association, Journalism Education Association and other organizations.

His writings have been published in *Tennessee Press*, *Chattanooga News-Free Press*, *Chattanooga Times, World* magazine and other publications. He also teaches journalism at Bryan College and advises campus media. He and his wife, Karin, have four children and live in Dayton, Tenn.

Teddy Roosevelt may have had some encouragement[58] with his rough ride

By John B. Carpenter

Herald-News Editor

Used with permission

The United States sent about 300,000 soldiers, sailors and Marines into battle against a much smaller, technologically backward country. The fighting would be relatively quick and bloodless but the rebuilding and occupation of the invaded country would last much longer. The war was covered closely by war correspondents traveling with the soldiers. The year was 1898.

No one now living in Rhea County, Eastern Tennessee, was alive in 1898 when Jasper Newton Dills charged up San Juan Hill with Teddy Roosevelt's Rough Riders, but Dills' wife still lives here, and she is a member of an increasingly exclusive sorority: Spanish-American War widows.

Opal (Flood) Dills, 93, lives quietly in a neat little home in South Dayton, Tenn. There are American flags everywhere and she flies two large flags outside her home every day, carefully taking them in every evening at dusk.

Opal has a bit of an independent streak. Her son, James Dill of Dayton, was only able to persuade her to give up her home in Dalton Ga., and move to Dayton so he could better care for her in February 2002. Her daughter and son-in law, John and Anna Lee Osborne, also live in Dayton.

She and her son have fond memories of her husband and his father, even though Jasper was 42 years older than his 22-year-old bride and 73 when James was born.

---

[58] Carpenter, J. (2003, April 27). Dayton woman is one of the few living Spanish-American War widows. *The Herald-News*, pp. A-1, A-9.

"Because he was older, he wasn't working full-time when I was a kid," James said. "We hunted and fished together. I guess I got to know him better than most kids know their father."

Opal prominently displays an old black and white photograph of her husband taken years before his death in 1961 at the age of 94.

Jasper was born in 1867 in Franklin, N.C., just two years following the end of the Civil War. One of 13 children, he soon had to learn to fend for himself after his father died. As a child he acted as a hunting guide for a doctor from Dalton, and when he was 13 he traveled to Dalton to ask the doctor for a job because his mother couldn't afford to feed her large brood anymore. Instead of giving him a job, the doctor took him in and raised him as his own son.

Times were hard and jobs difficult to come by. Jasper was logging giant redwood trees in Oregon when the USS Maine exploded and sank in Havana Harbor and the U.S. declared war on Spain. He figured joining the Army couldn't be any more dangerous than logging. Teddy Roosevelt resigned as assistant secretary of the Navy and raised a regiment of cavalry made up primarily of cowboys and frontiersmen who were spoiling for a fight. Jasper fit the bill. He and his fellow Rough Riders headed for Cuba by way of Florida in order to free the Cuban people from the "Dons," as they called the Spaniards.

The romantic painting of the Rough Riders riding up San Juan Hill with Roosevelt in the lead is based more on legend than fact. Jim said his father always told the story quite differently.

The Spanish soldiers outnumbered the Americans 8,000 to 5,000 and were firmly entrenched on top of San Juan Hill. The "Dons" had snipers in the trees picking off the unprotected American soldiers, according to Jim. Only the officers and the artillery had horses, so most of the Rough Riders were on foot.

"Dad said that when a colored sergeant (probably from the 10th Cavalry, an all-black regiment) saw that the Dons were picking off the high-ranking officers, he jumped up, raised his sword and yelled, 'follow me!' His men started up the hill, and so Teddy Roosevelt pulled out his sword and ordered his men to charge up the hill."

Jasper told his son several stories about his famous commanding officer. He said that Roosevelt, during the battle for San Juan Hill, spotted a black sergeant running back down the hill, drew his pistol and told the sergeant to halt. The sergeant stopped and said, "I'm not running away; I'm going for more ammunition," Jim said.

Shortly following the battle a Red Cross unit was serving coffee and donuts to the exhausted men, but they were charging a nickel for a cup of coffee and a donut and some of the men had no money, as Jasper told the story. "When Roosevelt found out, he drew his saber, charged the Red Cross tent and chased them back down the hill," Jim said. "Then he put his own men in charge of handing out the refreshments. His men really loved him after that."

Of the 306,000 American soldiers who fought in Cuba, only 385 of them died in battle. By comparison, more than 2,000 soldiers died of malaria while waiting in Florida during the seven-month long war.

"The only thing I got out of Cuba was malaria and tuberculosis," Jasper told his son.

He mustered out of the Army around 1900, shortly after serving in China during the Boxer Rebellion.

Jasper became a Baptist preacher and missionary in North Carolina but couldn't find work and joined the Salvation Army in Atlanta.

Opal was born in Eton, Ga., in 1909 of a prominent family. Eton was often referred to as Floodtown after her family, James said.

After the Stock Market Crash of 1929 and the onset of the Great Depression, jobs became even harder to find in the South. Opal hitchhiked to Atlanta in 1931 to look for a job. In need of a place to stay, she spent the night at the Salvation Army.

Jasper was 64 and Opal was 22, but from the beginning that didn't matter.

"I thought he was cute," Opal said.

The couple was married in 1932, and three children followed. Jasper Jr. was born in 1934 and Anna Lee was born in 1936, both in St. Petersburg, Fla., after Jasper and Opal moved there after their wedding to start a new Salvation Army operation. Already suffering from malaria and tuberculosis, Jasper had a heart attack in 1934. James was born in 1940 after the family moved back to Cartooga Jay Mountain, N.C.

Jasper continued to work as a part-time pastor and farmer in spite of his health problems and preached every Sunday morning for many years. Eventually the family moved back to Dalton.

Opal received a flag at Jasper's funeral, which was held with full military honors. She still collects and displays flags to this day. James Thurman, commander of American Legion Post 203 in Spring City, provides Opal with the large flags she flies outside her home and stops by from time to time to visit.

On Sept. 1, Opal will turn 94. She is one of an increasingly small number of Spanish-American War widows. According to the Veterans Affairs Administration, as of October 2002 there were just 262 widows of Spanish-American War veterans still living, and that number likely diminishes drastically with each passing year. She is apparently the only living Spanish-American War widow in Tennessee. The last Spanish-American War veteran, Nathan E. Cook, died in 1992 at the age of 106.

Interview with John Carpenter

Q: Did you use the Internet for any background?

A: I visited about a dozen or so web sites on the day that I wrote this story. I went to several sites for information or verification of historical details about the Spanish-American War, the Sinking of the Maine, Teddy Roosevelt, the Rough Riders, the Buffalo Soldiers and the battle for San Juan Hill or San Juan Heights. I went to several Veterans Administration and American Legion sites to gather information about Spanish-American War veterans and their wives. I also tried to verify the existence of a Cartooga Jay Mountain in North Carolina. I never could find anything on that, but I didn't have a lot of time to look.

When I first started in this business, the World Wide Web was just a twinkle in Al Gore's eye. For research purposes we had an encyclopedia, a biographical dictionary, an atlas and the phone book. Now, the world is literally at our fingertips.

Q: Was it difficult to get your source to provide the color? What did you do to help her recall vivid detail?

A: In truth, most of the interview was conducted with her son, James. Opal would interject some things and clarified a few points for her son, but she wasn't always following the conversation. She's 93, so you can't really blame her. I don't know that I did anything special to get the detail. I had an outline of questions I wanted to ask, but the real key was that we were talking about something that both of them are deeply interested in. When you are interviewing people about their great passions, you pretty much just have to prime the pump and then try to keep up. Generally, the more passionate they are for their subject the more descriptive their detail will be.

Sometimes I had to ask leading or clarifying questions to elicit some additional detail, and I guess I called back once or twice after the interview to get some more information. We sat around the kitchen table, which really did have a ceramic bowl of apples and bananas on it, and talked for a couple of hours. People generally feel most comfortable in their own home. Then too, families do most of their talking around the kitchen table. It's just a good place to do interviews. Don't ever expect to just do a telephone interview and then turn it into a great feature. It's not going to happen.

Q: Did anyone dispute the narrative as it related to Roosevelt? What can a writer do to help prevent disputes?

A: Are you referring to historians or our readers? If readers, then, no. No one called to dispute the account. I skimmed a couple of historical sources on the battle and didn't find any glaring discrepancies with the Dills' account, but, as with most stories, I didn't have a lot of time for research. The newest research tends to support Dill's portrayal of the role of the Buffalo Soldiers and TR's bravado. Whether the hill was actually San Juan Hill or not is in debate (à la Bunker Hill vs. Breed's Hill). Apparently the soldiers referred to it as San Juan Hill.

Reducing or eliminating disputes requires research, research and more research. The more sources the better for any kind of a story. The more sources that actually agree with one another, better still. While living, authoritative sources are the best kind, in this kind of a story, pretty much all you've got to work with are written sources. The Internet has plenty of historical resources, but you have to be choosy about which ones you rely on. Consider what the Web site's agenda is and who is funding it. As a very general rule of thumb, rely on .edu and .gov sites before .coms and .nets.

Q: Who do you most admire as a feature writer?

A: I think John Camp has to be my favorite feature writer, even though he's no longer in newspapers. In 1986—the same year I graduated from college—he won the Pulitzer Prize for feature writing for a series of five articles he wrote the year before on the plight of the small farmer in the Midwest. He has since gone on to become a best-selling mystery writer. His "Prey" series, written under the pseudonym, John Sandford, now has 13 novels. He's also written a number of mysteries under his own name and even a couple of nonfiction works. His work is still quality narrative sprinkled liberally with descriptive detail; he just gets paid a whole lot more for it now.

His series, "Life on the Land: An American Farm Family," which he wrote in 1985 for the *Saint Paul (Min.) Pioneer Press & Dispatch*, is a classic of descriptive narrative. His writing is simple, almost transparent; it never gets in the way of the story. He plays the role of narrator, and his style is familiar, almost as if he were talking to the reader, one-on-one, across the farmer's kitchen table. His descriptions are vivid without being overdone, and he has a gift for weaving in lots of quotations—letting his characters tell the story—while still keeping the story on track.

I particularly enjoy the first piece in the series. Its descriptive passages have an almost hypnotic rhythm that not only paints a picture for the reader but gives him a feeling for what the pace of life is like in farm country.

The landscape is not quite flat—it's a landscape of tilted planes, fields tipped this way or that, almost all showing the fertile loam of recent plowing. The black fields dominate the countryside, interrupted here and there by woodlots, by pasturage where lambs play in the fading sunlight, by red-brick or purple-steel silos, Grant Wood barns and Sears-Roebuck sheds, and by the farmhouses. There's a turn-of-the-century farmhouse here. Gray with white trim, it could be any one of a thousand prairie homes. There's a single rural-route mailbox on a post across the road from the end of the driveway. It says Benson on the side, but the paint has been scoured by the wind and the name is almost illegible.

There is a tire swing hung from a cottonwood with a yellow rope, and a kid named Anton kicking a black-and-white soccer ball in the driveway.

The walk to the porch is guarded by lilacs and lilies of the valley and a patch of violets. A tortoiseshell cat named Yin lounges on the porch, watchfully making way for visitors; a familial tiger-striper named Yang watches from the side yard. Just before the porch is a strip of iron set in a concrete block: a boot scraper, and well-used.[59]

That's detail and rhythm artfully combined. The reader feels like he is actually there down on the farm. All that's missing are the mouth-watering smell and the crackling sound of chicken frying in the pan.

Q: What are the three tips you give new writers?

A: I encourage my new reporters and students to never fall in love with their words. The story's the thing. The words need to be transparent. It doesn't matter how great you think the words are, if they don't tell a good story well, they are worthless. I think Camp does this particularly well. If you read his stories closely you notice that none of his words are flowery, his choice of vocabulary is basic and his sentence constructions simple. But his stories are powerful. One of my favorite quotes is from Samuel Johnson. It's a little heartless, but it illustrates this point most clearly: "Read over your composition, and when you reach a passage that is particularly fine ... strike it out." Now that's a tough editor!

---

[59] Camp, J. (1985). Life on the land: An American farm family. *Saint Paul Pioneer Press & Dispatch*. It is also reprinted in Friedlander, E. J. & Lee, J. (Eds.) (2004). *Feature writing for newspapers and magazines: The pursuit of excellence* (5th ed.). pp. 46-51. Boston: Allyn & Bacon.

Secondly, just like they say you can never be too rich or too beautiful, the feature writer can never be too observant or collect too much detail. While strong, active verbs give a story motion and realistic quotes give it life, it is the detail that gives it depth and makes it three-dimensional. Detail. Detail. Detail. What did it look like, sound like, feel like, taste like, smell like? Descriptive detail places the reader at the scene, whether it's in a firefight in Baghdad or on the bench at the Final Four. Then the trick becomes to keep your story from becoming a heavy-handed regurgitation of detail. Detail must be used artfully. Thousands of carefully placed brush strokes create a masterpiece; don't throw the whole bucket of paint at the canvas and expect to get the same results.

Finally, unless God made you one of the chosen few to whom He gave the gift of writing, the only way to become a good writer is to read, read, read and write, write, write. Don't read indiscriminately: to become a good writer, read good writing. I think the *Wall Street Journal* is probably the best-written newspaper in the country, and the *New Yorker* is a very well-written magazine. Dissect the writing; find out what makes it good. Then write. Don't try to imitate the writing of others, but use their techniques to experiment with things like rhythm and pace, descriptions, quotations, dialogue, even word selection, word order, sentence and paragraph length. Find an editor or friend who cares enough to be brutally honest, then listen ... hard.

Exercises

Re-read the article on kibbutzim and the Spanish-American War and think about the SHOP formula. Do the following tasks for each article.

1) Identify the **Selection**, the angle.
2) Which paragraph contains the most **History**?
3) Give three examples of **Observation** in this piece.
4) Identify the **Perspective** in this piece. How is perspective different from **History**?
5) How many sources are quoted in this article?
6) What bit of color is most memorable to you? What does that insight tell you about good writing?

Student story

At this point in this book, you may be thinking that the cited writers are the professionals and new writers can't achieve this level of writing. Not true. I've worked with hundred of writers in all parts of the nation, and they applied basic journalistic principles to their craft and earned a byline.

248

In some cases, the writer didn't speak English as a first language. Joseph Conrad is often cited as the best writer who spoke English as a second language. In the story below, Sweden's Hanna Wadefalk wrote a piece for a feature writing class and the Baptist Press wire used it. The link during late-2004 was: http://baptistpress.org /bpnews.asp?ID=17354.

Collegians recount how they handle homesickness[60]
By Hanna Wadefalk
Used with permission

BUIES CREEK, N.C. (BP)--Hiroki Mikado poured milk into his bowl of chocolate puffs and sat down in front of his computer. He clicked on the Internet Explorer icon and chose "Yoshinoya" from his folder of favorites. After he had spent a couple minutes looking at the Japanese restaurant's website, he slowly dipped his spoon into the bowl of puffs.

While Mikado, 27, a senior at Campbell University, was eating his not-so-eccentric meal, he stared at the screen, pretending the food was a tasty fare of beef, onions and rice from home. Until he can return to Ibraki, Japan, again, the World Wide Web is as close as he gets to his mom's cooking and everything else he misses about his native land.

Research suggests that nearly 70 percent of university students feel homesick at some time or other.

In other words, Mikado is not alone. He handles being so far from home pretty well. He said he thinks that can be explained by the fact that he is older than most college students. He has been away from home for eight years now, two years in the Tokyo area, two years in Hawaii and then three and half years at Campbell in Buies Creek, N.C.

"My family is just a 14-hour flight away," Mikado said. "If I made the decision to go back home, I could have tomorrow's breakfast in Japan with mama," he said and smiled.

Mikado said soccer has helped him a lot. He joined the Campbell soccer team last year. "When I made the team," he said, "my whole life at Campbell changed."

---

[60] Copyright (c) 2004 Southern Baptist Convention, Baptist Press. Visit www.bpnews.net. BP News -- witness the difference! Covering the critical issues that shape your life, work and ministry. BP News is a ministry of Baptist Press, the daily news service of Southern Baptists. Hanna Wadefalk is a journalism student at Campbell University.

He said he still has trouble with English and sometimes has difficulty finding passion and motivation to study.

"Only soccer can make me forget my difficulties," he said. Being a part of a team has helped Mikado to get motivated to improve his English so that he can understand better what his coaches and teammates are saying.

When Mikado needs someone to talk to outside his team, he talks to his Japanese roommate or gives a friend or a family member in Japan a call.

One of the toughest times away from home was when his sister called from Japan when his grandmother nearly died.

That time, and whenever a problem occurs, he turns to Petra Carlzen, Campbell's assistant director of international admissions. For Mikado, as for many international students, Carlzen functions as a "Buies Creek stand-in parent."

Carlzen has worked in international admissions for three years. She has learned that students tend to come to talk primarily when they first arrive in the United States and at Campbell as they try to adapt to a new country, culture and language.

Sergio Tejada, 21, from Armenia, Columbia, for example, arrived at his first school in Virginia without speaking a word of English.

"It was very tough," he said. "I took an American history class my first semester and had no idea what the teacher was saying."

Tejada left Colombia three years ago and since then he has only been home once – two and a half years ago. He can't go home due to the difficulties in getting a new visa to return to the United States.

Tejada saw his parents this summer when they came to visit him and his brother who lives in Florida.

"Whenever I'm sad about being so far from home or if I have a problem, I give my brother a call," he said. "If that doesn't help I'll call my mom."

Like Mikado, Tejada mentioned that being a part of a Campbell athletic team has helped.

"Everybody in the tennis team [is] from different countries and [they] know how it is to be far away from home," he said. Around his friends on the tennis team he can forget everything and just have fun.

"It is when I'm by myself that I start thinking," he said. "As long as I keep myself busy, I'm alright."

Carlzen said what students struggle with most is missing their families and that if something happens to someone in the family they are not around to help. The students ask themselves, "Why am I here when I should be at home?" As in Tejada's case, international students often do not have the option to go home, either for economic reasons or because of passport and visa issues.

So what does Carlzen tell students who miss home so much?

"It is not so much about saying anything," Carlzen said. "It is all about listening."

Carlzen's experience has taught her not to start a conversation with a homesick person saying everything will be alright.

"You have to listen, listen and listen and then talk," she said. "And when you are done talking, you can finish your conversation saying it will be okay."

Most of the time, Carlzen knows firsthand how to make a student feel better. In 1997, she was a freshman in college missing her home country of Sweden.

If her international admissions office cannot help, Carlzen sometimes recommends that students talk to campus minister Terry-Michael Newell Jr.

However, Newell has never had an international student come talk to him about being homesick and he has a theory on why: "I think the international students have already made the big decision when they decided to come this far," Newell said. "They knew that they could make it over here."

Like his counterpart, Newell always keep his door open for students in need. Having been the campus minister for seven years, he is well-acquainted with homesick students. Being away from home can be as tough for a student who is a two-hour drive from home as for a student from another part of the world.

He has found that the typical student coming in to talk is the one living as close as 90-100 miles away.

"It seems to me, many times the student that is homesick a lot is also the student that chose to go to school close to home," Newell said. For these students, he said, the home environment is typically very important and its absence has a great effect. After all, they have lived with the same people, possibly in the same place, and with the same routines for 18 years.

Junior Jennifer Hadra, 20, does not live quite that close. From Gladstone, Mich., she said her homesickness was worst when she first started school.

"I was really miserable the first month of school," Hadra said. "I missed having my parents right there to talk to, or if I was sad about something, have my mom there to pat me on the back."

For Hadra, as with most college students, college was her first experience being away from home for an extended period. After a while, she adjusted and learned how to function and do things by herself. The more she learned, the less she noticed that someone was not there to help.

Yet, whenever something bad happens Hadra said she always wants to go home because she misses the security of knowing that if she needs her family they are literally right there.

"If I am sad or upset, the best thing I can do is give my parents (a) call," Hadra said. "But a phone can never make up for a hug or a shoulder to cry on," she added.

Hadra is a Christian and said she would turn to the campus minister if she really needed to talk to a nearby adult.

Newell will gladly speak with any student of any faith. However, sometimes students might need the touch of a physician. All Campbell students have access to a professional counselor at student health services.

If a student contacts the infirmary with a problem, he or she can make an appointment with a doctor who may refer him or her to a counselor. The student also has the option to ask to talk to the counselor right away. All meetings are confidential.

Even if avenues of comfort and help can be found on campus, whether a telephone call, a friend, international admissions or the campus minister, that feeling of something missing will always be there. Home, whether Japan, Colombia, Sweden or Michigan, can never be replaced.

Summary

Some writers find it helpful to have a mnemonic, a device to aid you in remembering. For feature writing, the formula of **SHOP** stands for **Selection, History, Observation** and **Perspective.** Selection is the idea of the angle that you will use to write the story. History is the background that is essential to tell the story well. Observation includes sense impressions, and Perspective is the comparison that you can use to help readers appreciate the scale of the topic. This chapter included an interview with writer Wesley G. Pippert, who urged writers to plan ahead in preparing for articles, to collect lots of color while on the scene, and to ruthlessly check information for accuracy. This chapter also included ideas from editor John B. Carpenter who says he tells writers to focus on the story above all. The chapter ended with a student story that proves all of us can write if we apply the ideas that work.

Chapter 11

The ABCs of timeless ideas for feature articles
FeatureWriting.Net/Dial-a-Lead

Chapter at-a-glance

> ➢ Using SHOP to guide your Internet searches
> ➢ Reading what others have written before you write
> ➢ Collaborating with editor on the right angle

The following are sure-fire ideas for snagging an assignment for general-interest and specialty publications. The ideas are meant to be timeless and suitable for a wide variety of geographical locations. When interviewing for a full-time writing or reporting assignment, review this list. Many editors will test your understanding of audiences and the culture of writing and reporting by asking for a list of story ideas. The editor may prod a potential writer about his or her ideas on stories to determine if you have that elusive spark of curiosity and creativity that makes writers so quirky and fun. This list of timeless feature article ideas may help you get the job or a fistful of assignments or both.

In time, you will develop your own nose for assignments, and you will lean less and less on the cooked-up variety, but you'll have a few squirreled away when you are asked to contribute an idea. Ideas tend to

The relentless search for ideas will lead to spying an idea that may have gone overlooked by others, but not you.

stimulate other ideas, so this list's greatest use may be to jumpstart fresh ideas and approaches for you and your writing colleagues.

A
A day in the life of ...

Do the unpredictable. A day in the life of the lawyer's secretary, bank president's secretary, a professor's secretary, an elected official's secretary. These gatekeepers know where the bodies are buried. Does he or she have a job that can be left at the office at the end of the day? How about an ice cream vendor, sanitation worker, golf driving range ball collector? How about a mailman, pet storeowner, road worker? Interview a dogcatcher, mortician, shampoo person as you spend a day with them. This idea could be stretched into a series. For the SHOP approach, think secretaries. Remember SHOP stands for Selection, History, Observation and Perspective.

S – Select a secretary as a primary source and mention
 Secretaries Day.

H – Contact American Society of Corporate Secretaries
 521 5th Ave.
 New York, NY 10175-0003 USA
 Phone:(212) 681-2000
 Fax: (212) 681-2005
 URL: http://www.ascs.org
Or
 Association of Certified Professional Secretaries
 P. O. Box 89301
 Tucson, AZ 85752 USA
 Phone:(602) 650-2659

O – Spend a day with the primary source and observe that person at work and play. Talk to co-workers, friends, the boss and the clients, citizens or customers.

P – For a different angle, mention the naughty secretary. Remember Anamarie Giambrone of Queens, N.Y.? In 2002, the court sentenced her to up to six years for pillaging $800,000 from her boss, a senior managing director at Bear, Stearns. Giambrone used an erasable ink pen to write out personal checks for the boss to sign.[61]

Allergies
Find out the most common allergies in various geographical regions.

---

[61] (2002, Dec. 2). Taking letters, and a lot more. *Vancouver Sun*, p. C1.

S – Start with a physician or pharmacist, but the main event will be interviews with patients who sneeze their way through ratty facial tissues and over-the-counter remedies and exotic medicines that can leave the user in a swoon.

H – American Allergy Association (AAA)
3104 E Camelback, Ste. 459
Phoenix, AZ 85016 USA
Fax: (480) 368-1238
E-Mail: allergyaid@aol.com
Founded: 1978. Description: Allergy and asthma patients and their families, health care professionals, and others interested in problems created by foods, allergies, and asthma. Disseminates information on diet, environmental control, and other facets of allergy and asthma advice.

Or

American Academy of Allergy, Asthma and Immunology
611 E Wells St.
Milwaukee, WI 53202 USA
Phone:(414) 272-6071
Fax: (414) 272-6070
URL: http://www.aaaai.org
Founded: 1943. Description: Professional society of physicians specializing in allergy and allergic diseases. Sponsors annual two-day postgraduate course and three-day scientific session. Conducts research and educational programs. Maintains speaker's bureau; operates placement service; compiles statistics.

Or

American Academy of Otolaryngic Allergy Foundation
1990 M St. NW, Ste. 680
Washington, DC 20036 USA
Phone:(202) 955-5010
Fax: (202) 955-5016
E-Mail: aaoa@aaoaf.org
Founded: 1941. Description: Otolaryngologists who are interested in the study, research, and practice of otolaryngic allergy.

O – Spend time with the people who endure a reaction and describe their day-to-day life. What must they avoid? Are there any benefits to allergies? What are the trade-offs?

P – The American College of Allergy, Asthma and Immunology sponsors a Get Smart about Allergies national education campaign. The campaign informs allergy sufferers about how to better manage their disease with help from a family physician or an allergy specialist.

The campaign also features an easy-to-navigate Web site www.smartaboutallergies.com.

Arm wrestling

United States Armwrestling Association grew from the World Wristwrestling Championships televised by *ABC Wide World of Sports*. Arm wrestling is organized in 50 countries with 57 different weight categories, right- and left-handed competition, men and women. It is also known as U.S. Arm Sports.

S – Arm wrestle the champ and write about it.

H – World's Wristwrestling Championship (WWC)
423 E Washington St.
Petaluma, CA 94952 USA
Phone:(707) 778-1430
URL: http://www.armwrestling.com
Founded: 1953. Description: Conducts wristwrestling championships in divisions ranging from bantamweight (under 130 pounds) to heavyweight (unlimited). Conducts contests for both men and women. Maintains hall of fame.

O – Observe before, during and after the match. Note the reaction of the fans and non-fans. You may choose to write about your own experience; however, the experience of someone who is a novice may make a fun feature.

P – New York Arm Wrestling Association
200-14 45th Dr., Ste. 713
Bayside, NY 11361 USA
Phone:(718) 544-4592
Fax: (718) 261-8111
Toll-Free: 877-NYC-ARMS
URL: http://www.nycarms.com
Primary Contact: Gene Camp, Founder/Pres. Founded: 1977. Description: Sports-related group dedicated to the promotion of arm wrestling in the state of NY.

B
Best

Who is the best TV news anchor? Who is the best hairstylist? What is the best cup of coffee? What restaurant or person makes the best pizza? What is the best cup of coffee, ice cream dessert or hair stylist? What restaurant or person makes the best chicken wings or French onion soup?

Pick a town, region, state or nation and find the answer. It may be fun to do the article on an annual basis. You may have to create a poll to measure your picks or use figures from the chamber of commerce.

S – Who has the best cup of coffee? Try the chain coffee vendors and conduct your own contest using your taste buds.

H – Contact the National Coffee Association of U.S.A.

15 Maiden Ln., Ste. 1405

New York, NY 10038-4003 USA

Phone:(212) 766-4007

Fax: (212) 766-5815

URL: http://www.ncausa.org

Founded: 1911. Description: Green coffee importers, jobbers, brokers, and agents; instant coffee and liquid extract processors; roasters and allied coffee industries; exporters; retailers. Promotes sound business relations and mutual understanding among members of the trade, and to increase coffee consumption. Collects and publishes consumer, market and technical information on the coffee industry. Libraries: Holdings: 600. Subjects: coffee, caffeine. Additional Web sites: http://www.coffeescience.org.

O – Note the routines people use when making coffee. Observe the people who drink black coffee. Do they have similar behavioral quirks? Fashion? Do men or women put more additives into their coffee?

P – As you do your search for the best coffee, make a list of the cost, the name of the product if it is exotic (such as "Gut buster"), and the cost for one cup. You can compare places and values and provide your audience with a helpful guide on the best coffee for the money. A sidebar can examine the steps to a good cup of coffee.

Bus and rail system

Millions of Americans use buses and rail to commute. What is it like to ride day after day? Do riders forge friendships, or is the assumption that the commute is temporary and an unlikely place to make friends? What do people do while they travel? What is the etiquette for using a cellular telephone, personal stereo and food? The best interviews may come from drivers, dispatchers and mechanics.

S – Spend a day riding the bus, train or subway.

H – Bus History Association

965 McEwan

Windsor, ON, Canada N9B 2G1

Phone:(519) 977-0664

Fax: (519) 977-5781

Founded: 1963. Description: Historians in seven countries interested in motor buses and bus transportation; employees of bus companies; transit and intercity operating bus companies; motor bus manufacturing firms. Collects and preserves historical data relative to buses including photographs, equipment lists, and manufacturers' specifications. Cooperates with the bus industry to preserve historical archives such as biographies of pioneers in the field.

O – As people board a bus, train or subway, note their traffic pattern. Do they take the first empty seat, angle for a window, or stand morosely to one side? If you had to classify the passengers into categories, what classification principle would you use? List all the activities in which passengers engage. Notice anything humorous? Scary?

P – Terrorism is often associated with aviation, but what about mass transit? The Transportation Security Administration is to assume responsibility for mass transit security including buses, trolleys, commuter rail, van pools, ferry boats and light rail. U.S. mass transit has largely been spared from terrorist attacks, but worldwide systems, including Israeli buses, the Bologna train station and Paris metro, have been hit. How do passengers react to the threat? Perhaps a sidebar can offer suggestions on ways to be safe. A sidebar could suggest ideas for making the trip on the bus, train or subway more enjoyable.

I once read of a man who put his name and address on the handle of his umbrella with a note that said, "If found, keep the umbrella and send me $5." Periodically, he'd open the mail and find a check with a note that said, "Found your umbrella. Here's $5. Thanks." Unfortunately, the new owners failed to change the note and address.

C
Cemeteries

In Paris, on Oscar Wilde's monument in the Père Lachaise cemetery are the words from his poem, The Ballad Reading Gaol: "Mourners will be outcast men, and outcasts always mourn." Visitors continue to troop to the grave more than 100 years after Wilde died in November 1900. Colorful people, both honorable and not, sometimes attract attention even after death.

S – Visit the famous graves in an area and note the epitaphs. Interview visitors and the grounds keeper. Talk to the visitor's bureau and the chamber of commerce and get their anecdotes. Consider making a map and creating a car tour that unites some of these graves by theme.

H – International Cemetery and Funeral Association
1895 Preston White Dr., No. 220
Reston, VA 20191 USA

Phone:(703) 391-8400
Fax: (703) 391-8416
Toll-Free: 800-645-7700
URL: http://www.icfa.org
Founded: 1887. Description: Owners and managers of cemeteries and funeral homes; related suppliers and professional service firms

O – Watch the people who visit a gravesite. Do they whisper among themselves? Leave flowers? Take pictures? Sing? Note the condition of the grave. It may be maintained well, but the grave may be indistinct from the others. Note how the famous grave blends in or stands out in the cemetery.

P – Graves are sometimes leased in some countries. What about the United States? Hear about the Mount Rainier woman who sued a northeast Washington, D.C., cemetery claiming that the gravesite of her son was moved without her knowledge? How often does that happen? What do cemeteries do to prevent this kind of problem?

What makes a cemetery popular? Is the trend to buy now and die later? A sidebar could explore pet cemeteries.

Accredited Pet Cemetery Society
3426 Brush Rd.
Richfield, OH 44286 USA
Phone:(330) 659-4270
Fax: (330) 659-4254
URL: http://www.accreditedpetcemeterysociety.org
Founded: 1993. Description: Pet cemeterians. Promotes highest standards of professionalism. Endorses deed restriction of pet cemetery property and meaningful pet cemetery legislation. Offers educational programs on pet bereavement, support groups, and professional business management. Observes National Pet Memorial Day, the second Sunday in September.

Children, classrooms and conflict

Ever wonder if children consider the big questions? With permission, school authorities may allow you to talk to students about the edgy questions facing them. Suicide, drugs, vandalism, jobs, even terrorism may be on the radar. Interviews with students at both private and public schools would help make the article more representative.

S – Spend a day in the classroom. Ask permission to attend class to do the assignments. Perhaps, you can make an exception and use the gonzo approach from Chapter 7, *The ethical picture*.

H – Association for Childhood Education International
17904 Georgia Ave., Ste. 215

Olney, MD 20832 USA

Phone:(301) 570-2111

Fax: (301) 570-2212

Toll-Free: 800-423-3563

URL: http://www.acei.org

Founded: 1892. Description: Promotes good educational practices for children from infancy through early adolescence. Conducts workshops and travel/study tours abroad. Conducts research and educational programs; maintains Hall of Fame and speakers bureau. Maintains liaison with government agencies, cooperating organizations, teaching institutions, and manufacturers and designers of materials and equipment for children.

O – Becoming a fly on the wall can lead to valuable observation that will make your article fun to read.

P – Consider the debate over national standards tests for children. In addition, some regions want more programs for children who are considered gifted. University educators can provide a glimpse into the approaches used by other countries. The private-public debate will provide additional perspective into the state of early childhood education.

Celebrity

Consider working with a partner, a radio station, a TV station or an Internet service provider on a celebrity look-alike contest. This idea may work in a church if the congregation is large enough. A college or university may be another venue. A sidebar could examine the names ordinary people share with celebrities. Do you know how many times I am asked if I am Michael W. Smith? I just want to know if he is asked if he is Michael R. Smith!

S – Peruse a telephone book for the names of famous people. Call them and interview them on the amusing, silly or embarrassing comments they receive. Mine for those great anecdotes.

H – For anecdotes and history, try contacting the Association of Celebrity Personal Assistants

914 Westwood Blvd.

PMB 507

Los Angeles, CA 90024 USA

Phone:(310) 322-4495

Founded: 1992. Description: Individuals acting as personal assistants to celebrities. Promotes professional development of members. Serves as a forum for networking, job referral, and information exchange among members. Conducts educational programs; compiles statistics.

O – Spend some time with sources who have a celebrity name. Do they work to enhance the confusion by wearing clothing or using language that may mislead someone else into thinking they may be the real Phil Donahue?

P – Consider the angle of persuasion. Do people who look like celebrities or share the name of a celebrity receive preferential treatment? Do celebrities have more persuasive appeal than ordinary people? In a 2002 *USA Today*/CNN/Gallup poll, almost one-third of the people said they felt celebrities were "somewhat" effective in influencing the views of the president and other elected officials. Let your celebrity look-alikes or sources who share the name of a celebrity talk about influence. Allow a source in advertising to offer an opinion.

Christmas presents

Write a holiday article on gifts for types of people. For women who work out, create a gift basket that includes the items she would need at the gym. For the film buff, consider a popcorn box with a movie guidebook, a classic DVD of a favorite movie and a gift certificate to a cinema café.

S – Decide on four packages for men, four for women and four for either gender.

H – Gift Association of America (GAA)
172 White Pine Way
Harleysville, PA 19438-2851 USA
Phone:(610) 584-3108
Fax: (610) 584-7860
URL: http://www.giftassn.com
Founded: 1952. Description: Retailers, wholesalers, and industry affiliates of gifts, china, glass, and decorative accessories. Sponsors seminars at gift shows and European market tours.

O – Pick some high-end retailers and check for variety and prices. Be sure to do some interviews with shoppers and clerks. Then check some one-of-a-kind shops. Online web sites often have company email contacts that can provide additional information. The people who work this area are often chatty and good interviewees.

P – Consider the tension in giving gifts at work. Check with a source such as Susan Bixler of The Professional Image, a corporate image consulting firm. She found that people who don't think through the implications of giving a gift to someone at the holidays can accidentally insult the person.

Classified advertisements for babies

Some people use the classified columns in print and online to adopt a baby.

S – Get permission from the newspaper or online service to contact a person who has bought a classified advertisement and interview these people. Work for a variety of sources including single people who want to adopt and conventional adoption agencies.

H – Gift of Love International Adoptions
7405 University Blvd., Ste. 8
Des Moines, IA 50325 USA
Phone:(515) 255-3388
Fax: (515) 279-3017
Toll-Free: 877-282-8015
URL: http://www.giftoflove.org
Founded: 1994. Description: International adoption agency.

O – Visit with your interviewees and watch them interact with others. Are other children around? Is there a nursery? Check with a social service agency that handles adoptions and secure a checklist for the kind of environment that the state considers suitable for an adoptive child. How well does the family or person that you interview fit the requirements?

P – Countries such as Canada are exploring open adoptions, a verbal contract between birth parents and adopting parents declaring that both intend to keep contact with the other. The families plan to stay in touch. The Adoption Council of Ontario provides information on this practice, noting that it is becoming more acceptable in private adoptions.

Community events

Some newspapers and magazines include a section on events in the community. Monitor these community calendars for ideas. Journalists and writers are accustomed to reading the legal advertisements in the classified section of a newspaper, but other gems can be found by reading the community calendar for coming events.

Exercising to music provoked an article on a ministry where participants exercised to Gospel music. For this article, the writer arrived early, scoped out the gymnasium where the group exercised, listened to the leader describe her goals and the origin of the idea, watched and even participated in a workout. Following the workout, the writer interviewed participants and collected telephone numbers and email addresses for follow-up questions. The writer provided perspective by interviewing others involved in traditional exercise for their opinions.

A variation on this theme is to do a round-up article on all the novel exercise programs in several areas. Fitness centers offer step aerobics, kick boxing, cycling, Tae Bo and several other classes. Round-up articles include a number of examples on the same topic, such as the most popular exercise programs in different regions in the nation or different parts of the region.

S – Find an inexpensive activity that is offered to the community as recreation and attend, even participate. Try a ballroom dance class for mature adults.

H – United States Ballroom Branch of the Imperial Society of Teachers of Dancing

68 Centennial Rd.

Warminster, PA 18974 USA

Phone:(215) 491-9696

Fax: (215) 957-6067

Founded: 1904. Description: Teachers of dancing. Has established a uniform method of teaching various forms of dance; encourages higher education among teachers; prepares graduated syllabi for techniques; arranges medal tests in various types of dancing for adults and children; conducts professional examinations. Sponsors area competitions and championships in the international style of ballroom dancing; conducts lectures and professional training programs.

Or

See the United States Amateur Ballroom Dancers Association at http://www.usabda.org.

Or

Try http://www.ipl.org/div/aon, a web site that calls itself the Internet Public Library and includes a number of categories including "Entertainment and leisure, activities of amusement and diversion."

O – Dance. Describe the way it feels to coordinate motion with mind. Listen to conversations. How do students behave as they wait, as they practice and succeed? How do students dress? Is the atmosphere clubby or awkward?

P – Ballroom dancing is now recognized by the International Olympic Committee as an athletic activity. In ballroom dancing, the four main categories: American rhythm (cha-cha, swing, rumba), American smooth (tango, waltz, foxtrot), international Latin (rumba, samba, paso doble) and international standard (waltz, quickstep, tango).[62] Compare

---

[62] Garcia De Rosier, T. (2003, February 7). Simply ballroom: From the foxtrot to the tango, the dancing boom shows no sign of slowing down. *The Times Union* (Albany, NY), p. D1.

this style of dancing with the more interpretative style of college dance clubs.

Complain

What's the most effective way to get results? In this case, the issue isn't about complaints within the family, but those vexing problems with municipalities, garages and the other hallmarks of modern life. To narrow the arena of complaints, focus on your city, county or local government and its attempts to keep residents informed. Often these groups publish a list of offices that residents can contact for information on problems with storm water, animals, litter, small claims, zoning issues and so on.

S – Spend time with the people of these organizations and develop a list of ideas for strategies to get the job done.

H – International Customer Service Association (ICSA)
401 N. Michigan Ave.
Chicago, IL 60611-4267 USA
Phone:(312) 321-6800
Fax: (312) 245-1084
Toll-Free: 800-360-ICSA.
URL: http://www.icsa.com
Founded: 1981. Description: Customer service professionals in public and private sectors united to develop the theory and understanding of customer service and management. Goals are to promote professional development; standardize terminology and phrases; provide career counseling and placement services; establish hiring guidelines, performance standards, and job descriptions. Provides a forum for shared problems and solutions. Compiles statistics.

O – Visit the municipal building and observe the interaction of residents on issues of concern to them. What approach seems to work and what approach seems to fail? Help your audience see and feel the tension or the efficiency of the organization. For comparison, visit a retail shop and watch the interaction. Do discount stores with a high number of returns seem more or less helpful to customers than the more prestigious retail stores?

P – Among the best strategies for getting a complaint resolved is to talk to the manager, not a clerk, waitress, counter person or whomever is in the first line of interaction.[63] The secret is to be judicious; avoid complaining about trivial things. Often, the written complaint works

---

[63] Complaining: Ask the family. (2002, November 17).*Observer Magazine*, p. 99.

best. For comparison, talk to experts on ways complaining backfires and leads to hurt rather than a sense of restitution.

Catastrophes and crime

Ever wonder what intersection is the most dangerous in your area? In the state? In the nation? Police monitor these issues and can offer suggestions on avoiding problems and recommend solutions for improving the traffic pattern. In addition, police have figures for the most crime-infested block in the area. It is grim business, but a feature article that examines the intersection or block may help your audience avoid trouble when on the road.

S – Visit your local law enforcement office to learn about the most dangerous intersection in the area. Have the person who helps plan streets and traffic flow explain the problem and give recommendations to improve the situation. Explore the budget issues and the problems of local vs. state and federal funding for road projects. Ask about the safest intersection in the area and determine if volume of traffic necessarily translates into inevitable accidents.

H – American Driver and Traffic Safety Education Association
Highway Safety Center/IUP
Indiana, PA 15705 USA
Phone:(724) 357-4051
Fax: (724) 357-7595
Toll-Free: 800-896-7703
URL: http://adtsea.iup.edu
Founded: 1956. Description: Professional organization of teachers and supervisors interested in improving driver and traffic safety education in colleges and secondary and elementary schools. Awards honorary memberships to retired persons distinguished in the field. Provides assistance to state departments of education, colleges and universities, state associations, and local school districts. Divisions: Adult Traffic Safety and Driver Improvement; Education of Special Populations; Elementary Traffic Safety; Higher Education Traffic Safety; Secondary Traffic Safety; Traffic Safety Administration and Supervision; Traffic Safety Research.

Or

Alliance for Traffic Safety
Safety Center
Humphreys Bldg., Ste. 201
Central Missouri State University
Warrensburg, MO 64093 USA
Phone:(660) 543-4830

Fax: (660) 543-4482

Founded: 1960. Description: Educational, trade, and professional organizations having an interest in highway traffic safety. Acts as a forum for exchange of information among members and as a source of contact for state and federal safety officials for reaching participating organization safety personnel at both the state and national levels. Coordinates activities of member groups.

O – Visit the intersection, and watch the traffic patterns. When possible, interview some of the drivers including commercial drivers, and learn about their strategies. Watch the kind of drivers or vehicles that tend to be vulnerable.

P – Traffic experts often use a severity index where accidents are ranked by points. For instance, in Oklahoma an accident that causes injuries or fatalities scores six points, while one causing property damage scores two points. Totals are tabulated for six months or one year. Compare this approach used by traffic officials to other methods.

A sidebar on this idea is to explore crime and punishment. Courthouse records will describe the crime and the penalty. How often does the punishment remain the same for a crime? Does one county vary dramatically from another? Does one state vary dramatically from another state?

D

December graduates

What are the advantages of mid-year graduation?

S – Interview students from a variety of area colleges on their strategy for graduating in December. Talk to career counselors and headhunters. What are the trade-offs?

H – Academic advisers and school counselors can explain the popularity of the trend, which includes strategies to enter the job market before the May competition, an opportunity to travel before the academic year begins anew, and the avoidance of a sense of waste known as "senioritis." Examine the juxtaposition of music, from holiday favorites to traditional graduation music.

O – Meet with a family or a peer group who is graduating early. How are they preparing? Are graduation parties rolled into Christmas parties? Are spirits effervescent?

P – For a different perspective on graduation, contact the following group.
Graduation Pledge Alliance
Manchester College
Box 135
North Manchester, IN 46962

Phone:(260) 982-5346
Fax: (260) 982-5043
URL: http://web.mit.edu/mit-cds/gpa/
Founded: 1987. Description: Participants include students, faculty members, school administrators, and other interested individuals. Promotes social and environmental responsibility by encouraging students to pledge upon graduation that they will investigate and consider the social and environmental consequences of any job opportunity they consider or work at. Seeks to: develop a network of people interested in instituting a graduation pledge program at their respective schools; encourage employers to alter their policies and practices to reflect the social and environmental concerns of their employees; increase the role of school activities in developing an informed, democratic citizenry. Holds forums and workshops; sponsors essay contests; maintains speakers' bureau; offers consulting services.

Dirty work

We need custodians, nurses for the terminally ill and others to do the work of the unsung heroes. Who are they?

S – Develop a list of people who are essential to the society, but who are often faces in the crowd. Interview them on their philosophies and the reaction they receive from co-workers and the public.

H – Environmental Management Association (EMA)
56 Linden Sq.
Wellesley, MA 02482-4709 USA
Phone:(781) 237-3200
Fax: (781) 239-0200
URL: http://www.emanational.org
Founded: 1957. Description: Individuals administering environmental sanitation maintenance programs in industrial plants, commercial and public buildings, institutions, and governmental agencies. Conducts educational programs; operates placement service; compiles statistics

O – Spend a day with the people in the trenches and observe the rhythms of their job. One of the most rewarding feature articles I found was spending a day with a crew who collected garbage. I found out their nicknames come from Star Wars movies and heard more anecdotes than I could use. The sanitation workers developed their own classification system for matching trash to household, and offered commentary on the state of the union.

P – A slightly different angle is to compare the work of the private sector to that of the military, many of whom are required to do grunt work.

Ask a military public affairs officer to arrange for you to interview and observe soldiers doing their duty with little fanfare or glamour.

Driving test

What state has the most difficult driving test? How hard is it to transfer a license from state-to-state post the 9-11 tragedy? How tough is Minnesota's driver's test?

S – Check out the driver's tests in your area. Interview people who are new drivers and those who are coming from other areas.

H – Check AAA at www.aaa.com and call your local or regional office.

O – If possible, monitor a real driving test. You can read a typical examination in most states using an online version, but the real observation will come when you watch a new driver get behind the wheel.

P – For fun, see the driver's examination online for various states including the Commonwealth of Virginia at www.dmv.state.va.us. Contact the state department of motor vehicles at three states and ask the source what he or she considers the most difficult part of the examination. Ask for suggestions on succeeding for safe driving. One instructor told me that he always drives with his headlights on to help other drivers see him.

Dumpster divers

Author Philip Gulley says his boyhood home was on the road to a landfill.[64] Pick-up trucks would carry a load into the landfill, but they usually returned with a new load. One person's junk is another person's treasure. Not all trash is without value – just ask the people who rummage through those dumpsters behind retail stores. Some just want aluminum cans, but some bold collectors find usable building materials, products, even food.

S – Interview a team of these collectors to discover the benefits and disadvantages of the chase. Is it worth it? Do the police or store managers object?

H – Contact an organization such as Pack Your Trash to learn about the benefits of recycling. According to Pack Your Trash, their mission is to educate, encourage and impact our youth to take responsibility and promote a strong sense of pride in their community. Their ultimate vision is to establish PYT as *the* national anti-litter campaign and have an annual Pack Your Trash™ Day across the country.

---

[64] Gulley, P. (1999). *For everything, a season.* Sisters, OR: Multnomah Publishers, p. 157.

Pack Your Trash
c/o Ray Conti
2965 Pleasure Point Dr.
Santa Cruz, CA 95062-5407 USA
Phone:(831) 475-6171
Fax: (831) 475-5953
URL: www.packyourtrash.com
Founded: 1964. Members: 2,000.

O – Contact your municipal authority to find out the best place for dumpster diving. Check with law enforcement to see if they can connect you with a group that monitors trash. Many of these groups have earned good reputations because they leave the site better than when they found it. For instance, they sweep the area clean.

P – Some people restore discarded furniture. That's the story of Patch Canada, 31, who decorated her Arlington townhouse with items that she collected from a number of places.[65] Canada found that better furniture makers often identify their furniture with their logo and use tight tongue and groove couplings, rather than being glued or bolted together. Interview owners of thrift stores and second-hand furniture stores and write a sidebar on suggestions for shopping for the inexpensive but valuable piece of discarded furniture. Consider writing a first-person account on your personal adventure shopping for a treasure.

E
Engagements and wedding

The wedding industry is more competitive than NASCAR. What are some of the more unusual features?

S – Identify three businesses that print announcements, and determine some of the more novel ones.

H – Get some sense of the background on all things pertaining to weddings by contacting:
American Society of Wedding Professionals
268 Griggs Ave.
Teaneck, NJ 07666 USA
Phone:(973) 472-1800
Fax: (973) 574-7626
Toll-Free: 800-526-0497

---

[65] Toto, C. (2002, November 13). Use for used items; Furnishings from yard sales, dumps restored to beauty. *The Washington Times,* p. B1.

URL: http://www.sellthebride.com
Primary Contact: Brian Founded: 1992. Members: 100. Description:
Professionals in the wedding industry. Promotes the wedding
professional and educates brides on the experience of working with a
consultant. Provides trends, etiquette, marketing, consulting
information, directory listing, referrals, networking, and co-op
advertising. Offers local forums for information exchange among
members. Compiles statistics and conducts educational programs and
seminars.

O – Visit stores that cater to the wedding industry. Interview owners,
managers and clerks along with the customers and members of the
wedding party. Watch them interact. Does it remind you of a military
exercise or the work of duty-bound, cost-conscious consumers? What
makes everyone laugh? Cry? Get angry? Put the audience there and
help them live the moment.

P – Talk to couples about trends in weddings. Recently destination
weddings attracted couples. They're private but can include a church
service. The difference is that the location is somewhat exotic.
Remember when Madonna married Guy Ritchie at Skibo Castle in
Scotland, and Sarah Michelle Gellar and Freddie Prinze Jr., both from
Los Angeles, went to Mexico to wed? Check with couples in your area
and see what is planned. Consider a sidebar on the etiquette for paying
for travel and other expenses.

Entertainment on the cheap

What you can do in your area for $10 or less?

S – A coffee date is possible. The bean scene may be the most inexpensive
venue for a date. According to a survey sponsored by Starbucks,
coffeehouses are attracting daters with seven in 10 respondents (72
percent) saying coffeehouses provide "a quiet and convenient place to
talk" and that "the atmosphere is open and friendly."[66] Monitor the
coffee shops, not the taprooms, for an inexpensive date.

H – Interviews with Chamber of Commerce types may help you identify
places that are inexpensive but enjoyable. Parks offer free recreation
and a good value. Zoos and other tax-subsidized diversions can be
enjoyable and inexpensive with a season pass.
Or try
International Association of Amusement Parks and Attractions

---

[66] (2003, February 12). Contemporary couples kindle courtship over coffee.
Canadian Newswire.

1448 Duke St.
Alexandria, VA 22314
Phone:(703) 836-4800
Fax: (703) 836-9678
URL: http://www.iaapa.org
Founded: 1918. Description: Operators of amusement parks, tourist attractions, water parks, miniature golf courses, and family entertainment centers; manufacturers and suppliers of amusement equipment and services. Conducts research programs and compiles statistics.

O – Visit the coffee shop, zoo or walking path and study the troops. Be sure to interview a sample and get their suggestions on the best of the most inexpensive places to go in town. Make the article possess a regional flavor by calling other areas and getting their best picks. You may find that a family of four will get more enjoyment from sitting through a car wash than a night at a concert.

P – Homemade gifts can be had for $10 or less and can be quite memorable assuming the occasion is right. A sidebar on inexpensive gifts could include a list of suggestions such as including the date and occasion written somewhere discreetly on the prize.

Now that you have the SHOP idea, see if you can develop the suggestions below using the formula.

Exercise, suburban style

Mall walkers. Who walks and why?

F
Facials

Go to a beauty salons that specialize in facials, massages, pedicures and total beauty makeovers. Get the works, and write about the experience.

Family woes

What happens after a divorce? Talk to counselors and professors, find out what kinds of troubles this can lead to and what can be done to alleviate the tension.

Father's Day

For Father's Day, ask children to tell what makes their dad so super, asking for drawings done with black pen on white paper, as well as the written word.

Favorite restaurant, coffee shop, waffle house

As a take-off from the TV sitcom "Malcolm in the Middle" or a show of your choice, ask the names of favorite places around the nation. Ask why.

Favorite holiday

What are your favorite Christmas memories, favorite Hanukkah memories, and favorite thanksgiving memories?

Follow-up features

Readers enjoy what-ever-happened-to-so-and-so stories. They are called follow-up news stories, or folios, so why not attempt a follow-up feature? Remember C. Everett Koop, the surgeon general? Whatever happened to him? Do a follow-up article on what is happening with him, his anti-smoking campaign, and his advocacy of condoms. For instance, after writing about one of the groups mentioned above, take a second look somewhere down the road. Does it still exist? Has it grown? Are the members getting something out of it?

Food

Where are the best hamburger and the best breakfast? (Yes, this assignment is just a variation of the "Best" category, but this entry may give you some ideas that vary slightly.) Sample the fare of fast-food chains and write a review. Provide a chart outlining the calories and fat, protein, sodium and carbohydrate content of two selections apiece from each restaurant. Round out the package with a sidebar that examines what nutritionists have to say about fast-food breakfasts.

Funeral directors

Examine the funeral industry. Examine the funeral director's role in the grieving process, and how that is changing, the origins of the businesses in this area, the training required and why it often becomes a family business.

G

Gingerbread house

Assemble a gingerbread house and then do a first person piece on how this delightful chore works.

Golf

Examine the game of golf since Tiger Woods' winning streak popularized it when he hit the tournament circuit. Check on local schools for student golf teams and competitions. Talk to golf course owners about the influx of budding golfers. Get tips from golf pros for new golfers on getting started. What are the best kinds of golf clubs on the market? What are some of the best golf courses around?

H

Heroes

Who do children have as heroes? Teachers had elementary-aged students answer that question in writing. While most picked mom and dad, your article may find that children choose Batman, Leomny Snicket or Brittany Spears.

"Time, the magazine whose annual "Person of the Year" award is seen as a worldwide cultural barometer, has gone one step further by defining a new breed of heroes. Valor against appalling odds or sacrificing one's life in conflict – the actions that elevated Gordon of Khartoum or Joan of Arc to heroic status – are out and good works are in. The magazine's eclectic list of 35 names shows that service to the downtrodden is the new route to heroism."[67]

Historical features

Looking way back at the beginnings of towns, local places and local people can be a good way to put the present in perspective. These stories require a good deal of library research and exploration for photographs.

Other historical stories might explain how area towns and roads got their names. Interview retired people for clues.

Hi-tech fitness

From computerized rowing machines to no-sweat exercise tables, what do local fitness centers offer?

I

Investigate standing features

Review the standing features in the area and regional press. Some of these articles can be parlayed into features for a magazine. Use them as starting fodder for your own article.

---

[67] Morrison, J. (2003, April 20). Icons: Soft, caring and marketable, a new breed of hero for today, the 21st century. *The Independent on Sunday, London*, p. 3.

Ice cream

Locate popular ice cream places, particularly the mom and pop homemade type, and list their unique flavor combinations. Interview ice cream makers who concoct the crazy flavors and find out how they come up with ideas. Draw comparisons to the national chain store fare. Interview ice cream establishments and find out what flavors are most popular with customers. Talk to customers and poll them on what flavors they like. Do they opt for their old stand-bys? Or do they savor the flavor of the month?

Inventions

People patent some pretty weird and wacky ideas. Find out about some of these quirky inventions and interview the inventors. Contact the US patent office. Interview school children and showcase their inventions during the school's annual imagination celebration event or science fair.

J
Jail

The jailhouse rocks. Old jails are being recycled and used in new ways. Spotlight jails that now function as museums and restaurants.

Jewelry

Are diamonds really a girl's best friend? Find out from jewelry stores what the hottest trends are in buying jewelry. What gemstones are popular? What should consumers look for when choosing a diamond ring?

K
Kindergarten

Talk to parents and their children on the first day of kindergarten. Interview kindergarten teachers about what it's like in a classroom of first time students. Provide tips for parents to prepare their children for kindergarten. Find out about the history of kindergarten and where and when the first kindergarten took place in the US.

Kite

Vibrant kites are a summertime symbol. Contact kite flying organizations. Go to a rally or a kite flying contest and interview participants. Talk to kite manufacturers and kite store owners. Is kite flying a popular past time or has its popularity waned?

L
Llama

Dairy farms, beef cattle and sheep farms used to be the mainstay. Now llama farms are on the upswing. Why llamas? Find out what the draw is. Interview a llama farmer.

Locksmith

How many times do people lock themselves out of their car or house? What with panicked mothers trying to comfort crying babies locked in the car or salesmen late for that critical appointment with a new client, the locksmith surely has some tales to tell. What is life like for a locksmith who arrives on the scene to save the day? What are his tools of the trade? How does one become a locksmith?

M
Meeting notices

Sometimes the meeting notices that run in the paper can be turned into solid features. How about a Bible class that meets each Wednesday in a junkyard, and a group that helps parents deal with children who are at risk for drug abuse? In both cases, a writer can attend the meetings and stay in the background, letting the participants go on as they normally would

Mother's Day

Canvas a number of mothers and obtain their favorite recipes for a round-up article about Sunday dinners and holiday meals.

N
Names

I have always been curious about other communities in the United States that have the same name. A check of Rand McNally revealed several names in common. Become an armchair traveler and explore towns with the same name. Sources to check include local Chamber of Commerce, newspapers, and government officials. Among the topics covered include what are their problems, how are they resolving them, what is great about their towns and what isn't so great, what are the people like, what are the major industries, what is the school system like, and what is the history of the area.

Night life

Write about the nightlife. Roller skating? Stargazing? Skipping stones? What are the top three nighttime amusements in your area?

Not favorite

Who are the people you love to hate? Face it, there are a lot of folks out there who rub you the wrong way. A lot of them are just doing their jobs. But sometimes that doesn't make it any easier. Take a lighthearted look at some of these people we love to hate. The list can include parking meter attendants, assistant high school principals who dish the discipline in public schools, workers at the department of motor vehicles and soooo many more. This kind of article can help readers understand the reason some of these people seem boorish.

O

Oscars

Tell us the Oscar picks now.

Opera

Go to the local opera house and showcase the current season's operas. What goes into the production of an opera? Find out what kinds of programs are available that teach children and attract them to the world of opera.

P

Paralysis

Spend time with a quadriplegic. Chart the struggles and successes of a person with paralysis.

Parents without Partners

Visit your local Parents without Partners group. Find out what the group is doing. Are they finding partners within the group? How many couples meet and marry through PWP? Compare life before Parents without Partners with life afterwards.

Pets

Look for evidence of the cutest pet.

Plant closing

What happens to people when a company goes out of business?

Poverty

Hang out with the poor and write about it. Look at the plight of the poor and homeless in the community. Look at the system that exists to provide food and shelter for families. Explore the ways people exploit the system. Learn how churches and other institutions help.

Q
Quiche

What makes a good quiche? Find out what kinds of quiches are available from area restaurants. Sponsor a quiche-baking contest by inviting restaurant owners and area residents to offer their wares to an organization's luncheon such as a church group or PTA and have luncheon participants vote on their favorites. Winners will have their recipes featured in the article.

Quilt

Who doesn't love to curl up in a cozy quilt on a cold winter's night? Contact quilt makers and find what goes into making a quilt from start to finish. Tell about the different quilt patterns and their names. Talk to store owners who specialize in quilting fabrics and products. Visit the county fair and interview quilt contest judges. What do they look for? What national quilting organizations are there? Talk to organization heads.

R
Recipes

Write about people who cook foods native to other countries. Include stories and recipes from a variety of countries. Run a portrait photo of each and a story about them. At the end of the stories, publish the cooks' favorite foreign recipes.

Recollections

When an ancient local landmark is slated for demolition, collect recollections about the building. Did anyone become engaged or married there? Is anyone still around who helped with the construction? Imagine the contrast of juxtaposing the builder's memories with those of the demolition crew.

Recreation during droughts

Lake water levels have dropped because of the lack of rain in the area. What does this mean to people using the lake for water sport and water-related activities?

Relax

Ask ordinary people what they do to relax. Fishing, entertainment such as movies, shopping come to mind, but mine this idea for that novel approach to nirvana.

Rental properties

What are the problems with owning and leasing in town, out of town, high-rent, low-rent, condos, sink holes?

Restaurant woes

Restaurant workers never know what it's like to get clobbered until they work at the hot spot after the big game has let out. Check the golden arches or the ice cream store—if you can't get near the door, you're in the right place. Find out how the workers handle it. It's almost a suicide ritual. Also, listen to the hordes of 16-year-olds. Some are just boisterous, but some are looking for trouble.

Roller coaster

Where is the best one?

S

School

Go back to school. Sit through an elementary school class and do the work. Write about your experiences.

Singing telegrams

Ever wonder what it would be like to receive a singing telegram, a visit from the fairy, an actor in a cartoon character costume or a belly dancer?

Single

Who is the most eligible single person in the area?

Small-town care

Visit your community hospital and take its financial health. Compare the quality of this institution to the evaluation from the community and state departments of health. Be sure to talk to employees, patients and others to understand if the finances are problematic or not.

Smoke

How hard is it to start smoking? Instead of writing about those trying to quit on Great American Smokeout Day each November, talk to someone who may be considering the habit. In addition, spend a day with an older smoker, and talk to him or her about the issue. Consider visiting a tobacco outlet store, and chat informally with the customers. Do these people share other interests that can provide a snapshot into their world?

Soul food

A soul food potluck dinner during Black History Month can be a meaningful article or a routine recipe story. Contact the church about some of the best cooks and get pictures of them with their finished entrees.

Summer camps

Are there any summer camps in the area? What do they offer and where are they located? What parts of the country are represented by participants? Why are parents sending their kids to camp? Why do kids want to go? This feature lends itself to a chart that highlights location, cost, director, activities, web site address, actual web, telephone number and other information for each camp.

Survival in the city

Surviving the Big Snow: This article should tell readers the best items to keep on hand for emergencies; however, the best part of the article will tell readers ways to avoid cabin fever when the blizzard brings an unexpected day of vacation.

Surviving work

What's a strategy for surviving an office get-together? What should be avoided?

T
Teenager news

Spotlight a teenager and issues for teenagers including making the most of a part-time job.

Theater

Attend plays-in-the-park and concert series sponsored by county departments of parks and recreation or community arts organizations. Profile some of the local talent. Interview families in attendance with their picnic suppers. Why are they drawn there? Who are their favorite artists? Talk to event organizers about what kind of planning is involved and how talent is selected. Find out how local artists can audition for a spot on the play list and write a sidebar.

Tomato

What is the oddest looking tomato? What is the largest?

Tourism

With the threat of terrorism abroad and people choosing to spend their summer vacations in the United States, where are people going? What areas are being promoted and advertised? Is tourism in the area expected to be up? What part of the country is the best destination spot? What part of the country is the worst? Make a list of vacation spots and rate them by region. Where are the deals for packages?

TV

How do TV shows relate to their real-life counterparts? Ask doctors what they think of medical shows. Ask lawyers what they think of legal-eagle shows. Ask law enforcement what they think of police shows. Ask judges (if you can get one to talk to you) to comment on TV shows.

Tubing

What makes a sport? Is tubing the non-sport on the order of chess? Your article can provide tips for riding the current and a list of tubing supplies.

U
Umbrella

Contact umbrella manufacturers. Are umbrella sales up? Down? Interview people walking in the city on a rainy day. Do people rely on umbrellas or do most just brave the weather and run from car to building? What is the history of the umbrella? Talk to someone wearing a quirky mini umbrella that sits on top of their head.

Ushers

They keep order when throngs come into stadiums, concert halls or auditoriums to be seated. What is it like to be an usher? How do ushers settle disputes before show time when two people claim they have the same seat? What is it like to deal with the public who clamor for the best seats in the house?

V
Valentine's Day

How do you love me? ... Save the poetry, let's talk cash. For Valentine's Day price an evening out on the town that would make any heart grow fonder. The evening may include candy, roses, a card, and a singing Valentine's dinner at the finest area restaurant, a movie rental and candlelight.

Vintage clothing

Mission stores. Second-hand stores. Many places sell nearly new clothing. They also sponsor activities in which they could wear their vintage clothing.

W
Water slides

Where are the nation's best water slides? Rate them on the basis of comfort, safety, speed, cost and all-around enjoyment.

White collar messes

Interview people who do the clean-up. Get their war stories about the trash left in the waste can. It ranges from nearly-full coffee cups, uneaten sandwiches and candy wrappers. Ask about the restrooms and the other high-traffic areas.

White meat

White or red? Even the fast food restaurants are pushing the sale of chicken – nuggets, sandwiches, strips – and fish. Health experts are saying chicken and fish are better.

Women

Farmers. Mechanics. Short-order cooks.

Worst pothole

Where's the worst pothole in the area? On a related topic, consider writing about your area's list of "worst" features. Where is the "worst" intersection, the worst downtown eyesore and so on?

XYZ
X marks the spot

Examine the letter X. From the legality of signing one's name with an X to television's X-files and the movie X-men, the letter X stands as a unique letter of the alphabet. Cite the history behind the letter "X" in X-mas. X has the shortest entry in the dictionary. List some of the words and their meanings. Using an X to sign one's name is for people who can't read or physically sign a document, but it must be witnessed!

Xylophone

Cite toy manufacturers of xylophones. Find information about the musical awareness a toy such as the xylophone brings to toddlers and young children. Talk to a xylophonist. What kind of musical background does one need to be a xylophonist? Interview a master xylophonist. For what kinds of songs or musical scores is a xylophone best suited?

Yesterday's headlines

Readers sometimes complain that the press doesn't follow-up on articles with fresh updates. Use that idea to examine the big news from yesteryear. Explore an article from yesterday's headlines and follow it up. Every community has its share of skeletal remains that are found but remain unidentified. Do a folio and find out if the person could be found.

Youth

Baby boomers are aging but based on the billion dollar age-defying industry most are fighting wrinkles, bags and sags to maintain that fountain of youth. What kinds of products are on the market? Do they work? Talk to cosmetology experts and cosmetic surgeons about what boomers are doing to stay younger looking. Do a before and after profile on women who volunteer to use a particular product for six months and examine its results. Profile a woman undergoing a facelift. Examine the psychological effects aging has on women whose self-image is wrapped up in looking young and beautiful.

Zamboni

The Zamboni ice-resurfacing machine is more than 50 years old. Go to your local skating arena and talk to a Zamboni driver. How does the machine work? How long does it take to resurface the rink and how often does a busy rink need to be resurfaced? Interview the machine's inventor. Did you know that the Zamboni company has a driver of the year contest? What is the relationship between Zamboni and Snoopy?

Zucchini

Zucchini. It's one of the most prolific summertime vegetables. After eating their fill of fried zucchini and zucchini bread, what else do gardeners do with all that abundance? Talk to gardeners and country cooks. Find recipes for zucchini soup, sandwiches, casseroles, chutney, omelets and fritters.

Bill Newcott

Biography of Bill Newcott

Bill Newcott is the Features Editor for *Modern Maturity*, a magazine published by the American Association for Retired People.

A graduate of Rutgers University, Bill Newcott began his journalistic career on a small Los Angeles daily. Within four years, he inexplicably found himself Associate Editor of the *National Enquirer* in Lantana, Fla. After 11 years on the legendary tabloid – where he wrote the gossip column and about half of the paper's front-page stories – he took his next quantum leap to the venerable *National Geographic* magazine in Washington, D.C. As Senior Editor, he wrote articles ranging from Mars to Las Vegas. At the time he left in 2000, he was Expeditions Editor, organizing explorations from western China to Baja.

Now one of the top editors at the highest circulation magazine in the world with 23 million readers, Bill serves as travel and entertainment editor and has had the pleasure of hiring some of his own favorite writers, including Ray Bradbury and Ben Stein. He has contributed to the texts of several books, including the *National Geographic Expeditions Atlas,* David Allen Harvey's photograph volume *Cuba*, and *The Last Climb*. A founding board member of the worldwide Christian journalist fellowship Gegrapha, he is a frequent lecturer and is writing two new books: One about the solar system and another about Satan.

Interview with Bill Newcott

Q: From tabloid news to prestige journalism, your career is about as varied as it can get. As a writer working in so many different venues, do you find that your style has changed dramatically over the years? How?

A: I have always had a lively style of writing – for example, I'll never settle for a common verb when an evocative form of the word will do (The one exception is, of course, "Said." When you quote someone, "Said" is the word to use. Avoid at all costs the temptation to try "interjected," or "enthused," or "exclaimed." "Muttered" is okay on occasion). I cut my professional teeth as a stringer for the *New York Daily News*, and my editor there, a dwarfish fellow named Alex Michellini, insisted that all stories max out at 200 words. So that imposed a style that required exactly the right word at all times. I carried that acquired skill throughout my career; on a daily paper, where I filed four to five stories a day, to the *Enquirer*, where the unique demands of tabloid writing commandeered every trick of vocabulary and style in the book. I was hired at *The National Geographic* largely as part of an effort to liven up its writing, which was historically somewhat stodgy. So rather than reign in my tabloid tendencies, I found myself adapting and polishing them. Now, as an editor, I find myself encouraging my writers to take chances with style and structure. There's no reason a 2,000-word story cannot be every bit as energized throughout as a 200-word *Enquirer* piece.

Q: In the following piece on South Dakota, did you do much research ahead of time using the Web? How much do the publicity handouts help a writer?

A: The inspiration for the South Dakota story came only as I was actually making the trip, which I had piggybacked on a story I was writing for *National Geographic*. So my down-and-dirty research came after I'd returned. It's pretty much an experiential piece, but I did use web sites about the area to confirm bits of information I'd picked up on my own. The history of the Rapid City dinosaurs, for example, was greatly supplemented with web sources, which I then, of course, double checked for accuracy.

Q: This piece reads a bit like a letter from the field to a friend. You didn't include quotations but the reader gets the sense that she is getting inside information. Is this approach one that you, as an editor, want to approve ahead of time?

A: I'm glad you noticed that. One hallmark of our travel coverage here, we hope, is that readers come away feeling they've had an insider's look at a destination. That's why we often hire writers who have a strong personal attachment to the place in question. They know the back road restaurants, the off-beat museums, and the extra cozy hotels. I think any writer who can convince an editor he or she has a unique, insider's take on a place should have a great advantage.

Q: *Modern Maturity* accepts freelance submissions. What are two tips you can give first-time writers?

A: Two ideas come to mind.

1) Come up with a one-of-a-kind approach to the story you're proposing. Don't just say, "I'm going to New Jersey and I want to write about it." Say, "There are ice caves in northwest New Jersey, no one knows about them, but they're a day trip you'll never forget." (This is, incidentally, true).

2) Show me you're a writer. Published stuff is best – but please, not court reporting you did for the local paper. Send me something that reveals the heart and soul and unique voice you'll put into any piece you write for me.

Take a three-day tour of South Dakota and the West
By Bill Newcott
Used with permission

DAY 1. The first thing you'll notice about Rapid City is, of course, the brontosaurus.

High atop the tallest nearby hill, silhouetted against the endless South Dakota sky like some prehistoric wonder horse, Rapid City's bronto is visible all over town. He (or she; genetic data is not available) presides over the millions of tourists who each year speed right past, each of them anxious to arrive at one of the several world-famous destinations just a short drive from here.

They seldom take the time to turn off the main road and head up to Dinosaur Park. But you, you will be different. You will follow those little dinosaur-logo signs through the business district, past a hillside neighborhood, and up a winding road to the top. And you will be rewarded.

It was in the mid-1930s that FDR's Works Progress Administration decided that Rapid City ought to have its own collection of life-size concrete dinosaurs. The bronto dominates the scene, but as you mount the stairs to its feet you'll pass, on a terrace below, a 20-foot-tall toothless Tyrannosaurus Rex threatening a spunky little triceratops. Just like that scene from the 1939 movie "Fantasia," except these guys came first.

From the bronto's feet, turn slowly and soak in the 180-degree vista that confirms your conviction that Rapid City is the perfect home base for a three-day stay. To the south and west roll the Black Hills, sacred to Native Americans and treasured by people who like to carve giant Presidents' heads into solid rock. To the east is Rapid City airport – a single change of planes away from virtually every major airport in the country. And beyond that, across the prairie and barely etched against the horizon, ripples the bumpy profile of Badlands National Monument. Over to the northeast sprawls Ellsworth Air Force Base, home to a first-rate air and space museum.

And at your feet spreads Rapid City itself, a ranch town that got swept up in the tourist influx created 70 years ago by nearby Mount Rushmore.

There are a few ways to drive to Mount Rushmore. The quickest is to get on Eighth Avenue, also known as the Rushmore Road, and head out of town. It's four lanes most of the way. Lots of folks like to meander a bit and take Iron Mountain Road. It's narrow, winding, and dotted with tunnels and "pigtail" bridges with steep approaches that loop over themselves. You can get some amazing views of Mount Rushmore framed in the tunnels. And you can also get a nasty case of motion sickness aggravated by elevation. You've been warned.

No matter what approach you take, you'll see the gigantic heads of Washington, Jefferson, Teddy Roosevelt, and Lincoln from miles away (The lighting is best in the morning). Still, they charge you eight bucks to pull into the new parking structure. Old timers still mourn the passing of the old parking lot, and of the tree-lined path that once led from the lot to the viewing area. Now you walk along a granite-pillared causeway, past snack bars and souvenir stands, a grandiose monument to a monument.

Psst. You can bypass the mall—and park for free—if you turn off the road just north of the pay parking lot entrance. This smaller, shaded National Park Service-operated lot does require you to walk up about 60 steps. It fills up fast, though, so get there early.

Despite a bad case of over development, there is no ruining the exquisite effect of the sculpture itself, its angular, vaguely art deco portraits somehow in perfect harmony with the mountainside, as if they were miraculously formed by forces of nature. The best feature of the recent development is a one-mile boardwalk leading from the visitor's center to the very foot of the mountain. You walk right to the edge of that curtain of slag, massive squared-off boulders. Beneath the heads, you'll notice a little spur trail that disappears into the rock field. Take it. A very short walk takes you into a kind of grotto. Look up through a gap between two huge chunks—and hold your breath as you view the sculpture perfectly framed.

Afternoon thunderstorms often rumble through here in the summer, but don't let that stop you from continuing past Rushmore on Route 16—stopping to admire some truly amazing "profile" views of George Washington—to a project that, when completed, will make Mount Rushmore seem more like a quaint little chip off the old mountainside.

The Chief Crazy Horse memorial, now taking recognizable shape after more than 50 years in the making, is so huge that the chief's face covers more ground than all four of Rushmores heads put together.

When I first headed up the road to see Crazy Horse 25 years ago, the approach was made of dirt, and it took a little faith and a lot of imagination to make out the profile of the chief and his horse in the distant rock. But today the monumental face is completed, and the horse's head, contorted downward in full gallop, is clearly taking shape.

Despite the scale of the project, you might never have heard of it. The family of sculptor Korczak Ziolkowski, who died in 1982, has continued his work—and like him they refuse to accept government money to finish. So they collect donations from those who visit. Thus, there's no built-in National Park exposure, and not much of a publicity budget. But you must make the trip, if only to tell your great-grandchildren you were there when old Crazy Horse was still taking shape.

On DAY 2, say hello to Bronto and head east from Rapid City. It's 35 miles to Badlands National Monument, but with the official speed limit 75 on Interstate 90, it'll feel like a spin to the neighborhood grocery store. First stop: the town of Wall, gateway to the badlands.

Now Wall, as anybody who's driven within two or three hundred miles of the place knows (thanks to the areas of billboards that precede it), is the home of the Wall Drug Store. Wall Drug Store is to drugs what the American Telephone and Telegraph Company is to telegraphs. There may indeed be some corner of Wall Drug where you can actually buy drugs, but its true trade is in hot dogs, pizza, souvenir hand towels, miniature Rushmore's, steer horns, novelty thermometers, card tricks, t-shirts, flip-flops, sunglasses, bumper stickers, plaster prairie dogs, instant film, naughty post cards, and vending machines. Oh, yes, and free ice water. Since 1939, the signs say.

You will stop at Wall Drugs, as everyone else does. Here's what you do. Wend your way through the maze of shops. Stroll across the courtyard where you can take a friend's picture on a dinosaur. Duck into the shooting gallery near the snack bar, and note the sign that reads "no flash photography." Take careful camera aim at the gallery targets, and take a flash picture. You'll thank me later. Get a five-cent cup of coffee before you leave.

Now head down Route 240S, the lonely, dusty road to the Badlands. Like a range of candles dripping in the South Dakota sun, the peaks and valleys of the Badlands seem to flow like liquid rock. An extinct sea floor of dried mud, the landscape has been carved by rain and runoff over the eons. Mud sediments trace horizontal lines across the water-worn walls, which retreat into small canyons, giving the appearance of a colorful, undulating curtain.

Most visitors stick to the overlooks, emerging briefly from their cars to get a peek at the vista. But you'll be more adventurous. Trudge out a bit along one of the marked pathways. You'll find yourself walking along a high ridge that slopes off to your right and left, revealing dramatic new aspects with every step.

Shortly after you enter the park at the Pinnacles Entrance, you'll notice a gravel road that turns off to the right, called the Sage Creek Rim Road. The 30-mile road is not a loop, so you'll have to double back to see the rest of the park, but along its length is your only chance to see up-close the 600-strong bison herd that the National Parks Service has reintroduced to the area. If you're a bit less adventurous, stay on the main park loop road, stop at the Pinnacles Overlook, and gaze west through a good pair of binoculars. You may get a glimpse of the herd.

As you exit the park at the eastern gate, you may be tempted to hit the gas and head for your hotel. But slow down, pardner. Or you might miss the sign that reads "Helicopter Rides, $15." It seems too good, too cheap, to be true. But no, Helicopter the Badlands does, indeed, give you a heli-lift ($15 each, double occupancy). Sure, the flight lasts all of four minutes. But you'll get an unforgettable eagle-eye view of the Badlands. And if you ask, your pilot will even point out where several movies have been shot.

DAY 3. Today marks your most distant trek from Rapid City, a two-hour drive across the border into Wyoming. Duck off the interstate at scenic Route 14, click off 25 miles—and hold your breath as you drive over a rise and see Devil's Tower National Monument. Thrusting 865 feet into the sky, the core of an ancient volcano is still sacred to many Native Americans. You can hike all the way around the thing, but visitors are asked not to disturb prayer banners tied to sticks at various spots along the way.

Up close, the tower is almost too big to take in. Your best view is back on the main road just beyond the park's entrance. Pull over for a moment and admire the monolith, set like a sculpture atop a sloping green hill. Just before you rejoin the interstate, stop off at one of the little diners in the town of Sundance. Order the mashed potatoes and sculpt them into a mini-Devil's Tower, muttering the lines Richard Dreyfus made famous in "Close Encounters of the Third Kind"—"This *means* something!" Then imagine how often the waitress has heard that one.

Back in South Dakota, get off at Spearfish and follow the signs to the D.C. Booth Historic Fish Hatchery. You have never seen so many trout in your life—and best of all, there's an underwater viewing window that showcases fish so big you'd swear the thing was a huge magnifying glass. Despite the town's name, there's no fish spearing allowed.

Now head back toward Rapid City, stopping at the town of Sturgis. If you're there the second week in August, you'll be smack in the middle of the largest motorcycle gathering in the nation. Each year, some 100,000 bikers descend on this little burg for a week of, well, let's be charitable and call it merry-making.

Any other week, park on the lazy main street and duck into one of Sturgis' premiere dining establishments, the Road Kill Café ("From Your Grill to Ours!") Sad to say, they serve only regular dinner fare, although the menu does feature such fanciful names as Smear of Deer, Pig in a Blanket, and Guess That Mess.

As the sun begins to settle behind the Black Hills, double back to Spearfish for the world-famous Black Hills Passion Play. For most of the 1900s, local folks and a handful of professionals have staged this three-hour drama recounting the last week in the life of Christ in a vast outdoor amphitheater. One night as I sat in the audience, at the moment of the crucifixion, a spectacular shooting star streaked across the sky. For a moment, at least, everyone there was a believer.

Well, that's three days in Rapid City, and we haven't even touched on the area's great kitschy wonders, like the Cosmos Mystery Spot (where "the laws of nature seem to have gone completely berserk"), Reptile Gardens, Pan for Gold or the World's Largest Prairie Dog. And you really shouldn't miss The Journey, a classy new museum right in Rapid City chronicling human habitation in the region.

Then there's Yellowstone, just a day's drive away. But that's another story.

Marita Littauer

Biography of Marita Littauer

Marita Littauer wrote her first book at 23. She went on to write nine more and took on three more book projects for the 2003-2004 season. She is the founder of CLASS, a program that men and women use to enhance their personal and professional communication skills in speech and print.

A professional speaker with more than 20 years of experience speaking to women's groups, church conferences, conventions, and businesses, Marita is known for motivating others to succeed. Some of the groups she has addressed include the National Christian

Women's Conference, the National Religious Broadcasters Convention, the Chickasaw Indian Nation, Loma Linda University Dental School Auxiliary, and Sam's Club Managers Meeting Spouse Program. Marita is a member of the National Speakers Association.

Her first book, *Shades of Beauty*, ultimately led to her most popular book, *Personality Puzzle*, and two of her newer titles, *Getting Along With Almost Anybody* and *Talking So People Will Listen*, co-written with her mother, Florence Littauer. *Come As You Are* was written with Betty Southard. *Love Extravagantly* was written with her husband. In 2004, Marita worked with her mother, Florence, to write *Journey to Jesus*.

Under Marita's direction CLASS has grown from its foundation as a speakers' training seminar to a full-service agency for the established and aspiring Christian speaker, author, and publisher. She serves as President and has created CLASS Speakers Service, the Media Publicity Service, the CLASS Reunion, and CLASS Chats.

Marita and her husband, Chuck Noon, have been married for more than 20 years. They live in Albuquerque, N.M., where Chuck is a marriage and family therapist.

Interview with Marita Littauer

Q: What question do new writers ask the most often?
A: Most of the people who seek my advice are speakers and the hardest lesson that they have to learn is to nail themselves to a chair and write. I tell them to create a deadline and stick with it. I'm working on three writing projects, and I give myself rewards as I complete a portion of the work. For instance, I may tell myself that I won't have lunch until I finish a portion of a chapter.

Writers have to sacrifice. I don't do holidays; I write. I look at the calendar and plan my writing. There's no magic pill. It is like dieting. It takes work, but when that book is finished, it is exhilarating. I hold the book up and revel in the finished product. A writer can gain that same sense of fulfillment with the publication of an article.

Q: What holds people back the most?
A: Most new writers are afraid of not doing it right. They are too concerned with punctuation and grammar and think: What if I don't like the result? I tell them that the computer will liberate them to *brain dump*. Get the ideas down. Once the ideas are in a computer file, the writer can move the paragraphs around and revise the ideas until the ideas make sense.

Q: Do you have a suggestion for getting started?

A: Writers and speakers have to pay their dues and sometimes that means working for the experience alone. For writers, I suggest that they seek out compilation books such as the popular "Chicken Soup" series. These books seek a variety of writers who can tell their personal story. The trick is to follow the directions. My book, *But Lord, I was Happy Shallow* is a compilation book, but I had to reject nearly two-thirds of the submissions because the writers didn't follow the instructions. Many of the articles had potential, but they didn't meet the main criterion – humor. My advice is to study the submission guidelines and produce the kind of copy the editor is seeking. This success will lead to other successes in writing, and, perhaps, in speaking, too.

Q: Where do you suggest that speakers get started?

A: Again, new writers and speakers may have to work *pro bono*, but the opportunities exist. Whether it is a church or a corporation, the venues are there. Many places won't have a budget but will give the speaker a gift certificate or a meal. You find these places by working your own network and volunteering to speak. In addition, you must develop a flyer on yourself that tells a bit about what qualifies you to speak. It doesn't have to be your education. Most likely it will be about your personal experience that people want to hear about. It is a promotional piece on yourself.

Georgia Shaffer is mentioned in this book on feature writing. She may have a degree in psychology but people want to hear her speak because she has overcome three bouts with cancer. Speakers have to ask themselves what qualifies them to speak. Georgia is qualified because she knows how to overcome loss and people are hungry for the personal lessons that she has learned.

Next, study the coming events section of the newspaper. Often newspapers list organizations that have monthly meetings using local or regional speakers. Get the program chairman's name and offer to speak. Use the one-page flyer that promotes your messages to give to the program chairman. You may even have a cassette tape of yourself that you can send that person.

When you speak, make and use a handout that lists the points of your message. (Use the PIER approach that I mentioned in my article below!) Make sure that outline includes your name, contact information, even your personal web site. Your audience will use that sheet to take notes and they are very likely to keep it for future reference. Then, when the need arises, they will have your contact information so they can suggest you as a speaker. Use one speaking assignment to hitchhike to the next one.

Author's note: Writers sometimes speak on the same topics from a writing assignment. Here's an article from a master of the writer-speaker dynamic.

Putting power in your presentation
By Marita Littauer
Used with permission

I have been teaching people how to speak though the CLASSeminar since 1981. As those in the audience watch me and the other staff members interact with each other on the platform, they can see we are having fun. They watch us flex with the schedule and add in stories of events, which just took place during the previous break. They see that we have little or no notes.

As the afternoon winds down and we are nearing the part of the schedule where each participant goes to their small group and prepares and delivers a presentation, their anxiety level rises. After comparing those of us who are up front and the attendees in the small groups, I am often asked, "Does it ever get fun?" Or, "When does it get fun?" The answer is, "Yes it does get fun." Admittedly, there are those of us who are more naturally hams, those whose personality type gravitates toward the stage. But everyone, regardless of his or her personality type, can be an effective speaker, enjoy being up front and put power in their presentation. After a while, it even becomes fun!

There are five parts to putting power in your presentation. These steps will make it easy for you to put it all together and make it easier for your audience to get your message and remember the key ideas you wish to communicate.

Passion

I often run into people who think being a speaker looks like fun or they think it looks like a glamorous lifestyle. They ask, "How can I become a speaker?" I believe you don't really become a speaker, rather it is an evolution. You don't one day decide "I'd like to be a speaker" and then check out books, learn jokes and use other people's material and then reprocess it all in a speech you call your own. Some people do try this approach. Some may have excellent acting skills and be able to pull this off. But, for most their message is empty. You can tell when you listen to these people that something doesn't ring true. You can probably think of people you have heard who have done this.

The first secret to putting power in your presentation is passion. Start by examining your own life. What are you so excited about that you can't keep quiet? For those of us who desire to be Christian speakers, what has God done in your life lately that you want to share? These are your passions. They are things that are a natural outpouring of who you are and what you believe.

You may have several topics that you feel passionate about. Take a few minutes now while you are thinking about it and jot down the topics or ideas that excite you or really get your adrenaline pumping. Here are a few ideas. Many people feel impassioned about restoring marriage, raising godly children, hospitality, recovery, the abortion issue or their personal testimony. There are, of course, hundreds of additional topics. Begin a list and keep adding to it as new ideas come to your mind and as you grow in your Christian maturity. When you start with a passion, the other important pieces fall into place much more easily.

Personal examples

Since I have been involved in teaching others to be more effective speakers for so many years, I listen to other speakers different from the average audience member. When I observe a speaker who is nervous or struggling, I want to go help them, to hold their hand. I have seen countless speakers who start out nervously, fidgeting with their pen or the change in their pocket and peppering their words with an abundance of "ahs" and "and ahs". As I watch, hurting for the presenter, I have discovered an almost universal cure for the pain -- both the speakers and mine. As soon as the speaker begins to share a personal story, something they know backwards and forwards, something they don't need notes to tell, they warm up. They become more natural and animated as they tell stories from their own life.

Personal examples add energy to your presentation. They let the audience know you have been there and that you know what you are talking about. Be sure to use them liberally throughout your presentation.

Preparation

This next point is the most important and therefore we will spend the most time here. Passion and personal examples are valuable tools, but if you don't prepare, you may gush on enthusiastically with no real point or purpose. The key to preparation is to know your subject well, know what ideas you wish to communicate but yet be flexible enough to adjust some of your material to fit the specific needs of each group and the required time frame.

Many novice speakers are afraid that when they stand up in front of all those people that their mind will go blank. As a result, they write out their speech word for word. When they stand up front they actually read the entire message. Most likely you have heard some of these types of speakers. It is obvious when someone is reading a speech. I always feel offended that I took my time to attend a program where the speaker is reading a speech. I feel like they could have just mailed out the script and I could have done something else with my time. In Toastmasters International, the group which meets weekly to help people improve their speaking skills, the last assignment in the first level program is to write out your speech word for word and deliver it following those notes exactly. This assignment is last because it is the most difficult, yet this is where many people start.

Instead, what I am suggesting in preparing your speech is a method that will allow you to have everything you need in front of you, in case your mind goes blank, yet offers that flexibility. Notice the term "preparing a presentation" rather than "writing." A good speech should not be written out word for word. It should be "prepared" with all of the key ideas, teaching, stories and scripture in the notes, all of which you follow for continuity. But, by not writing it out word for word, you allow for flexibility in timing, group make-up, and the leading of the Holy Spirit as to the needs for this particular group.

The PIER System allows for all of these factors. The speaker can be assured that you have all the ingredients needed for a "teaching" presentation is available, but they are arranged to allow for flexibility.

To help remember the concepts, think of yourself standing in front of an audience. You look out at them and they are looking back at you like a sea of faces. The desire is to make your presentation stick out in their minds like a PIER sticks out into the ocean. PIER is an acronym for Point, Instruction, Example, and Reference.

POINT - As you begin your speech preparation, start with the main ideas you wish to convey to your audience. These ideas become your POINTS which when collected together become the points of your outline. As you sit down to prepare your presentation, say to yourself, "What are the key things I want the audience to remember?" Let's say you get three ideas. On three separate pieces of paper write the idea across the top of each one. At this place in your preparation, your ideas may come to you in the form of a question, a single word, a thought, or a complete sentence. Don't worry about that yet. Simply write down the ideas as they come into your head.

Since you are writing each point on a separate piece of paper, it doesn't even matter if they are in the order in which you will ultimately use them. Often once you get into your preparation, you decide that the point you had as the first one should be somewhere else. Since they are on separate pieces of paper, you can just rearrange them as you see fit. These ideas become your points, the "P" of the PIER.

About two inches down from your point, write an "I" in the margin on each piece of paper. Another two inches down write "E" and another two inches an "R". This creates a simple "fill-in-the-blanks" form for your speech preparation.

INSTRUCTION - Think about your "Point". How are the listeners going to make that concept a part of their lives? These ideas become your instruction. For example, in your "Point" you may tell your audience that having a good prayer life is important. In the "Instruction" you will offer them several ways to improve their prayer life. Next to the "I" on your paper, write down the main techniques you want the audience to learn. Since these ideas are from your head and should be something you have studied or experienced, they will be concepts you know well. Therefore, you don't have to write out long cumbersome instructions. By listing just the key steps, you can glance at your notes and be reminded of the things you intend to communicate. This way you can be sure to include all the concepts while you are standing in front of the audience.

Depending on the time allowed for the presentation, you may give detailed instruction and even have the audience try your suggestions right there or you may simply give them the techniques to implement your ideas. Offering the listener an idea without equipping them to accomplish it will be frustrating to the audience and futile for you.

EXAMPLE - If you give the listeners a point and then tell them how to do it but quit there, you may come across as preachy and hard to relate to. To show the audience that you know what you're talking about, that you've been there, include a personal story that exemplifies the principle. You may share your own struggle with the situation and show how you overcame it or the example given may be that of a friend or family member. People remember stories better than just points. Again, these stories are usually things you have experienced so you won't need to write them out word for word. Next to the "E" on your notes, jot down a few key words to remind you which stories you intended to tell with that point. If you have a lot of time, you may want to include several stories to make your point. Or, if your time is cut at the last minute, which often happens, you can pare your stories down and just tell one or even use an abbreviated version if necessary. You can also adjust your stories so they are appropriate for the particular audience you are addressing at the time. If the group is made up of men and women, be sure to use stories that will relate to both. If it is all women, you may use slightly different examples. They will feel as though you customized the presentation just for them. The stories will give your points life!

REFERENCE - So far all we have discussed are your own ideas. The "Reference" allows you to back up what you are saying and give it more authority. If your presentation is being given to a Christian audience, it should include various scriptures. These would be your references. You may have one verse you will want to quote or even several which will validate your point. Next to the "R" on your notes list the address of the verse or verses you wish to use. If you are only using a couple of verses you may want to write them out completely in your notes, so you can quote them without having to fumble through your Bible while you are up front. If you time is cut, you can simply offer the audience the address of the passage you are using and paraphrase it to save time. If you have been asked to stretch your message, which does rarely happen, you could give the address and ask someone from the audience to find the verse and read it to the group.

In addition to the Bible there are many other references you can use to reinforce what you are saying. They may include newspaper or magazine articles, books, statistics or quotes from notable people. I recommend that every speaker have a good quote book such as Bartlett's Familiar Quotations in their resource library. When you do use these additional references, be sure to have their source in your notes. You don't have to include the source in the verbal presentation but you should have it in case anyone questions its validity.

After you have "filled in all your blanks," the next step is to make your points easier to remember. You as the speaker will have notes from which to work. Therefore you could give your presentation with one point being a question, another being a single word and another being a thought. However, when there is no continuity to your points they are not as clear for your audience to catch or as easy for them to remember. So once the hard part is done, you are ready to clean it up.

Go back over your points. If, for example, three are questions and one is a single word, can you rework the idea the single word represents into a question so the points are uniform? Or, if there is no obvious pattern to your points, try to boil the points down to one or two words that represent the main thought. Review your points again. Do several of them start with the same letter? Do a couple of them rhyme? Or, can you use the first letters to spell a word that summarizes the focus of your overall message? If you see an emerging pattern, try to make the words of the other points fit that pattern. This is where a Thesaurus or Synonym Finder is helpful. If you have one or two words which don't fit the pattern, look them up and see if you can find a synonym which will communicate the same point but fit within your pattern.

For example, here are three real points I often use to teach this concept. These points originally came from an article on father/daughter relationships by Gary Smalley. His points are: 1) A father should include meaningful touching as his daughter grows up. 2) A father who wants to develop a close relationship with his daughter should invest himself in her best interest. 3) A father should keep his anger under control.

Now quickly cover up that paragraph and try to repeat those points without looking. You can't, can you? While those are three excellent points, they are too long and cumbersome to be easily remembered. Lets look at the first point. 1) A father should include meaningful touching as his daughter grows up. Can you condense it down to one key word? How about "Touch"?

Now let's look at the second point. 2) A father who wants to develop a close relationship with his daughter should invest himself in her best interest. Now there are several key words you could pick out, but since the first word begins with a "T", can you think of a "T" word, which captures the heart of that point? How about "Time"?

Okay, the last point. 3) A father should keep his anger under control. What "T" word comes to mind for this one? Most people come up with Temper. Yes, that is a "T" word and it does capture the essence of the point, but does it work? To check your points once you have simplified them, they should all be the same parts of speech. They should be all nouns, all verbs, all thoughts, all sentences or all questions. To check this you can simply put a prefix before the point. You might say, "A daughter needs Touch." "A daughter needs Time." Those both work. Point number three, "A daughter needs Temper." How can you rework that so that it fits the context, is a "T" word and is the correct part of speech? Tenderness, "A daughter needs Tenderness." Now you have three easy to remember points -- Touch, Time and Tenderness. The message is the same, but now it is also easy to remember!

Presentation

Once you have filled out your "form" using the PIER formula, you have your speech basically prepared. When you are ready to actually present your message, you will need an opening, which may be a story -- the E in Pier, which will put you at ease. Or, it may be a question that helps to create a need in the audience for your subject. If you do begin with a question, be sure that it is a question with an obvious answer and one that everyone present can answer affirmatively, without embarrassment.

When I begin my presentation on *Personality Puzzle*, I always ask the audience, "How many of you have noticed there are people out there who are different from you?" Of course everyone has noticed that. So they can all answer by raising their hands in agreement. To indicate that I am expecting a response to the question and particularly a raised hand, I raise my hand as I lean into the audience and ask the question. By asking a question to which they can all respond, I have already done several things. First, I have created an atmosphere of interaction. Rather than having a sense of being preached at, the audience is already involved. Additionally since the question is something that applies to everyone, the communal response draws the audience together.

After your opening story, question or questions, move right into your points. Remember, PIER is a formula, not an outline in itself. By preparing your presentation, using PIER you have all the information you need. But, when you actually present it, you can start with the story – the Example – and then move into the Point you learned from the story, then teach the audience how to apply that in their own lives – the Instruction – and then wrap that point up with a quote or scripture. You can arrange the Point, Instruction, Example and Reference any way you want and you can present it differently each time. This flexibility allows each presentation to be unique, fresh and specifically applicable to each audience.

If you choose to use a handout for your presentation, which I suggest as it allows your audience to follow along and provides them with a place to take notes, use the Points of our outline to make up your handout. If you are using scriptures or quotes, you may also want to include them in a smaller font with the key points. This prevents losing people as they lean over to the person next to them and ask, "What verse was that?" If you do choose to use a handout, be sure to include your name, address and phone number to identify whose material the audience is taking home. This way if they want to quote you at a later date or use your ideas in some research of their own, they know how to find you to get permission. Plus, if they love what you said and want to recommend you to another group, they will know how to contact you.

Finally, you will need a closing which may include a recapping or a summary of your points and end with a challenge or call to commitment. Often a poem or other inspirational piece that exemplifies your message is an effective closing. The closing poem doesn't have to be an original composition. However, if you are gifted in poetry, this is an excellent place to incorporate it. If the closing quote or poem is not original, be sure to site the source.

Many people who are giving a Christian message in a church type setting feel as though they should close with prayer. Unless the presentation is an actual sermon, I suggest that you not use a prayer as your final words. Closing with a prayer in a non-church service setting confuses the audience. The way we show appreciation in our society to a person who is on the "stage," a performer, singer or speaker is by applause. This lets the person know they did a good job and is the audience's way of thanking you. However, closing in prayer creates a somber and quiet mood. We are not accustomed to breaking into applause at the sound of "Amen." So when you close with prayer, the audience doesn't know whether they should thank you with applause or keep quiet. It creates an awkward and uncomfortable moment for everyone.

If a prayer of confession or commitment is appropriate after your presentation, there are two effective ways to handle it. One is that you have the emcee or program chairman do it after you have finished. Or, you can offer the prayer that is on your heart. But then come back with your summary of points, closing poem or concluding challenge. This provides an effective transition from the prayer mood to a powerful closing and will leave your audiences on an up note.

Occasionally, the desired mood may be a quiet somber exit into a time of reflection or stillness. In such circumstances, the prayer may be the most effective way to close.

Practice

The last thing you need to do is practice. Once you have found the subject area of your passion, peppered it with the vitality of personal examples, prepared your message and gotten the presentation together, you are ready to practice. Start alone in your bedroom or office, preferably in front of a full-length mirror. Allow that passion to show and use hand gestures to clarify your points. Work on your message until you are comfortable with all the parts. Then tape-record it. Listen to how you sound. You are apt to find places where you have lots of gap fillers such as "ah" and "you know." These usually indicate an area where you are not as familiar with your material or are not comfortable with it. Make changes or study those areas more completely. While it is unlikely you will ever be completely happy with your finished product, the next thing is to give your speech in front of supportive, but honest friends and/or family. This may be three people in your living room, or it may be your Bible study group at your church. Ask for their encouragement and insight. Notice I didn't say criticism. Accept their praise and listen to their suggestions. If they suggested many changes, you may want to give your speech once more in a controlled environment before you venture beyond the safety of your support network. If they give you a thumbs-up, go on. Share what God has put on your heart with others and expect results!

When you prepare your speech using the PIER System you can be confident that you have included everything you need for a strong presentation and still have the freedom and flexibility that is the sign of a "Pro!"

Exercises

1) Re-read the articles. Look at the styles. Describe the tone. Would you say that the articles have a friendly tone? How did the writers do that? For instance, phrases such as "Psst" help convey that kind of tone. Identify three other devices that help the tone remain light.

2) Think back to Chapter 5, *Interviews that work*, and recall the section on "collaborative editing." Imagine some of the discussion that went on when Bill Newcott bounced the idea of a "quotation-free" feature article off a fellow writer. What are some of the trade-offs, do you imagine?

3) Think about Marita Littauer's idea of passion. What are you passionate about? List three topics related to that passion that could be parlayed into a presentation. How can those topics be re-cast as feature articles?

Summary

This chapter took an A to Z look at specific feature writing ideas and strategies. This is the "Net" in FeatureWriting.Net. The chapter also included interviews with Bill Newcott and Marita Littauer. Bill Newcott's entry included a light-hearted feature story, the kind that you can write if you clear it first with an editor. This chapter also included a piece by writer-speaker Marita Littauer who provides an example of the how-to article, a special type of feature. If you have persevered through this book, you now have a strategy that will make you a profitable writer. Now all you must do is write. Write in season and out of season and before you know it, you will have a quiver full of published pieces and a growing reputation as a freelance writer.

About the author

Michael Ray Smith

Author spends his days writing and teaching

Michael Ray Smith is an award-winning writer, photojournalist, academic and conference speaker. *FeatureWriting.Net* is his fourth book. University Press of America published *The Jesus Newspaper*, his third book, in 2002. Smith's other books examined local history. His academic journal articles explored people with disability and mass media, the early American press, editorial cartoons, C.S. Lewis and G. K. Chesterton, international mass communication and other communication topics.

In 1988 Michael began his teaching career at a state school in the South. Since then, he has taught journalism at a private college in Pennsylvania, directed a journalism program at a liberal-arts college in Indiana and served as chair of a graduate journalism program in Virginia. In 2003, he was named chairman of Campbell University's Department of Mass Communication in central North Carolina.

As a journalist, Michael spent a decade in newsrooms as a reporter and editor and penned more than 3,000 articles for publications such as *The Atlanta Journal-Constitution, The Baltimore Sun* and *The Philadelphia Inquirer*. In 2001-2002, his students recognized him as Favorite Professor of the Year for the college, recognition that he considers his highest honor.

His work in professional organizations such as the Association for Education in Journalism and Mass Communication resulted in the establishment of an interest group. He is member of Who's Who Among American Teachers and Who's Who in Communication.

Michael and Barbara Smith have two daughters, Shannon and Taylor. Barbara is a certified public school teacher and an avid speed walker. Shannon works in communication and Taylor is a ballerina. Michael provides most of the comic relief in the family, an honor that he'd sooner pass on to another family member someday. Wink.

Index

Michael Smith
910. 893-7528
smithm@campbell.edu